150 Best Companies for
Liberal Arts Graduates

150 BEST COMPANIES FOR LIBERAL ARTS GRADUATES

Where to Get a Winning Job in Tough Times

Cheryl Woodruff
Greg Ptacek

JOHN WILEY & SONS, INC.

New York • Chichester • Brisbane • Toronto • Singapore

In recognition of the importance of preserving what has been written, it is a policy of John Wiley & Sons, Inc., to have books of enduring value printed on acid-free paper, and we exert our best efforts to that end.

Copyright © 1992 by Cheryl Woodruff and Greg Ptacek
Published by John Wiley & Sons, Inc.

Library of Congress Cataloging-in-Publication Data

Woodruff, Cheryl
     150 best companies for liberal arts graduates : where to get a winning job in tough times / Cheryl Woodruff
          p.   cm.
     Includes index.
     ISBN 0-471-54793-X (paper)
     1. Job hunting—United States.   2. Vocational guidance—
United States.   3. Education, Humanistic—United
States.   I. Woodruff, Cheryl, 1944–   .   II. Title.
HF5382.75.U6P83   1992
650.14—dc20   92-13998

Printed in the United States of America

10   9   8   7   6   5   4   3

Acknowledgments

Considering the hundreds of phone calls and interviews and the enormous amount of library research required for this book, we could not have completed it without the help of the following people, most of them liberal arts students. We sincerely appreciate their hard work and dedication in performing research and editorial services.

Mary Arace, Research Director

Anne Clifford
Sharon Cohen
Laurie Collister
Debrah Giese
Larry Jerdef
Tien Lee

Laura Osborne
Athena Regala
Susan Shields
Jeff Silberman
Eric Stano
Aletha Weaver

We extend special thanks to Professor Bob McClory at Northwestern University, Medill School of Journalism, who supervised the following students in their research and editorial work for this book:

James Arndorfer
Kim Barker
Melissa Bigner
Josie Blumenthal
Mara Dionne Brock
Heidi Christensen
Mary Donahough
Lisa Elliott
John W. Ellis IV
Meredith Epstein
Anisha Frizzell
Heather Harding
Rachel Janutio
Brian Johnson
Anneke Leurdijk
Leticia Lopez

Laurianne McLaughlin
Juliette Pagliaro
Joel Palmer
Amy Reinholds
Scott Relyea
Kathryn Rospond
Stephanie Saull
Todd Spangler
Grace Tan
Sonya Turner
Imelda Valenzuela
Mike Watts
Dan Weinrib
Seretha Williams
Cynthia Wang

Foreword

We were first contacted about participating in this project when it was merely an idea in the minds of co-authors Cheryl Woodruff and Greg Ptacek. We did not have to think twice about the opportunity to participate in such an important undertaking.

Adding first-person accounts from young liberal arts graduates on corporate management fast-tracks in each company profile is a unique approach, and it provides excellent insights into the myriad opportunities that abound in business today.

A book that underscores the true and lasting values of a liberal arts education is an invaluable service to students and graduates who have made their commitment to a broad, humanities-based curriculum. Any book that exposes liberal arts graduates to the rewarding career possibilities in the world of business is an invaluable guide. We knew this well since both of us majored in liberal arts as undergraduates, prior to law school and life-long careers in investment banking. Our liberal arts educations have proven to be a broad foundation upon which we built our success in business.

This book is also a great service to companies like Goldman Sachs that need candidates of good character with integrity, honesty, high ethical standards and inquisitive minds that have had exposure to a sweeping range of subjects and disciplines.

We congratulate the authors on their ambitious undertaking, and we hope that readers will take seriously the sage advice offered on the following pages.

Robert E. Rubin & Stephen Friedman
Senior Partners and Co-Chairmen
of the Management Committee
Goldman Sachs

Contents

Introduction

Every year about one million college graduates enter the job market, half with a distinct disadvantage. It has nothing to do with race, creed, color, or gender. Rather it's what many employers consider an anomaly in the high-tech, specialized, profit-driven economy of the nineties—the liberal arts degree.

This is the first career book designed expressly for liberal arts degree graduates who face the prospect of (or are currently in) low-paying, ungratifying, unchallenging jobs. Both a reference book and a handbook, it lists the best companies to work for and how to get the best jobs. We also interviewed liberal arts graduates who work for these companies. Their comments appear in the "Report from the Trenches" that accompanies each profile.

The goal of this book was not only to find the companies that are hiring liberal arts graduates, but also to narrow the list to those with fast-track management training programs accessible to liberal arts grads. Many of the employers listed here actually prefer liberal arts grads over business, engineering, and computer science grads. Information was largely obtained through personal interviews with corporate human resources officers and other corporate executives; college placement officers; liberal arts grads *cum* corporate employees, and career planning specialists.

We obtained additional information by surveying several hundred companies that were identified by college placement officers as active recruiters of liberal arts graduates and by examining corporate annual and 10K reports, newspapers, magazines, journals, and speeches.

The Recession

When this project began in 1989, there were far more corporate employers who qualified for inclusion than there were a year and a half later. Some of these employers had long histories of hiring liberal arts graduates and promoting them to management positions. However, due to their current economic situations, they were not hiring college grads.

The impact of the recession is the primary reason for the scarce mention of many companies in financial services, advertising, and publishing—fields that normally are wellsprings of employment for liberal arts graduates. However, many of these companies do appear in the comprehensive list of likely employers of liberal arts grads in Chapter 5.

Indeed, some of the companies that made the final cut had just emerged from bankruptcy (Federated/Lazarus) or were still in bankruptcy. Carter Hawley Hale, the West Coast retail giant, was still protected by Chapter 11 bankruptcy status as the book went to print, but had recently returned to profitability and was planning to emerge from bankruptcy by the end of the year. In the meantime, its hiring of liberal arts grads was proceeding as normal.

Final Selection

If the first requisite for including a company in the book was the availability of jobs, then the second was access to information. Some companies with the reputation of being good employers for liberal arts graduates were simply uncooperative about the project.

The Gap, for example, was positively hostile about releasing the most basic facts about its corporation. We could have obtained the information independently of management's participation. However, our collective work experience has been that when a company is more secretive about releasing information than the CIA or FBI, then that attitude probably pervades other aspects of the work environment.

Likewise, research indicated that Pitney Bowes had hired a large number of liberal arts grads for sales positions. But management was too skittish to allow its employees to be interviewed, thereby automatically eliminating the company from consideration.

The list of employers who made the cut is not meant to be absolute. There are plenty of corporations that hire liberal arts graduates but simply don't have to recruit. Companies in the entertainment industry are prime examples. More often than not, you get a job there by *whom* you know, not *what* you know.

Latest Information

Finally, every effort has been made to provide accurate, up-to-date information. In a few cases, the employee interviewees requested anonymity, so pseudonyms were used. All the employers profiled were hiring or were poised to hire a significant number of liberal arts grads at the time the book was written. A worsening economy could curtail these employers' recruitment efforts. Nevertheless, we stand behind them as best-bet employment opportunities for liberal arts grads, regardless of the bullishness or bearishness of the market.

Hello, Out There

We are planning to update this edition regularly, so all feedback on the employers included in this book would be most appreciated. Furthermore, a note to all corporate employers: We'd like to hear from you. If you think your company deserves to be in future editions of this book, then tell us why. Please send all correspondence to our attention, care of our editor.

Cheryl Woodruff and Greg Ptacek
c/o Steve Ross
John Wiley & Sons, Inc.
605 Third Ave.
New York, NY 10158

ONE

Buy, Beg, Borrow, or Steal . . . but Read This Book

Considering that most college students spend four years preparing for a career, precious few of us who majored in the liberal arts had at graduation time even an inkling of how to go about getting one. Most of us had a rather abstract concept of job hunting: Read the classifieds, knock on a few doors, and consider the offers.

Unlike our business, computer science, and engineering counterparts, we smelled the coffee only *after* we graduated. And even after entering the job market, finding a better job was essentially the same process of stumbling around in the dark until you bumped into something better.

This book was designed by two liberal arts grads to be the kind of book we wish we had had when we hit the pavement looking for jobs. It's written with the assumption that you, the reader, are a fairly intelligent, mature person with certain innate job skills.

You don't need us to tell you not to wear surfer jams or bring your mother to an interview. Nor do we offer Machiavellian strategies on manipulating potential employers. (If you insist on using this kind of information, the Career Planning or Business shelves of your local bookstore are filled with these kinds of volumes, such as *Dressing to Look Like Donald Trump (Before Bankruptcy)* or *Chainsawing Your Way Through Job Interviews*, to mention but two.)

This book has been created with the specific needs of the liberal arts graduate in mind. First and foremost, this book tells you which companies hire liberal arts graduates and who are the best employers among them. Second, it shows how you can package your assets as a liberal arts graduate.

Before getting into that, we want to give you some perspective on the job market as it specifically relates to the liberal arts graduate. It's interesting stuff, but strictly background. So feel free to skip it. You already know why you need a job, or you wouldn't be reading this now.

Why should I read this book?

For only one reason: to give yourself an edge in the job market. Your own talents notwithstanding, it's a jungle out there and the competition is becoming increasingly cunning.

Consider the following:

- College enrollment has continued to rise in most states despite the recession, according to the American Council on Education. That means more recent grads chasing fewer jobs.

- Every year about 75,000 students graduate with MBA degrees.

- Less than one-half of the companies seeking liberal arts graduates recruit on campuses, according to a comprehensive study on liberal education and the corporation.

What about all those workers retiring? Someone's got to take their places.

If you are a college student now or a recent grad, then you're what demographers affectionately call "baby busters," the generation that succeeded the "baby boomers." Boomers, born of parents in the post–World War II decades, number about 76 million. Busters, born in the so-called birth-dearth years of the late 1960s and 1970s, number fewer than half that many.

There are no hard statistics on the job opportunities for busters, but common sense can tell you that busters face unprecedented competition in the job market. Pathways for advancement are clogged with boomers, the majority of whom will not retire for the next couple of decades. Even worse, there's now a recession to contend with.

Just how bad is the current job market for new college grads, particularly liberal arts majors?

It's not a pretty picture. In fact, it's the worst that most of us can remember.

"We've been through up-and-down cycles before, but this is the worst I've seen in 30 years. Firms that were trying to hire 2,000 new employees [in 1990] may be only hiring 200," said H. Edward Babbush, placement director at California State University at Long Beach, in a front-page article in the *New York Times* in April 1991. And that was *before* the government officially acknowledged there was a recession.

From June 1990 to January 1992, 4.5 million jobs were lost. And unlike previous recessions, a larger portion of the jobs lost in this recession belonged to white-collar management positions. Industries that have been particularly hard hit are those that traditionally have been sources of good jobs for liberal arts grads, including advertising, mass media, retail, and financial services.

Here's one more sobering fact: In recessionary times, businesses tend to hire more business majors and fewer liberal arts majors.

You mean business has a built-in bias against liberal arts grads?

Yes, for the last 20 years. In a 1983 Northwestern University survey, only 20 percent of the 260 companies responding expected an increase in the hiring of liberal arts graduates in the foreseeable future, while 40 percent expected a *decrease*. Contrast that to the 69 percent that expected to increase the hiring of non–liberal arts majors.

Three years later, a Research & Forecast study showed that only 12 percent of senior-level executives at 108 companies preferred liberal arts graduates, versus 51 percent who preferred computer science and engineering majors or 27 percent who preferred business majors.

Is it any wonder, then, that between 1970 and 1985 the proportion of first-year students professing interest in the liberal arts declined from 40 percent to 21 percent?

Does this declining interest in liberal arts justify business's bias against liberal arts grads?

No! Studies conducted by corporations consistently demonstrate that liberal arts majors perform as well as and frequently *better than* their business, engineering, and computer science counterparts. Here are two examples:

1. An in-depth investigation into educational competence traced the careers of corporate employees at AT&T for 27 years. The study revealed that nearly half—46 percent—of its humanities and social science graduates reached mid-to-higher levels of management after 20 years, but only 25 percent of its engineers and 31 percent of its business majors rose that high.

2. In the late 1970s, Chase Manhattan Bank, the nation's third largest, began tracking about 80 new BA and MBA graduates who entered the same specialized training course on the development of credit and risk analysis. One to four years later, their supervisors were asked to rate the trainees' performance, specifically in their "application of credit skills on the job with emphasis on quantitative analytic ability," an area one might expect the MBAs to perform better in than the BAs. On the contrary, Chase found that the BAs outscored the MBAs. Of the low performers, 60 percent held MBAs; of the high performers, 60 percent held BAs.

Here's one more fact that will raise your eyebrows: 38 percent of today's CEOs majored in the liberal arts, according to a recent report in *Fortune* magazine.

What kind of companies, then, *do* hire liberal arts grads?

As you will see in Chapter 3, companies in all kinds of fields hire liberal arts grads: accounting, advertising, agriculture, automobile renting/leasing, banking, building, computer services, fashion, financial services, hotel, health care, insurance, management consulting, office supplies, printing, telecommunications, and toys. And almost every other field is covered in the comprehensive list in Chapter 5 (as well as the governmental agency employers profiled in Chapter 4).

So why do some companies favor liberal arts graduates while others don't?

We'd like to chalk it up to matters of taste and breeding. It seems there are two types of companies in the corporate jungle, and they tend to cross all fields of business.

Researcher Rosabeth Moss Kanter in her 1985 study of 31 firms identified two types of companies: progressive and nonprogressive. Progressive companies were characterized by innovative programs, such as quality circles and flexible work schedules; in general, they strived to improve the quality of work conditions. Senior management of these companies was dominated by liberal arts graduates, and not too surprisingly, such companies tended to hire more liberal arts graduates and promoted them faster than nonprogressive companies.

All companies were created equal. But when it comes to the liberal arts graduate, some are more equal than others.

TWO

Getting Your Foot in the Door . . . and Keeping It There

Think of the information in this chapter as the requisite provisions in your job hunt. It's divided into five sections:

1. Red Hot Chili *Peppers*: These are shameless confidence builders. We like to think of them as EST—Excellent Scholarship Talk. You have a liberal arts degree and you're great!

2. *Attitude:* Now that you have the confidence to pick up the phone, the next step is developing the right job-finding attitude. A pinch of chutzpah, a spoonful of initiative, and voila! A recipe for success.

3. *Research:* Attitude will take you only so far. Information is the name of the game in business. Know thy (potential) employer.

4. *Resumes:* As in politics, putting the right spin on your life story can mean victory or defeat.

5. *The Interview:* Rehearsal's over: it's showtime. As in show biz, you gotta leave the audience with an impression (costume optional).

RED HOT CHILI *PEPPERS*

Of the hundreds of people interviewed for this book—from corporate executives and professional career counselors to recent liberal arts graduates—two ironic, conflicting ideas emerged with almost unanimous consensus: First, a liberal arts education is highly valued in today's job market; second, despite this fact, liberal arts graduates still lack confidence, clarity, and direction when looking for their first jobs.

If you're one of the millions of liberal arts graduates who are long on education and short on confidence, the following comments might give you a boost:

> *It will never be easier for you to find a job than it is right after college. You will never again be less expensive and not expected to have rigorous experience in your field.*
>
> Susanna Rabb Bailin, Career Counselor
> Rabb Planning Center, Inc., Cambridge, Mass.

> *Liberal arts graduates have a natural curiosity, further honed by their schooling, about the interests and motivations of others. It's this, I suspect, that leads many of those who are products of a liberal arts education to become such excellent business people.*
>
> William W. Adams, Chair and President
> Armstrong World Industries, Inc.

> *An employee who has the demonstrated ability to think independently is always of value, no matter how competitive the job market is. Liberal*

arts students are able to bring to a company like T.J. Maxx well-developed analytical and communication skills.

Richard Lesser, President
T.J. Maxx

We prefer liberal arts graduates over business graduates, because they are more open-minded as far as starting off a career.

Diane Petersen, Human Resources Manager
Benefit Trust Life Insurance Company

One of the advantages of hiring liberal arts graduates is the flexibility they bring to their career and job assignments. They are able to go into many areas instead of being highly specialized in one career field.

Harold McLeod, Director of Personnel Development
Burlington Industries, Inc.

Liberal arts students have an emphasis on communication skills. They're able to think on their feet because they've had a smorgasbord of academic challenges in their classes.

Chris Ryan, Manager of Campus Relations
EDS (Electronic Data Systems)

Liberal arts graduates have a broad-based background they can turn into a plus. They should approach their job search with the idea that they have something to offer as opposed to apologizing for their liberal arts degrees.

Bing Spitler, Manager
College Relations and Organization Development
Armstrong World Industries, Inc.

Just because you don't know anything about cars, don't turn down an interview with Chrysler. Liberal arts majors can look at something and see how it can be used in the best way. A lot of the skills you think apply only to a given field are really generic and have a wider application.

Jamie Butcher, Production Planner
R.R. Donnelly & Sons

Liberal arts students are well-rounded. That's what today's business wants to see. They are moving away from the specialized business person to ones who are more versatile.

Lee Adourian, Supervisor
Chubb Group of Insurance Companies

ATTITUDE

It's okay to show employers *attitude*—confidence, chutzpah, initiative. But unless you're auditioning for a Broadway play, a little attitude goes a *long* way when you're job-hunting. In other words, keep it to a minimum.

On the other hand, display even a flicker of the wrong attitude (arrogance, anti-business, I-want-it-all-now, laziness) to a college recruiter, and you've shot yourself in the foot.

Anti-Business/Anti-Sales

Whether or not you have planned a career in business, the reality is that most liberal arts graduates end up working for corporations. That's where most of the good jobs are. So even though you may have dreamed of going to law school, writing novels, or being a movie star, you are looking for a job in the business world. The worst thing you can do is think and act as if a business career is a consolation prize beneath your talents and principles.

> *One of the problems with liberal arts students is they are involved with ethical questions and they don't see a home for themselves in business. But they can have a great home in business. Many tend to think of sales with a misconception—that it's dirty. If they stop and look around, they see that the vast majority of people in business are professionals who are not doing anything unethical or against their personal values.*
>
> Bing Spitler, Manager
> College Relations and Organization Development
> Armstrong World Industries, Inc.

Arrogance

It's common for some people looking for their first real job to have a cocky, unrealistic attitude about their capabilities and what to expect. If you've ever been referred to as a know-it-all, repeat the following phrase 100 times before each interview: "I don't know it all now, so I can't have it all now."

> *At an early stage in their careers, most people anticipate they'll get as much out as they put in, and that's not true. A "paying-your-dues"-type philosophy is something that most liberal arts graduates don't want to*

accept. You have to ask how ambitious you are and do you have what it takes to be successful?

Craig A. Marr, Corporate Personnel Manager
Enterprise Rent-a-Car

If liberal arts graduates know how the real world works, they'll be fine. If they have the realistic expectation that their education is about to begin now that they're out of school, they'll be fine.

Carlee Cashin, Management Trainee
Enterprise Rent-a-Car

I kind of turned around what some people might see as a disadvantage: a liberal arts degree. I turned it around to make it an advantage. I stressed that with all the different types of courses I took, I could learn anything. I said, "If you try to teach me something, I can learn it and adapt to it."

Michelle Morrow, Inventory Control Specialist
J.C. Penney Co.

Student Mentality

Some liberal arts graduates have a hard time shaking the student attitude that you have to earn 90-100 points for an A, 80-90 for a B, and so on. If you've worked in a business atmosphere during college, you've probably already learned that business is more subjective and far less predictable than school. And if you're really smart, you've already picked up the idea that to even get your foot in the door in this economy (let alone ahead of the pack once the door opens), the game starts at 100 and goes up from there. Come in at 80 or 90 at some companies and you're not even in the game.

School teaches individuals a sustaining lifestyle. I exemplified that. I did just what needed to get done to get by. But it's where you go above and beyond that you are rewarded once you get into the working world. Some people are never able to break from that school mentality. That doesn't work here.

Kirk Johnson, Supervisor
Benefit Trust Life Insurance Company

Lack of Enthusiasm

Another fatal mistake you can make is showing up at an interview without knowledge or excitement about the job or the company. Here's where your college skills can pay off: do your homework. The only way to develop enthusiasm is by doing your research first. Then, if you don't get excited, cancel the interview. Don't expect recruiters to sell you on their company; they expect you to sell them on yourself.

Sometimes interviewers will ask the question: "Do you really want this job?" or "Why do you want this job?" If the student hesitates, we know they're not mentally sold yet. They should have done their research on our company. Researching for an interview is very important.

Bing Spitler, Manager
College Relations and Organization Development
Armstrong World Industries, Inc.

On the other hand, too much eagerness and too little finesse will blow you out of the water. Try not to seem desperate.

We had one person who called over and over again about a couple of jobs. We're looking for enthusiasm to a certain point. But you've got to know protocol.

Jean Lim, Employment Services Officer
Seafirst Bank

RESEARCH

One of the most often repeated pieces of advice you'll find when you read the profiles in this book is: "The more you know about our company and the job you're interviewing for, the better your chances of getting a job offer."

Lynn Nemser, a corporate human resources consultant with Partners in Performance, Inc., in Pittsburg, says liberal arts students who continue to use their good student approach to job-hunting are the most successful. "Research is absolutely critical. They should approach their job search the same way they approached their academic studies. If they start their career explorations the same way they start their courses, they are going to be successful."

There's no shortcut for research. Use all the sources available, including the profiles in this book. Basically, you have 50 prototypes right here under your nose; if the company you're interviewing with isn't here, you'll need to dig up the same type of information that we've included.

·Find out everything you can about the industry in general and a company in particular by scanning library databases for current newspaper, magazine, or trade journal articles. Also check reference books and the card catalog for any books that might have been written about the company.

Here are the sources and instructions we used in gathering information for this book:

Library Research

1. *InfoTrak*, a computer database that surveys most newspapers, magazines, and trade journals.
2. *Value Line Investment Survey*, a monthly publication that provides current information on major corporations.
3. *Business Periodicals Index*, a listing of publications that might pertain to the industry you're interested in.
4. *National Newspaper Index*

Call Company Headquarters

Ask the company's public relations office to send you a copy of the most recent annual report and a 10-K Report. These will provide information on the company's earnings, forecasting, competition, and products and services. Also ask for any recruitment or benefits brochures they might provide for college recruiting. (Your career guidance office may already have these.)

Call Your School's Alumni Office

Ask if there are any graduates who work for the companies you're interviewing with. It's especially important to talk to people who are doing the job you want. Call those people and ask to meet with them or ask questions on the phone. Your goal is to find out what they do, if you could do it, and if you're right for it. Also ask if they can help you in any way.

Questions to Answer

Company History

- How many employees?
- How old is the company?
- Where are the company headquarters? Are there any other locations?
- What business activities is the company involved in? What are its main products or services?

- Who are its customers or clients? Who are its competitors?

- What is its market share? Annual revenues?

- How is it weathering the recession? Have there been lay-offs?

Job Characteristics

- What qualifications in terms of grades, work experience, or curriculum and background are required or preferred?

- What personality traits are desired?

- What is the corporate culture and philosophy? Mission statement? Dress code? Working conditions?

- What types of jobs are available to liberal arts graduates?

- What is the starting salary or range?

- What types of training programs are offered?

- What are the benefits?

- What is the specific hiring process? (How many interviews, with whom, resumes, transcripts?)

- What are the drawbacks to working there?

- What is the interviewing process? How many? Where? What questions do they ask?

- What's a typical day or week like?

- Are there any advice and tips for getting a job there?

Make a Personal Visit

Visit the store, facility, office, or corporate headquarters before your interview, if you can. This will help you get the feel of what it would be like to work there. Don't be afraid to chat with a receptionist or other employees you may encounter. Be straightforward and ask them what it's like to work there and if they can give you any advice.

The information, knowledge, and insight you gather during this research process will give you confidence for interviews and crucial information to tailor your resume.

RESUMES

Most experts have different opinions about how to prepare a resume. We suggest that you consult some of the many career books that focus on resumes and make your own decisions about length, style, and form. Keep these things in mind:

On the first go-round, your resume will be scanned quickly, so design it with plenty of white space, no clutter and with the important items standing out (objective, hook, education, etc.).

The following are specific suggestions for shaping your liberal arts background into a marketable asset.

Put a Business Spin on Nonbusiness Experience

Forget the idea that you have no relevant experience. You do. The skills you have developed in school, organizations, or part-time jobs are the same skills you'll need when you work for a corporation. You just need to learn how to package them and express them verbally.

Consultant Lynn Nemser, who in addition to helping corporations find the right people, developed and conducted career seminars and workshops for liberal arts graduates at the University of Pennsylvania, says any liberal arts courses you've taken are relevant whether or not the subject matter is. "Ask yourself what you did in college. You read, researched, explored, analyzed, summarized, wrote. . . . Those are employable skills and talents. Those are things you do when you have a job."

Before preparing your resume, make a list of all the skills you developed in school, organizations, or other extracurricular activities in which you participated. Keep in mind that almost all employers we've surveyed and interviewed say they are looking for liberal arts graduates who have well-developed skills in communication, leadership, and teamwork. Be sure to emphasize these qualities when you prepare your resume.

Put a Business Spin on Your Skills

You've accumulated many skills from your school and extracurricular activities. Here are some words and phrases you might use on your resume, as well as in interviews, to describe your capabilities:

Analytical thought	Organize ideas, people, events
Analyze ideas and data	Meeting deadlines
Assessment techniques	Motivating
Budgeting	Multiple priorities

Conflict resolution	Planning
Creativity	Presentation skills
Critical reading	Prioritization
Delegating	Problem solving
Flexibility	Strategizing
Follow-through	Strategic planning
Goal setting	Team projects
Interpersonal skills	Time management

This list might seem intimidating, but if you have ever been on a team or worked in a group or on a project, most of these terms apply to you.

State Your Objective

After giving your name, the date, and your phone number, the first thing you'll write is your objective. According to Nemser, this is where you must frame your resume and demonstrate to the employer you know what you could do for the company. "This is the greatest difficulty with liberal arts students. They need to help the employer translate something. They have to narrow it down for the employer."

Here are some examples of objectives:

- Entry-level position in marketing, market research or other facet of consumer behavior

- To use analytical and research skills in a small-business setting

- Position in a management-training program in the area of . . . (sales, marketing, administration, customer service, manufacturing, management consulting, etc.)

If you've narrowed your interests down to a specific industry such as retail, insurance, fashion, management consulting, or financial services, add the particular industry. For example: *Entry-level position in marketing, market research, or other facet of consumer behavior in the advertising industry*

If you can't make up your mind as to which field or industry you would like to enter, make up several different resumes, each with different objectives and hooks if necessary.

Using the Hook

After the objective, the most important eye-catcher will be the "hook" that grabs the person scanning your resume. This should be your most outstanding quality, skill, or accomplishment—the one that the employer values most, and it should be the first item highlighted on your resume. It can also be a conversation-starter in interviews.

As mentioned before, your hook might be different for different employers, depending on their requirements. The point is to accentuate something positive that you know is of great value to a particular employer. Consider these hooks:

High GPA	Independent studies pertinent to
Prestigious school	a particular job
Academic or other relevant	Research project that relates to
awards	the job
Specific major or course work	Relevant job experience
valued by the employer	Campus leadership roles
	Teamwork activities

Translate Previous Job Experiences

Most liberal arts students merely list the summer or part-time jobs they've held without translating that experience for the employer. You need to make it relevant to the corporate employer and demonstrate that you get the big picture. Do this by using the skills list mentioned previously and by relating your experience to the field of expertise and to the particular industry. Some examples are:

- *Customer Service:* McDonald's, clerk . . .

- *Health Care Delivery:* Blue Cross/Blue Shield, receptionist

- *Leadership and Management:* County Recreation Department, life-guard and camp counselor

THE INTERVIEW

Everything we've told you so far in this chapter is a rehearsal for your interviews. Everything you've put into developing your confidence, attitude, knowledge (research), and resume will, in some way, be projected in your interviews.

There's only one thing we haven't mentioned: *The first impression is crucial.* Unfortunately, you'll have only 60 seconds to pass this preliminary test, and if you fail, you won't get another chance. So, do whatever you have to do to get the right outfit, hairstyle, or jewelry to fit the image of a particular company. Ask people who work in corporations, friends, even professional image consultants, if necessary, for their advice.

Here are some brief interviewing tips corporate recruiters and liberal arts graduates offer:

1. Think "final exam." Make a list of questions you'll be asked and role-play with a friend.
2. Relate your career interests to those of the company (e.g., computers, fashion, insurance, banking, finance).
3. Demonstrate your knowledge of recent positive news events relating to the company, especially those that appeared in industry publications (e.g., new products or services, industry awards, mergers or acquisitions, new management and so on).
4. Mention something you happen to know about one of the company's major competitors or clients.
5. Emphasize your teamwork orientation (find out what "quality circles" are, then discuss).
6. Ask the interviewer to describe a typical day or week in the job for which you're applying.
7. Use industry-specific buzzwords (and know exactly what they mean).
8. Use the phrases mentioned above to describe your skills and experience.
9. Don't be afraid to pause and summarize your thoughts before answering a thought-provoking question.
10. Ask specific, informed questions about the company's training program.
11. Look for opportunities to demonstrate your knowledge of current events, keeping these comments or asides brief and intelligent.
12. Describe how you managed your time and priorities by juggling many courses, activities, and jobs.

The Art of the Close

Conclude the interview just as a salesperson would close a sale. Give a quick summary of your qualifications and reiterate your hook, or what you can do for the company. Then ask, "Do you see any disparities between my abilities and what you're looking for?" Try to rebut any objections on the spot. Then, briefly state your qualifications again.

Don't Leave Empty-Handed

The least you should ever get from an interview is a referral to someone else who might hire you. Better yet, try to go away with an offer, an appointment for a second interview, an agreement of what the next step is, a promised call back, or a recommendation for another job within the company.

Follow-Ups

Follow up every interview with a call and a letter reiterating your specific qualifications or particular asset you bring to the company. But be sincere, and realistic in your abilities; don't overdo it.

YOUR FIRST YEAR ON THE JOB

Although the purpose of this book is strictly to help you find the right job and career, in the process of interviewing, we were told about some mistakes many liberal arts graduates make in the beginning. Revisit this section after you get your job.

Navigating Corporate Politics

- Get to know the important people in the company as soon as possible.
- Avoid getting caught up in gossip or in other people's conflicts.
- Be wary of giving out information or repeating conversations, even when it seems innocuous.
- Don't criticize your superiors (or anyone else for that matter). Assume your boss has more information than you have; decisions don't always have to make sense to you.

Forming Alliances

- Be careful who you form alliances with. Observe and don't participate until you're sure.
- Try to develop a mentor relationship with a respected superior as soon as possible.

Working Hard

- The first impression is the key to your success or failure. Begin by establishing who you are and what your work ethic is, because that initial corporate mind-set regarding you is very difficult to change.
- Get rid of the student mentality. Go above and beyond what is required.

THREE

The Best Companies for Liberal Arts Graduates

Here's a fact that many liberal arts majors may not enjoy discovering: whether they graduated this year or 10 years ago, 75 percent of all college graduates will find employment within corporations.

The companies in this chapter are the best of the lot for the liberal arts graduate who doesn't want to spend his or her career in the typing pool. These companies not only have a history of hiring liberal arts graduates, but they also continue to hire them in spite of a bad economy.

NO APOLOGIES NECESSARY

What's more, these companies value what the liberal arts graduate can bring to their organizations. You won't need to apologize for your chosen field of undergraduate study; these employers recognize that the "variety of ideas explored by the liberal arts educated person gives him or her a resourcefulness generally superior to that of someone who has had technical training only" (from a recent article in *Personnel Journal* entitled "Why Executives Need a Liberal Arts Education").

That's not to say that any of these companies is perfect. We're convinced the perfect company does not exist; however, these companies come closer to the ideal than any others.

PERFECT EMPLOYER, INC.

What would be the ideal company for the liberal arts graduate? We think it would be one founded by a liberal arts graduate whose current top management, most important the CEO, held liberal arts degrees. The company would be owned largely by its employees and offer above-average salaries and generous, merit-based bonuses.

The corporate culture would be open, informal, and friendly without being messianic or obtrusive. The management style would be team-oriented and open-door; employees would be encouraged to think creatively and offer ideas and solutions. White-collar employees could air their grievances to an independent ombudsman without risk of losing their jobs.

The work environment would be attractive, emphasizing individual expression rather than corporate uniformity. (No cubicles, and windows that open!) All employees would be able to use a large, in-house health club. Ongoing mental and physical health workshops would supplement the complete medical/dental benefits plan. An in-house child-care facility would make working parents happy and productive, and an employee cafeteria would serve healthful food.

Speaking of child care, our perfect company would allow for a four-month paid leave of absence for new mothers and fathers. It would also allow a parent to jump off the corporate fast-track for up to two years and return to the same position or another equivalent position.

Overtime would not be encouraged, and when necessary, employees would be paid accordingly. Three weeks' vacation time would be offered, with two-day increases for every year employed.

Ongoing training would allow employees to keep pace with the latest development in their fields. The company would pay for continuing education in the liberal arts, knowing that a true liberal arts education is a continuous, life-enriching experience. After five years of employment, the company would allow employees to take a six-month sabbatical at half-pay to explore any opportunity that will somehow enrich their lives.

Finally, our perfect company would be a member in good standing of its local, national, and international communities as well as a leader in nondiscriminatory hiring practices and ecological innovations.

CHECKLIST

When considering taking a job with a prospective employer, you might want to see how the employer measures up against our ideal company in terms of the following:

- Starting Salary
- Bonuses
- Medical Benefits
- Training
- Opportunities for Advancement
- Hours (official and nonofficial)
- Corporate Culture and Philosophy
- Work Environment
- Perquisites (health club, company car, etc.)
- Forums for Employee Grievances
- Child Care and Parental Leave Policy
- CEO (does he or she have a liberal arts degree?)
- Continuing Education (in the liberal arts or otherwise)

HOW TO USE THIS CHAPTER

The companies are arranged alphabetically, with three parts to every profile:

The Boilerplate: A thumbnail sketch of the company with particular emphasis on how to get a job there and the company's distinct advantages and disadvantages.

The Profile: An in-depth look at the company's history and its recruiting, hiring, and training policies as they relate to liberal arts graduates.

Report from the Trenches: A first-person account by an employee with a liberal arts degree about what it's *really* like to work at that particular company.

CONSIDER ALL THE POSSIBILITIES

You may not envision yourself as having a career in insurance or building products, but don't limit your options. Some of the very best companies in this chapter may not be in the most glamorous industries. You can use these profiles to get a glimpse of what it would be like to work in various fields.

AETNA LIFE & CASUALTY CO.

151 Farmington Ave.
Hartford, CT 06156
(203) 273-1350

Other Employment Centers
Offices ranging in size from 10 to 300 employees in about 40 states

Products/Services
Leading provider of insurance and financial services

Number of Employees
48,000 nationwide

Job Opportunities
Entry level positions in insurance underwriting, marketing, claims, and bond underwriting

Starting Salary
$21,000–$25,000, depending on location, position, and prior experience

Major Pluses

+ Training (employees are encouraged to participate in a wide variety of company-sponsored seminars, workshops, and courses to enhance their professional skills and advancement in the company; at the Aetna Institute for Corporate Education, a full-time staff of 60 teaches 200 to 400 students each day)
+ Incentive/savings program (employees can save up to six percent of their salaries; and the first five percent is matched by the company)
+ Excellent benefits, including noncontributory pension program, maternity and parental leave, work-at-home arrangements, and flexible work schedules

Drawbacks

− Company's enormous size tends to overwhelm many new employees

Corporate Philosophy

Company promotes enthusiasm among its employees and values initiative and self-motivation

Atmosphere

Very professional, conservative, and formal on the whole, although individual departments often have a much more laid-back feel

Working Conditions

Frequent changes are the norm here, so employees must be flexible and adaptable.

Tips for Getting a Job

- Show a strong academic performance.
- Demonstrate previous work experience and knowledge of business environment.
- Accentuate leadership ability and potential.
- Mention participation in campus activities.
- Research the industry before applying. Know the different career areas available.

Profile

Established in 1853, Aetna is not only one of the nation's oldest insurance companies but also one of its largest corporations. In 1991, Value Line Investment Survey listed Aetna's assets at more than $90 billion and projected its overall investment outlook to 1996 as excellent, giving it an A for financial strength.

Opportunities

Aetna offers a myriad of career opportunities, but few people outside the insurance industry know this. Much too often, college graduates apply for positions at Aetna without knowing anything about the insurance business.

"I think within our industry there are a lot of misconceptions about who we are and what we do," says Lorenzo Pace, administrator of college relations. "Oftentimes, the liberal arts major sees us as insurance salesmen, meaning that's the only type of career area we offer."

Room for Growth

Once you sign on with Aetna, there are many opportunities to try different career areas within the company after learning the specifics of the industry.

"When they have fully grasped the technicalities associated with an entry level position, including claims, marketing or underwriting, or they can avail themselves of other opportunities, such as a support role, such as in staffing, law, public affairs, communications, or training," Pace says. "Because they have industry experience, it's a lot easier for them to move into other areas."

More and More Liberal Arts Grads

In the past few years, Aetna has been hiring more and more liberal arts graduates. In fact, liberal arts and business grads are hired in equal numbers. Liberal arts grads traditionally start out in areas such as underwriting, marketing, and claims, although recently positions in the technology division and the bond underwriting area have been opening up. Flexibility and openmindedness are key traits Aetna wants in its employees. That's why liberal arts graduates are valued here.

Getting Hired

About half of the college graduates that Aetna hires contact the company directly. The other half are recruited on college campuses nationwide. In this case, the first step in the hiring process is an on-campus screening, usually followed by a second interview at the home office. In some areas, a panel interview is required.

Human resources personnel are generally responsible for the initial screening of job candidates, but the second interview is always conducted by the hiring supervisor.

What You Can Expect

Advancement hinges entirely on the individual and his or her performance. The first 18 months are typically spent in the training program. After about three years with Aetna, a formal position is almost always ensured.

At that point, there is an opportunity to move into other areas within the company. Management opportunities and supervisory positions are always future prospects.

Internships

Aetna likes employees who can take the initiative and who have some knowledge of the insurance industry and of Aetna. One way of getting a head start is by pursing the company's internship and college co-op programs. Internships are offered primarily during the summer after a student's sophomore or junior year. These paid positions offer a preview of the industry and the various career opportunities available. Interns work on specific company projects throughout the summer.

The co-op program is for students who take a semester off from school and work full-time in a paid position. Although for most schools no course credit is available, the company will surely look favorably on those students who show interest and ambition early on.

Report from the Trenches

DONNA BRODZINSKI

Position: Programmer Analyst
Age: 29
Earnings: Low 30s
School: University of Connecticut, Storrs, Conn.
Major: Math

When Donna graduated from college, she began working at Travelers Insurance as a systems analyst. After 3½ years, she decided to pursue a more technical career path as a programmer analyst. Because Travelers had no immediate openings in this area and Aetna offered more in terms of salary and training, she accepted a position as a programmer trainee at Aetna in 1989. Here's what she told us:

When I began as a programmer trainee, I went through a ten-week training course. As a trainee, you basically go through the motions, proving your abilities, coding, and working on various projects.

After a year, I became a programmer analyst. I stayed in the same area (claims), but I got more specific assignments and more responsibility.

My goal is to become a senior program analyst. In 10 to 15 years, my highest goal is to be vice president of the claims area.

Good Training

One of the best things about working for Aetna is its continuous on-the-job training. Each department is allotted money for in-house training. Right now I'm taking technical courses, but they also offer managerial classes. In your free time, you can listen to audiocassettes the company provides to get more versed in whatever subject you choose.

Competitive Salaries

Another advantage is that salaries are competitive. The company has tried to stay on top, a little above competitors.

A Typical Day

We run large volumes of claims through the system overnight. If there is any problem, I spend the morning troubleshooting. If not, I continue to work on assigned projects. For example, the business area might call and say they have a new client we need to get in the system. So I would do modifications for the business area.

Corporate Culture

The atmosphere is conservative. The majority of employees wear suits. There are lots of activities to get involved in to help the company. For instance, I volunteered for what they call the "high performance group." As part of the group, we conducted a survey to learn what employees felt about the company. We calculated the data and sent a letter to the whole claims area reporting the responses. (Results showed staff were on edge about their jobs because of recent changes and layoffs.)

Working Atmosphere

We have fun. There are lots of recreational activities, such as aerobics classes at the fitness center. We have a birthday club and a donuts club. Within our area we have a charity club. Every Friday at the end of the month, we donate a dollar to a charity and get to dress down for a day, wear jeans or something nonprofessional. That eases the pressure.

It's a very young atmosphere. Most of the staff are in their 20s to 30s. Managers are in their lower 30s.

Access to Management

The high-level executives know us personally. They hand out our checks. They're open to new suggestions. Before our monthly departmental meetings, they ask for feedback, either anonymously or with your name on it. So they do listen at times. The staff does have somewhat of a voice.

Main Drawback

At times it can be too stressful. Management deadlines can be unrealistic.

Advice

If you're aiming for a technical career, get as much programming training as you can. The more technical you are, the more favorably you'll be looked upon. Every company is going technical. If you don't want to be technical, you still need that background. Then you can work from that point.

Don't Be Naive

Liberal arts graduates are often naive; they don't know how corporations work. They don't know how to deal with a superior or how to ask for what they need. To become familiar with corporate life, I would suggest an internship or a co-op situation where work is part of your college curriculum. Basically, in college you work on your own. Here you have to work on a team—you have to be able to work with other people.

AGWAY, INC.
333 Butternut Dr.
De Witt, NY 13214

Mailing Address
P.O. Box 4933
Syracuse, NY 13221
(315) 449-7061

Other Employment Centers
Syracruse is Agway's headquarters and home to about 1,000 employees. The vast majority of employees, however, work at various locations scattered throughout the 10 northeastern states. Agway's petroleum division also has companies in Illinois, Wisconsin, and Kentucky.

Products/Services
Nonprofit agricultural cooperative that operates several different companies, including a retail chain that carries almost anything a farmer would need, an energy products division that provides petroleum and other energy products to farmers, a farm equipment leasing company, and an insurance company that specializes in insurance for the agriculture industry

Number of Employees
8,000

Job Opportunities
Assistant managers

Starting Salary
About $23,000

Major Pluses

+ Training (one-year, hands-on management training program that leads directly to manager or assistant manager position)
+ Potential earnings (after two to three years, from $33,000 to $42,000; after seven to ten years, from $48,000 to $55,000)

Drawbacks

− Willingness to move four or five times before reaching a general management position

Corporate Philosophy

Agway is a farm cooperative and goes out of its way to maintain a down-to-earth relationship with its customers and employees. This people-oriented approach is reflected in the working environment. Management places high emphasis on longevity, so promotion is almost exclusively from within.

Atmosphere

Dress is casual (don't look for any IBM types here); almost everyone is on a first-name basis.

Working Conditions

Relatively small company-owned and operated retail stores

Tips for Getting a Job

• Emphasize and demonstrate any activities, especially leadership roles.
• Show knowledge of or interest in agriculture.
• Emphasize internships or work experience.
• Know a good deal about the company before your interview. Do research and visit one of its stores.

Profile

With more than 95,000 farmer members, Agway is one of the country's largest farm cooperatives. It is listed among Fortune 500 companies and employs more than 8,000 people. Yet this is a far cry from the fast-track, high-intensity world of Wall Street. Agway's deep commitment to its customers is reflected in its emphasis on rural, down-to-earth, honest-to-goodness values. As an Agway employee, you don't become a small part of a large bureaucracy. You essentially become part of an extended family.

Training

Agway has a good reason for favoring longevity: it invests about $50,000 per trainee. You will start out in the management development program, which means committing yourself to a year-long, hands-on training program. This typically involves working side by side with the manager of the store where you are located, as well as attending some classroom sessions in Syracuse. After that, you can expect to manage a small (10-to-15–employee) store or petroleum company and move up from there.

Because almost all promotion is from within, most employees start at the bottom of the corporate ladder. Eleanor Rich, manager of recruitment and management development, speaks from experience: "I went through the training program. I was assistant manager for a year, then got my own store and managed a bigger store after that. That's pretty typical. Now, I'm in personnel, and a lot of people will move around like that."

It's an unwritten rule at Agway that once promoted, you remain in that position for at least a year. And more often than not, moving up requires moving away. Rich explains: "We have locations all over the place, and when we train people in a certian location, we do it with the understanding that at the end of the year they're mobile and able to go wherever we might need them."

Qualifications

You don't need to know a lot about agriculture to get a job with Agway, unless you plan to work for the leasing division, Telmark. But a strong interest in agriculture helps. Rich grew up on a farm and says working for Agway is "a way to maintain that farm connection and yet not be there on the farm itself."

Otherwise, Agway looks for people with high initiative and strong people skills. When recruiting on campus, Rich says she looks for people who have been involved in clubs and organizations; leadership and work experience are perhaps the two most important aspects. "Having an agricultural background is really a plus, but just having that alone is not nearly enough," she says. "They need to have good people skills, a good ability to talk to people. . . . The ones who impress me are the ones who are obviously interested in the company. If they've obviously taken the time to visit some of our locations and they've found out enough to ask some good questions, that's very impressive."

If you live anywhere in the Northeast, learning about Agway shouldn't be a problem. You may have already visited one of its 250 stores or 150 gas stations. Setting up an interview shouldn't be a problem either. Agway recruits on most major campuses in early spring. Second interviews are held at the end of March in Syracuse, and job offers soon follow.

Report from the Trenches

CHRIS FIVEK
Position: Personnel Membership Manager, Agway Energy Products
Age: Late 30s

Earnings: High 50s (est.)
School: Albright College, Reading, Penn.
Major: Psychology/Sociology

What has surprised Chris Fivek the most about Agway is the advancement potential within the company. During his 16 years with the petroleum division, Fivek has moved nine times and worked his way up from management trainee to membership manager. He says the moves were a small price to pay for the career opportunities. Here's why he has stayed with the company that hired him right out of college:

At the time I came into Agway Energy Products, the most I knew about petroleum was how to put gas in my car and how to change oil. That was it. Some people think, "Wow, what do I know about the oil business?" But that's easily taught to someone. Going through a liberal arts curriculum, people learn how to learn.

When I interviewed with Agway, one of the things that was very attractive to them was the number of groups I had participated in, both on-campus and off-campus. People skills are crucial in this type of company. After all, gas is gas, and diesel is diesel; the only thing that makes a difference between us and our competitors is the people.

Training

As a management trainee, no two days were ever the same. Sometimes coming out of school, people are used to being spoon-fed. The biggest change when I became a trainee was that I had to have a lot of initiative. I always thought there was a progression on how fast you moved that was beyond your control. I guess it surprised me that it wasn't up to someone else. It was up to me.

I started out in 1975 as a plant manager (after a year as management trainee). Six months later I became an operations manager at a different plant. Six months after that, I got my first plant manager position. After five and a half years with Agway, I became a district manager and had eight to 10 operations reporting to me.

Some companies will say it, but Agway really does promote from within. The president of pretroleum, the manager, and three of the executive vice presidents were all management trainees at one time.

Mobility

In the first five years with Agway I had moved four times. In 16 years, I've moved nine times. That's on the high side, but with Agway's promotion-from-within policy, it's very important to be mobile. Agway doesn't go out and hire a personnel specialist. It hires people to go into the training program, and through the training program I think you see the scope of what the company is all about. If I sit down with a manager now, I can say, "Look, I've been there."

Corporate Culture

This is a performance-based company. It's not who you know, it's your ability to motivate your people. It's also a very down-to-earth company. I can call up the president of petroleum and say, "This is Chris from the Harrisburg office," and he'll know who I am. Anybody in the plant system can call up any of the executives and not have to go through a screening process or have to talk to a subordinate. Executives make themselves available to people to answer their questions.

Rewards

You're not going to see any Agway employees on Time's *or* Forbes' *lists of the 100 richest people in the United States. But we're very competitively paid, and we have the ability to be paid a 25 percent management bonus.*

In a people-oriented business like this, the kind of rewards I look for are from coworkers or subordinates of mine. Just before I was promoted to this job, I remember announcing to a group of my employees that I was going to be leaving. I caught a couple of drivers with tears in their eyes. They said I had made a real impact on their lives. And for the short period that you're there, if you can make an impact on somebody, you know you've been successful.

The Future

I'd love to be the key personnel person for all of Agway. I know that's possible, and as long as it is, I have no plans to go elsewhere.

AMERITECH (American Informational Technologies)

30 South Wacker Dr.
Chicago, IL 60606
(312) 750-5000

Other Employment Centers
Chicago, Cleveland, Detroit, Hoffman Estates, Ill., Indianapolis, Milwaukee, and Troy, Mich.

Products/Services
Telecommunications

Number of Employees
More than 75,000

Job Opportunities
Management trainees in sales or marketing

Starting Salary
$25,000

Major Pluses
+ Fast-track training (Ameritech Development Program includes two year-long on-the-job-training assignments)
+ Stability (one of the most profitable and financially stable of the "Baby Bell" phone companies)

Drawbacks
- You're just one worker among 70,000.
- Overtime pay has become virtually nonexistent due to recent cash crunches.

Corporate Philosophy
Company tries to avoid "worker drone syndrome" and encourage empowerment by encouraging employees to take the initiative to improve the company, especially in the area of customer relations.

Atmosphere
Varies from company to company and department to department. It's generally comfortable, while professional and efficient. Bring in your favorite coffee mug, but don't put your feet on the desk.

Working Conditions
Comfortably corporate, depending on the department and the management

Tips for Getting a Job
- Demonstrate an ability to write and think critically.
- Prepare yourself as a complete package. The company might ask you point-blank: "What do you have to offer us?"
- Emphasize your background in management skills. You don't have to say you were a VP with ATT, but you can say you were the president of a university organization.

Profile

Ma Bell is alive and well in the Midwest. When AT&T was forced to divest itself of its local utilities, five of the Bell companies serving the Great Lakes region joined to become Ameritech. Today, the new corporate entity is the telephone comany for 75 percent of the population in this area, serving more than 13,000,000 businesses and residences. It also owns other information-related companies and is expanding operations overseas to such areas as New Zealand and Poland.

The Big Corporate Ride
Working for a huge corporation whose combined personnel could completely inhabit a medium-sized city can be daunting. Competition can be tough. Graduates who snag a position somewhere in the catacombs of

Ameritech should be ready to do things the *company way*. They should also have a strong stomach for bureaucracy.

But don't let that scare you off. As is the trend in corporate America (led by Japanese methods), entire tiers of management are being eliminated and even entry-level workers are being given more responsibility.

If you want to get ahead at Ameritech, be sure you have a team spirit, a storehouse of good ideas, and lots of energy. You'll need all of it to turn the tide started by its 1980s corporate culture.

Enlightened Employer

More than most corporations, Ameritech is aware of need to empower its employees as individuals. The company spends about $100 million annually in employee training, with each employee spending the equivalent of about 10 days annually in career development programs.

The company also has a number of programs that encourage and reward employees who come up with ways to reduce costs or increase revenues.

But keep in mind that work atmosphere, hours, pay, and job descriptions can vary wildly from department to department. You may have a blast in your own office while others down the hall are under high pressure and working the graveyard shift.

Many Roads to Success

Remember that getting work with a large corporation also means that you'll be eligible for countless career options. Advancement in a company this big can be not only vertical, but also horizontal as employees switch departments in midstream.

"Every career path is different," says Jan Peterson, manager of staffing. "It's set up that way."

Companies like Ameritech also provide a large array of resources, so you can take advantage of its tuition aid program and pursue new degrees while still maintaining your career.

A Changing Industry

The telecommunications industry changes rapidly because of technological advancements. The telephone company of yesteryear is quickly metamorphosing into the personal communications company of the future. Fiber optics and coaxial cables are "turning telephone networks into vehicles that will enable users to communicate any combination of voice, text and video," as Stephen Weinstein and Paul Shumate recently noted in *The Futurist* magazine. That means there will be many new areas of opportunity for open-minded employees.

Recruiting and Hiring

Much recruiting is done on-campus in the Great Lakes region that Ameritech serves, while some interviews take place in the corporate offices.

In some cases, students intern with the corporation and join the payroll after graduation. This gives them an early start, since the internship period is credited as employment time.

In most cases, the hiring process consists of completing the application packet and having three interviews—one with the campus recruiter and one employment interview. Later, you'll have an interview with a specific department head. You can expect a number of basic aptitude examinations that your university courses should have covered. Applicants sign a statement of truth certifying their grades; transcripts are requested later.

Ameritech Development Program

This is the best option for liberal arts graduates, but it's also the most competitive. Corporation-wide, only 20 to 25 new employees are hired into the program. Matriculants should show evidence of leadership, negotiation skills, and initiative. They must also have graduated with a minimum GPA of 3.25. It's a strict program, but worth it for the corporate attention and special care, which includes seminars and a core of employee programs.

The development program enables young management types to benefit from on-the-job training. Each individual path is planned differently, but most include one segment of lower-level supervisory work and one segment of staff or sales work. After the program, workers are evaluated and sent down the appropriate career channel.

Report from the Trenches

YVONNE TURPIN

Position: Associate Manager, Special Services Center
Age: 25
Earnings: Mid 20s (est.)
School: Central State University, Wilberforce, Ohio
Major: Psychology

As graduation time approached, Yvonne Turpin was unsure whether to continue with her education or get a start on her career. When Ameritech expressed interest in her after her internship, the choice became easier.

Now she's thinking about going back to school. But she doesn't have to take time out for that—Ameritech will help her pay for it while she works part-time with the company.

That's just one way Ameritech is changing workers from robotic company men and women to happy, empowered workers.

Here's Yvonne's view:

A Talk with the President
I would say the upper management is very open-minded to suggestions and concerned about people's feelings.

I'm enrolled in the Ameritech Development Program. Recently my peers and I began planning our next semiannual meeting, and we decided to have the president of the company come and be our guest speaker.

I went to talk with him about what it is we wanted to hear from him—what our theme for the day was and what was on our agenda. He asked me, "What would you do differently if you were CEO of this company?" He said, "I want to you distribute that question to all of your peers so that when they come to the meeting, they will be able to answer that for me."

He's actually going to sit down with the nine of us and listen to our input! I understand that's the way he is with everyone.

A Slice of Atmosphere
We know when to have fun and when not to. But it's not very strict. Being in Cleveland, everyone here is a Cleveland Browns fan. I am a Cincinnati Bengals fan, and they are archrivals. On Fridays we have dress-down day. This past Friday, Cleveland played the Bengals, and I wore a Bengals sweatshirt—I was Bengals from head to toe. And everyone else here was Browns, so they razzed me all day. Monday it was my turn to dish it out, because the Bengals won.

Empowerment in Corporate America
Historically, the picture has been that you have a boss and the boss tells you what to do and you do it. When you finished you let them know so they could tell you what to do next. What we're trying to do in this office and in the company on the whole is allow personnel to feel empowered—to allow them to feel that they have the authority and autonomy to pick up a project and do it.

If I'm empowered to help you and you're empowered to help me, then we can help each other when one of us is swamped.

The Future
It's a good corporation to work for and it has firm footing in corporate America. I don't feel as if I'm just a peon. I feel that no matter what I want to do, I can. I have friends working for companies who think, "Gosh, this is it. This is all I'll ever be," because that's the atmosphere the corporation breeds. I don't feel that or sense that here.

AMES DEPARTMENT STORES

2418 Main Street
Rocky Hill, CT
(203) 536-8234

Other Employment Centers
450 Ames stores in 17 states; 15 Crafts & More stores in 8 states; and a wholesale sporting goods company

Products/Services
Ames Department Stores offers discounted general merchandise; Crafts & More sells (what else) hobby and home crafts on a retail level; take a wild guess at what the wholesale sporting goods company does.

Number of Employees
Approximately 35,000

Job Opportunities
Management trainees

Starting Salary
Low 20s

Major Pluses
+ Automatic pay increase after five-month training period
+ 15% store discount, stock purchase plan, student loan program, retirement, and savings programs
+ Comprehensive relocation cost coverage for training and all relocations

Drawbacks
− Unwise expansion led to Chapter 11 bankruptcy in 1990 (company is in process of closing 250 stores).
− Advancement nearly always requires relocation.
− On average, it takes a good five years to become a store manager.

Corporate Philosophy
Strong emphasis on local community involvement—not only does Ames take an active part in national charities, but the company regularly invites Boy Scouts to the company to raise funds through bake sales and the like.

Atmosphere
Although this is a retail department store chain, the Gilman Brothers, who started the company, emphasize a family atmosphere among its employees. Everyone is on a first-name basis, and even hourly associates have a low turnover rate.

Working Conditions
Imagine a homey, personable K-Mart.

Tips for Getting a Job
- Be outgoing, enthusiastic, confident, and very communicative.
- Research the company and try to check out a nearby store.
- Spotlight extracurricular activities beyond a good grade point average.
- Show how you can be flexible in a variety of roles or situations.

Profile

Ames would best be described as a retail chain on the rebound. It caught Reaganomics' corporate acquisition fever in 1988 when it bought out Zayre. Unfortunately, it created huge losses, a Chapter 11 bankruptcy, and major layoffs. Fortunately, a new management team came in and stabilized the situation. And its human resources people now tell us the company is doing business as usual and hiring again.

What They Want

Ideally, Ames wants some evidence of your time management skills, decent grades, any involvement as a leader in campus groups and activities (panty raids excepted). "Some business class experience is a plus," noted Sandy Spencer, Ames' college relations specialist. "But good interpersonal and time management abilities are better than a specific course." Examples of acceptable retail experience could be working in an amusement park, as a shift supervisor in a fast food outlet, or anything related to customer service. The bottom line is that Ames wants open, friendly, and flexible people. A 4.0 grade point with no outside experience isn't as important as a well-rounded background and the ability to communicate, be enthusiastic, and get along well with people. So while retail experience helps, Ames' training program will accept the unexperienced—as long as they have the desire to learn.

The Hiring Process

A completed application, an initial interview, and two letters of reference are all you need to get a training assignment. "Training assignments are on a first-come, first-serve basis, with those responding earlier generally getting their first or second choice of placement," Spencer said.

Training

The five-month, hands-on training program covers all the bases. Trainees spend eight weeks in operations and 12 weeks in merchandising. They study a workbook and standards manuals and take spaced tests throughout. The training covers everything from learning about receiving and financial control to working four weeks on the front line in the various departments. Graduates become assistant managers in a store, overseeing several departments with $1–$5 million in sales a year under their immediate control.

Career Path

From assistant manager, you'll probably be moved into apparel or hardline operations and eventually move up to become store manager. Promotion, based solely on performance, typically takes five years. With each promotion comes a pay increase.

Expect to be relocated. Applicants are expected to pick three states of preference when hired, and they'll be trained and placed in one of those locations. Fortunately, Ames covers most relocation costs, including temporary housing and transporting your car to the new location.

Report from the Trenches

DAN BLACKMAN

Position: Hardlines Manager
Age: 23
Earnings: Mid 20s (est.)
School: University of New Hampshire, Durham, N.H.
Major: Communications/Economics

Dan Blackman wasn't exactly wet behind the ears when he was recruited on campus for a position at Ames. Beginning in high school, he had worked at (of all places) Zayre as a runner, and also gained experience at Caldor retail outlet, Bradley's and, ironically enough, the Somersworth Ames store, where he worked as a supervisor. So he really wasn't too surprised with working retail and the way Ames did business. Here's his story:

The Training Program

The program covered everything in 20 weeks. It entailed every section of the store from your frontlines and your registers to upstairs with mainframe computers, doing invoices and knowing both the hardlines and softlines side of the store.

It was an intense, self-training program. The manager was there to help you along, but you had to teach yourself and go through each phase of the program. There was a self-test at the end of each phase.

It was an excellent program, although someone who doesn't have the experience might be a little rushed.

Career Progress
After the training program, they send you out once a position opens. I was sent out about three days after my 20 weeks were over. I was placed right away because there was an opening to be put into official management.

I was given a portion of the hardlines department when I first came here as an assistant manager. Since we lost some management and reshuffled things (after the bankruptcy), now I have the entire department. A raise came with an increase of duties. They compensate automatically out of the management training program—in my case, it was a $25 per week raise.

Promotions are never in-store. It's open to a lot of transfers. I had three days' notice about my transfer, although they did pay for everything.

The Typical Day
It's mainly customer service. Secondly, it's making sure we have enough merchandise in stock for the flyer ads we send out each week.

My responsibility is to make sure the warehouse sends us the correct merchandise. I try to ensure that my associates keep the store orderly, make it look full, and set what we call a plan-o-gram, which is how each aisle is laid out with merchandise. Almost everything is pre-programmed so all Ames stores look alike.

The Work Environment
There has been a lot more tension here since the bankruptcy and buyout. The home office has put us under a magnifying glass to make sure we can pull out of it and we're doing our best.

One of our biggest problems are internal theft and a stressful work load. Teamwork and competitiveness vary from store to store. Fortunately, the store I'm at now is excellent. We all get along extremely well, thanks to the store manager, who has done an excellent job at building camaraderie. Also on the plus side, my colleagues are very capable.

Best And Worst
I really enjoy the variety; the days are never the same. I need change, and I certainly get that here.

What's tough is the scrutiny from the district and region. I realize that it's necessary at some of the less well-run stores, but they even come to well-oiled stores and shoot you off in different directions. We also don't have enough help, which I hope will change.

The Future
I'm very happy in my position. The management camaraderie keeps me going, but I don't like the [geographical] area. It's very difficult to establish new ties outside of the store. My roots are near Boston and the University of New Hamp-

shire, so I have asked that my next transfer be to southern New Hampshire or Massachusetts.

Advice
This is one of the highest-rated occupations around in terms of stress. You're not going to be sitting around a desk all day, and no two days are ever the same. Be sure to do something you like or are interested in. Don't just do it for the money. I like retail and knew what I was getting into, and I have learned to adapt to the unexpected—and enjoy it.

At Ames, you need good communications skills and you need to be very open. With customer service such a high priority, they have to see openness in an interview. Ambition is a primary factor, as is your willingness to relocate.

ARMSTRONG WORLD INDUSTRIES, INC.
P.O. Box 3001
Lancaster, PA 17604
(717) 397-0611

Other Employment Centers
Regional offices scattered throughout United States

Products/Services
Manufactures and markets interior furnishings, including floor coverings, building products and furniture

Number of Employees
25,000 worldwide

Job Opportunities
Sales and marketing

Starting Salary
Upper 20s, plus bonuses

Major Pluses
+ Outstanding training program
+ Security (solid, old company)

Drawbacks
− Working alone
− Lots of travel

Corporate Philosophy
People are the company's greatest assets; all management positions are filled from within the company.

Atmosphere
Conservative dress, informal attitudes (everyone is on a first-name basis all the way to the president)

Working Conditions
Most sales and marketing reps work from a home office fully equipped by the company

Tips for Getting a Job
- Do your research prior to the interview and be certain you're interested in sales and marketing.

- Know why you want the job. If the interviewer asks, "Do you really want this job?" don't hesitate. If you aren't quick to respond in the affirmative, they assume you're not mentally sold yet.

Profile

If you're interested in sales and marketing, this Fortune 500 company has much to offer in training, security, and advancement opportunities.

Well known and respected for its outstanding sales-and-marketing training program, Armstrong provides an environment conducive to learning in its 8-to-12 week formal training program. Armstrong Manor, a renovated farmhouse near the company's corporate headquarters in Lancaster, Pennsylvania, has traditionally been the temporary home where trainees live, work, learn, and develop camaraderie.

The training apparently translates well into other industries as well; companies with lesser programs are known to go after employees who have been through the Armstrong program.

The Meek Need Not Apply

If you're not good at working alone, forget about this company. Armstrong marketing reps work from home and spend lots of time alone on the road. That's why the company is adamant about hiring graduates who are self-starters.

You will need self-discipline, goal orientation, and independence, because, says Bing Spitler, manager of college relations and organizational development, "There will be no one there to tell you to get up at a certain time and get started."

Why Liberal Arts Grads?

You can be sure your education is valued at Armstrong, which was one of the first companies to begin recruiting liberal arts graduates on campus at the turn of the century. The prevailing company attitude is that because liberal arts graduates come out of school with no specific career or craft, most of them have the attitude that they need to learn a skill or a trade.

The Wrong Attitude

What they don't like at Armstrong is the anti-business attitude some liberal arts graduates possess. Students with a bias against business or sales rarely get past the first interview with Armstrong—or with any company for that matter.

"Many liberal arts students tend to think of sales with a misconception that it's dirty," says Spitler. "If they stop and look around, they see that the vast majority of people in business are professionals who are not doing anything unethical or against their personal values."

Upward and Onward

Most liberal arts graduates start as marketing rep-1s. These are sales-related positions working with primary customers, usually wholesalers. Marketing reps work out of their own homes in assigned areas with assigned customers. They are responsible for achieving sales figures either alone or as a part of a team. This includes keeping the wholesaler advised on new products, promotions, advertising campaigns, training, and perhaps market research.

The next step, which takes up to two years to reach, is marketing rep-2, then senior marketing rep, executive marketing rep, and territorial manager. All of these are marketing positions in which the individual receives increases in pay and responsibility. At any of these positions, from marketing rep-2 up, the employee has the opportunity to move from marketing into advertising, market research, human resources, or other management positions within the company.

The next promotion would be to line manager in the field or regional manager or to a staff position in marketing management, where one would direct a specific marketing element of the division.

Hiring Process

Before getting a job offer from Armstrong, you will go through at least three interviews: one on campus, a second one at the home office with a specific department head, and a final one with the sales or marketing manager you would be working with.

The company brings in four or five candidates at a time to tour its facilities. Fewer than 50% of those invited to corporate headquarters are ultimately given an offer.

Report from the Trenches

ERIK J. CHRISTENSEN
Position: Assistant to Manager, Recruitment and Training
Age: 27

Earnings: Low 40s (est.)
School: Grove City College, Grove City, Penn.
Major: International Affairs

After graduating in 1987, Erik was hired as Marketing Rep–1 in a Wisconsin territory. After a year and a half, he was promoted to Marketing Rep–2 and sent to a higher-volume territory in Cleveland, where he remained for another year and a half. He was then promoted to assistant to the manager for recruitment and training at corporate headquarters, where he is now. Erik describes his five-year career with Armstrong:

How I Got the Job
The one-on-one campus interview was normal but it was unlike some of the other companies I went to in that there weren't structured questions. It didn't feel rigid. It was very flowing and easygoing. Other companies had a set of questions and tests you had to take and it was impersonal. This was a real personal experience. That's the reason I took this job.

Career Progress
I was hired for a Marketing Rep–1 position. Whenever you come into that position, you are put into one of the different divisions. It could be floor division, architectural ceilings, residential ceilings, which are under the building products division, or ceramics.

Then you go into a division's training program. At that time, it lasted 12 weeks. About 9 weeks of that were in Lancaster in a classroom environment where you'd go to the laboratory and to the plant. The marketing and sales managers train you. It's really an excellent training program. Really strong. You then go into the field, and maybe six months later you come back for two more weeks of training. You go out for a year, then you come back for two more weeks of training.

I stayed in the Marketing Rep–1 position in Wisconsin for a year and a half. I had a distributor or wholesaler for whom I was responsible for helping to increase the sales of Armstrong products. You travel with their sales people, help coach them and develop their selling abilities for Armstrong. At the same time, you're learning a lot from them, because those guys have been out there for a while and they know how to sell.

You're responsible for development of some of your top 30 accounts. This position is for someone who is an initiator. There is a relaxed structure, but you have to be pretty mature to go into this job, because there's a lot of responsibility and no one is there telling you to get up every morning and get out there and do this job. You just have to do it or you're not right for the job.

We have computers in our homes, cars provided by the company, car phones. We have interoffice mail we send through the computer. All of our accounts are on the computer and you kind of have your own little business out there. I was in the office about once a quarter for developmental purposes, but frequently the regional managers would come up and travel with me, to help coach and develop me.

First Promotion
The next step was into a Marketing Rep–2 position when I moved to Cleveland, which was a territory with greater level of competition and complexity. I remained in that position for another year and a half and then moved into the position that I am in now.

Second Promotion
This progression was kind of a jump. It's definitely a great job. I was interested in this job after I went through the training program and saw that it would be a coveted position. When I was offered it I was very, very happy. It was something I really wanted.

I'm here all the time training these people, helping them after work hours and spending a lot of time with them. Then after they leave, I go out and coach and travel with them in the field to help them take what they've learned in the classroom out into the field and into their own territories.

They Keep Me Motivated
The thing that keeps me motivated the most is that somehow, some way, they know when I'm ready for additional responsibility. They've never let me get stagnant. I go out there, and just when I think I've got everything under control and I might be able to sit back a little, it is time for something new. The managers are very in touch with your development and that is what keeps me going. That's what gets me up in the morning.

They Backed Me Up
When I'd make a decision out in the field, my managers would fight with me to the end with a customer or a wholesaler. This sounds kind of corny, but I've never really been disgruntled. That's why I'm still here. Other companies have talked to me, but I'm not leaving.

Advice
I think, for the right person, it's a great job. You've just got to know that it's going to be challenging. I remember when I walked out there (into the territory) I said, "Holy Cow! $2 million of volume and they want me to manage this and run it." Coming right out of school, that's pretty big. When you come out of training you're swimming with the rest of them, so just dive in head first.

ARTHUR ANDERSEN & CO.
69 West Washington St.
Chicago, IL 60602
(312) 507-2150

Other Employment Centers
Major offices in New York and Geneva; branches in most major American cities

Products/Services
Accounting and business consulting

Number of Employees
60,000

Job Opportunities
Auditing and tax accounting (will train on the job to become CPAs and/or MBAs) and business consulting

Starting Salary
$25,000–$30,000 plus overtime

Major Pluses
+ Specialized training/education (company spends more than $300 million annually on training-related activities)
+ Sponsored CPA/MBA programs
+ Overseas assignments
+ Tremendous advancement and compensation potential

Drawbacks
− Long hours (50-hour work-weeks are normal; 80-hour weeks not unusual)
− Client politics—you must prove yourself again with each new client relationship

Corporate Philosophy
Code words: career-long training; teamwork

Atmosphere
High energy, buttoned-down conservative, constant change. Client demands require quick response, creativity, and adaptability.

Working Conditions
Long hours, often hectic and high pressured

Tips for Getting a Job
• Be prepared. Know the company.
• Know how your interests relate to the company.
• Choose an area of specialty.

Profile

The last place most liberal arts graduates would expect to find a job is in one of the biggest CPA firms in the world—Arthur Andersen. It is also the world's largest business consulting firm and ranks 30th in *Forbes* 400 US Private Companies.

However, this company happens to be one of the most active recruiters of liberal arts graduates in the country. It hires about 350 of them annually and offers some of the best opportunities for training, advancement, and compensation that we've encountered.

Where Do You Fit In?

Since 1989, the company, which was founded in 1913 as a CPA firm, was more or less split into two separate divisions: accounting and consulting, both of which offer opportunities to liberal arts graduates.

On the accounting side, new graduates are expected to have an interest and aptitude for accounting and will eventually become CPAs and/or MBAs.

On the consulting side, most of the client work involves designing, installing, or changing technological information systems. No certification requirements are required, but many employees still go on to get their MBAs.

Most MBA and CPA candidates are enrolled in work study programs, either taking courses and working simultaneously or going to school on and off, earning salaries as they learn. Whether it's formal education, on or off the job, in both divisions there is extensive and continual internal training for skills and professional development.

Don't let the accounting or technical aspect scare you away. According to Dennis Reigle, managing director of recruiting and college and university relations, "We hire liberal arts graduates with the assumption that what they need in training they can get from us."

What They Want

On resumes and in interviews, recruiters look for solid academic achievement, motivation, a good range of interpersonal communication skills, extracurricular activities, poise, leadership abilities, and a team orientation. Beyond that, work experience or interests that mesh with those of Arthur Andersen might also help you get your foot in the door.

Career Path

First of all, the prevailing attitude here is up or out. Apparently, almost no one stands still or gets stagnant. All new employees, regardless of their jobs, take immediate training before they begin to see clients. Then, they work in a team, reporting to senior consultants or managers. As your career develops, you also become an instructor in some courses. You start as a staff consultant, then after two or three years become a senior staff consultant where you run parts of engagements and do some supervising. After five or six years, you will become a manager, and in 10 to 12 years, a partner.

The Hiring Process

Most recruiting is done on college campuses where recruiters host receptions and give presentations prior to interviewing. Later, the campus interview serves as a major screening device. If invited back, you will meet at one of the company's offices for a daylong meeting with several employees and managers.

Report from the Trenches

BOB LONG
Position: Senior Consultant
Age: 26
Earnings: Mid 40s (est.)
School: Williams College, Williamstown, Mass.
Major: History

Bob decided before his senior year that he wanted to go into the business consulting field in the financial services area. Arthur Andersen was one of his top choices from the beginning. After an on-campus interview, he was invited to the New York office for a second round. When he arrived a month later, the recruiter who had seen him at Williams took him aside and made him feel welcome and comfortable. That really impressed him.

After a series of interviews with staff people, managers and partners, Bob was offered a position on the spot. That was in 1988. Bob remained in New York until 1990, then accepted a two-year assignment in Zurich. Here's what he told us about his career with Arthur Andersen before leaving for Switzerland:

Training

All new hires begin as staff consultants. You receive four weeks of training in the office. Currently, unassigned partners run the programs. The first half of the first week you learn about things like benefits, insurance, payroll, internal stuff. During the next three and a half weeks you begin internal self-study courses in what Andersen Consulting calls "green books." (There are approximately 60.) You read 10 during the first two and a half weeks with tests each week.

The last week you begin to work on the computer learning COBOL and similar programming languages. The company has acquired what used to be a campus outside St. Charles, Illinois. At capacity, it holds 3,000 people. Here you attend three weeks of CAPS (computer applications practice school). All trainees worldwide are trained here. It's hard work and hard play. In classes you are learning COBOL, getting acquainted with different programming languages and computer systems. Classes are run from 8 A.M. to 10 P.M. with an hour for lunch and two for dinner.

Socializing

After 10 P.M. you can hang out at a bar on campus that stays open until 1 A.M. There are also some bars and bowling alleys in St. Charles. There is usually a group of 150 to 200 in each class. On Thursday nights there are buses available if you want to go to Chicago. There is a golf course and several sporting facilities on site as well. Socially, it feels like a college atmosphere. What stands out in my mind is the number of friends you make from around the world.

First Assignment

After training, you go back to your original office, and hopefully, your assignments are there. Or you may be in the staff room from one to three months working on internal projects. After the first day, I went out to a client. During the first year you are always part of a team (you generally are later as well). They are very demanding but you are never without a support network. There are often 20 people on a team.

My projects have all been in New York, mostly with investment banks. At my first assignment a number of senior consultants and managers were giving a big presentation, so I helped put slides together. There are two typical first assignments: (1) helping set up programs and (2) an assignment of your own. Generally, during the first six months you do programming. They are generally good about not having you do programming for more than a year. You start your career in the heart of detail and work your way out of it.

My first client assignment lasted two to three months; my second one almost three years. There, my role and function changed dramatically as time went on. It's more typical to do one type of work for a type of client. My smallest project had 20 people; the largest, 60. When that happens there are generally as many of us as there are client personnel.

Becoming a Supervisor

Next, you become a program supervisor designing systems. Instead of creating a program, you step back and ask what needs to happen. As time goes on your job becomes more functional, and often after the first year you begin to specialize. My area is financial markets, so I must learn investment banking and apply that knowledge to new systems.

Liberal arts has a strong presence here. Liberal arts majors may struggle initially, but after the first year it becomes much easier for them when the job becomes more functional.

A Typical Day

In my last assignment I helped design a system for pay-out dividends. For six months, I probably spent two to four hours each day talking to users, brokers, and systems people to find out how they process now and how we can build the new system. I ask questions, such as: What do you do now to process? Why do you do it that way? Can we automate? Is there a better way? The rest of the day I research on areas, look at standard industry guidelines, and then bounce ideas off an Andersen manager.

Employer Expectations

I'm always amazed at how quickly they put responsibility on you. They expect a lot immediately. One time, I reported to the client—not to my manager. They put in the parameters and said "Go."

Corporate Politics

There is a political element here. There are some managers to whom you basically have to say, "Yes, you are the manager and you are better than I." But I think this comes with any corporation of this size. You need to learn how to play the game and who the players are. A lot of times you need to take the initiative and make sure they know who you are.

I have two suggestions for beginners. One, get to know the important people in the company during your first year. Two, focus on a specialized area from the start.

The Future

Will I spend the rest of my career with Arthur Andersen? Probably not. The further you go at Arthur Andersen, the harder you work. I'm very happy with all I've done so far. It still boggles my mind how many people I graduated with who hate their jobs and are not happy. I have been extremely happy at Andersen Consulting, and I would recommend it to others.

BAIN & COMPANY, INC.

Two Copley Place
Boston, MA 02117-0897
(617) 572-2000

Other Employment Centers

Dallas, San Francisco, Toronto, Brussels, Geneva, London, Milan, Moscow, Munich, Paris, Sydney, and Tokyo

Products/Services

Management consulting

Number of Employees

1,000

Job Opportunities

Associate consultants (ACs)

Starting Salary
High 30s, plus bonuses

Major Pluses
+   Outstanding training with early responsibility for important client work and a wide variety of assignments
+   Opportunity for quick advancement (within three years, many ACs become full-fledged consultants earning around $70,000 per year)
+   Opportunity to go to business school ("Bainies" who have worked for the company for a few years have a 95% acceptance rate at top business schools)
+   Possibility of becoming an entrepreneur with financial backing from Bain Capital
+   Three weeks of vacation after one year of employment

Drawbacks
−   Long hours (50 to 55-hour weeks are the norm; during crunches you might work 18 hours a day for 3 or 4 days at a stretch)
−   Occasionally dealing with client politics

Corporate Philosophy
Stated purposes: To create *measurable* results for its clients and to strengthen the client's organization

Atmosphere
High-energy, youthful, teams of typically three to six people at different levels in the organization; Open communication between ACs and senior management

Working Conditions
Depends on individual clients, as much of the work is done on-site. Work often requires travel.

Tips for Getting a Job
• Demonstrate analytical and problem-solving skills. (Read following employee first-person account for examples of interview questions.)
• Discuss team involvement, whether on or off-campus.
• Demonstrate enthusiasm and an interest in business.
• Display an eagerness to learn everything you can about business; arrogance will get you an automatic rejection here.
• Show you can organize and articulate your ideas and opinions.

Profile

Bain & Company was founded in Boston in 1973 by William W. Bain. Beginning with just a handful of consultants, the company now has 1,000 employees and has consulted with more than 300 clients in 125 industries in 58 countries.

William Bain is no longer involved in the company. According to David Lord, editor of the highly regarded trade publication *Consultant News,* the company went through a serious ownership crisis when he left.

Now owned by its officers and employees, Bain & Company is secretive about its profits, client roster, and inner workings of the company, perhaps less so about its training program and job opportunities. Although the company enjoyed many years of rapid growth (about 50 percent per year), in recent years, revenues have fallen dramatically. Lord estimates that revenues have dropped from a high of $242 million in 1989 to $206 million in 1990.

"They have been through a great deal of trouble," he says, "They laid off roughly 15 to 20 percent of their staff in late '90 and '91. But they have started to rebound and I am told they are recruiting and hiring again."

Training

Bain's training program is recognized as among the best in the consulting field, and the firm prides itself on preparing young graduates for almost anything they want to do in the business world, from consulting to starting companies. "Our training is the single best badge of honor you can get," says Ralph Poole, director of training.

Most training is on-the-job, but especially helpful to liberal arts graduates is the classroom work that precedes any client contact. The business curriculum includes financial analysis (cash flow, accounting, investment appraisal, ratio analysis), industry analysis, and what Bain calls the 3Cs: cost, customer, and competitor analysis.

Recent undergraduates typically begin as associate consultants (ACs) and work as members of teams made up of consultants and managers from various levels of the company. After a few months of classroom training, ACs are assigned to a client. Working with their team, they come up with solutions to serious business problems. The tasks assigned to ACs include researching, interviewing the client's customers or personnel, serving on client task forces, and preparing the final analysis and recommendations.

During your AC training period you'll also work hard on developing a business vocabulary. "They may not have the vocabulary of business," explains James G. Allen, manager and director of consulting in the Moscow office. "But we get around that problem. It's not difficult for someone with a liberal arts background to learn the vocabulary of business. They will talk like CEOs after a month. We work hard on that."

Career Path

Within two years, most ACs become consultants-in-training (CITs), at which time they receive a raise and additional or more advanced responsibilities. This varies with the individual's capabilities.

Within three or four years, many CITs become consultants, again receiving pay increases and more advanced assignments. At this time many opt to go to business school and then back to Bain, to nonprofit organizations, or to other companies. Some even become entrepreneurs.

Interviewing

To get a job with this company, it's essential to have good analytical and problem-solving skills, as well as a team orientation. Tailor your resume to this and demonstrate it by the way you answer questions in the interview.

"We look very hard at their analytics," says Allen. "How they approach the whole act of problem solving. Typically, you ask 'How many square meters of pizza were sold last year in the United States?' You force the candidate to think about how they would answer that question. What kind of quick analysis could they do? How do they go about analyzing the problem? They think out loud and tell you how they approach the problem. We want to know if they are good, clear, conceptual thinkers, because that's all that business is."

What They Want

Getting a job at Bain is very competitive (1,000 resumes typically produce 35 offers). Between 50 and 100 ACs are hired each year, more than half of whom are liberal arts graduates.

Although the company seeks out the top graduates of the most prestigious schools, recruiters say they will look at anybody, but rarely consider anyone with a GPA below 3.0.

What They Don't Want

One automatic killer in interviews is rambling or reticence. You must demonstrate your ability to summarize your thoughts and talk about what you know.

Likewise, one of the worst qualities you can demonstrate to Bain recruiters is arrogance. "Any perception that this person is self-confident to the point of arrogance is a quick deal breaker," says Allen.

Report from the Trenches

JON McNEILL
Position: Consultant-in-Training
Age: 24
Earnings: High 60s (when promoted to consultant)
School: Northwestern University, Evanston, Ill.

Major: Economics

John McNeill could be the envy of thousands of liberal arts graduates who have found themselves in frustrating, unsatisfying careers; he gets fulfillment and satisfaction from his work, he's been promoted twice in three years, he's being paid exceptionally well, and he is exposed daily to such a variety of business challenges that he feels he will have the skills to be a successful entrepreneur in the not-too-distant future. To top that off, he will very likely get financial backing from his employer. Here's his story.

Bain didn't recruit at Northwestern, so I sent a resume during my senior year in response to some material they had sent to Northwestern.

Must Be Analytical
In my first round of interviews they were trying to get at my analytics (analytical abilities). They give you several business situations and they are straightforward. They start out with something like, "How many corner windows are there in a building with eight floors and two towers?" Then there are more with different business situations. For example, "If you were in the meat industry, could you brand hamburger the way Purdue brands chickens?"

They were not intimidating. They were just trying to get a feel of how I would fit. Bain has a strong team culture. Team spirit is everything here. They want to get a feel of what kind of a team player a recruit would be. New recruits are the lifeblood of a consulting firm.

Our recruiting operation is set up as separate from human resources. My first round of interviews was with the consulting staff. The second round was more in-depth questions concerning my background.

Associate Consultant
As an AC, I was given one case with five other team members. The other half of my time was spent on training. Some classroom work was involved. Then we were given a company to analyze its strategic position. We dug out all the information we could on this company and what its situation was. Then we prescribed what we would do. We presented it to a group of senior managers and they gave us feedback. After that I spent all my time on client work.

First Client
Our clients tend to be Fortune 500 companies. My first client was a consumer products line. I came on a team with five other people who had been working with this client for six months. I was the only new one so I had a lot of good coaching. I also started a relationship with the manager on the team and he's still a mentor to me.

We were trying to help this company with its sourcing strategy, consolidating its vendor base, their suppliers. One of the great things about being an associate consultant is that you can be a generalist and you can learn to focus on the key problem in a company and how you would go about fixing that. Then you help the client implement that. That's where the rubber meets the road. We are generalists by industry, but we are quick studies.

Other Clients

I worked on strategy for a beverage manufacturer and on a marketing strategy case for a paper goods company. I also worked on an acquisition case for a waste management company and helped them increase their business. I also worked on a manufacturing strategy for a semiconductor company.

Generalist or Specialist?

You have a choice of staying as a generalist or developing specific skills. Practice groups operate on two dimensions: on a specific industry or on a particular function such as manufacturing. Some decide they want to specialize.

If a manufacturing case comes up, I will lean toward that first. This is an interesting twist. I came here leaning toward finance and started doing manufacturing work and really fell in love with that.

Future

Most of us tend to gain business skills [in business school] and then go back to Bain and then into industry. The minority tend to go into industry. Some go into the nonprofit sector. Others become entrepreneurs. Bain Capital is a venture capital firm, and quite a few "Bainies" will go out and start companies and find capital through Bain Capital.

We've found that a lot of the skills that we were using to turn around other companies were skills that we could use ourselves to start companies. That's why Bain Capital was formed. After I leave Bain I want to start a company or work in a smaller start-up situation. I'm an entrepreneur at heart.

I spent a year and a half as an associate consultant and was then promoted to consultant-in-training (CIT) and given increased responsibilities. I will stay with Bain probably at least another year and then will make a decision about whether business school fits with the entrepreneurial heart in me or not.

Challenges

One of the challenges of this job is delivering on the results of the analysis that we've done. You do airtight analysis and the real trick comes in implementing it, making it work. For example, refocusing the entire organization of a client can be a tricky situation. Those are delicate situations at best and present interesting challenges.

Bain is the visionary and we've built a lot of expertise. When we leave the data and introduce the human element there is resistance. People inherently resist change. So, motivating them, then sustaining it is the challenge.

Most of my clients have been open to us because they see us as an earpiece to senior management.

Corporate politics with clients are difficult. I lean on our senior managers to help me. I watch them operate in those situations and learn from them.

Intense, Satisfying Work

The work I do is not real stressful, but it is definitely intense. We work within short time frames facing big problems. It requires intense thinking and immediate and aggressive action. I usually work 50 to 55 hour weeks. But as I compare with people I graduated with, there is a significant difference. Some went to be product managers, others to investment banks, and most of them haven't had the experience I've had.

If you want to go into business, this is the chance in three years to get concentrated exposure to a disciplined way to think through business situations. It's an interesting experience for folks who like variety and not a lot of routine. A strategic consulting firm offers that exposure. When you come in here daily, there is not a set routine. That's the main thing I like. I like the usefulness and the youthfulness. It's exciting, high energy.

Tips

Candidates should demonstrate that they have problem-solving and analytical skills. If they've been leaders in organizations on campus or off campus, that's a great thing to present. Finally, for folks who've worked during summers or during school, don't be afraid to talk about it. That shows initiative.

BENEFIT TRUST LIFE INSURANCE COMPANY

400 Field Dr.
Lake Forest, IL 60045
(708) 615-1300

Other Employment Centers
Three major claims offices in South Bend, Ind., Youngstown, Ohio, and St. Louis. Thirteen smaller branches nationwide

Products/Services
Life, medical, dental, and disability insurance

Number of Employees
1,100

Job Opportunities
Claims processing or customer service representatives in group or individual insurance

Starting Salary
Low 20s

Major Pluses
+ Very secure; no lay-offs in 79 years
+ Four and a half–day work week year-round
+ Pension plan funded 100% by the company
+ Free life, health, dental, and disability insurance
+ Credit union
+ On-site fitness center
+ Dining room and cafeteria offering subsidized lunches

Drawbacks
− Things tend to move slowly, especially the first couple of years.
− Lots of competition for every management opening

Corporate Philosophy
Teamwork . . . quality

Atmosphere
Conservative. Because this is a mutual company owned by the policy holders, there's not a lot of pressure or corporate politics.

Working Conditions
New, beautifully designed, landscaped corporate center with all the amenities

Tips for Getting a Job
• Be prepared by researching the company and the insurance field beforehand.
• Demonstrate professionalism—that you have a work ethic and can organize your time.
• Show eagerness to learn everything there is to know about insurance.

Profile

This is one company at which business graduates won't have an edge on you, and if you take advantage of the training, you will have plenty of advancement opportunities.

"We prefer liberal arts graduates over business graduates, because they are more open-minded as far as starting off a career," says Diane Petersen, human resources manager. "When they come to our company they are willing to go into training, and we can develop them into what they want to become."

Getting Started

Recent college graduates usually start in claims and go through a training program to become a claims processor. They learn all the necessary medical terminology about policies and paying claims. Some employees, however, start in customer service and deal directly with claims problems. Others start in the contracts area where they learn in detail about insurance contracts.

After working in claims, the next step would be to customer service, then in a supervisory position. However, it's also possible to move laterally to obtain more knowledge and then into a technical postion such as auditing or underwriting.

There's a lot of opportunity to move up in Benefit Trust, but it isn't automatic; it's competitive and the movers are the ones who've taken advantage of every opportunity to learn all facets of insurance. This means working in different departments and taking formal insurance education courses.

Training

Training classes are held three or four times a year for new employees going into claims. Those employees going into the contracts area are trained on the job.

Progressive training is offered to employees through the Life Office Management Association twice a year. After a succession of about 10 courses, an employee becomes a certified fellow, a prestigious designation that makes the employee eligible for higher-level positions. To encourage employees to take such courses, the company pays all enrollment fees and gives the employee a $50 cash award for every class.

Internships

Liberal arts majors in their sophomore and junior years have an opportunity to get valuable training as summer interns by working in Benefit Trust's various departments. Many summer interns end up as permanent employees after graduation and can be hired at a higher level than their counterparts who begin after they graduate.

Requirements

There are no GPA requirements, because, says Peterson, "We're more interested in what they *want* to learn than in what they already know."

Company History

The company was founded in 1913 by a group of railroad workers who wanted to find a good income protection program—sort of an unemployment policy—to take care of the commonplace deaths, injuries, and disabilities among railroad employees. The company's success led it to eventually offer life insurance and group health insurance to employees outside the railroad industry. With assets today in excess of $400 million, Benefit Trust is still mutually owned with all profits going back to its policy holders.

Report from the Trenches

KIRK JOHNSON
Position: Supervisor, Group Benefits
Age: 26
Earnings: Low 30s (est.)
School: North Park College, Chicago, Ill.
Major: Biology and Psychology

After graduating in 1987, Kirk took a volunteer job in Alaska for a year and a half. When he came back to Chicago, he decided to go into the insurance field because of the variety of opportunities. After researching and interviewing with several companies, including Allstate and State Farm, he decided that a smaller one, Benefit Trust, seemed to be the most promising. He started with the company in 1989.

Career Progress

I started here as a claims processor trainee. I went through the claims processing class, a formalized training program. In the training class, there were areas with regular testing, but at the same time, it was very interactive. I was actually working on the claims that I would be processing. It was not a simulation.

Through the next two years I basically moved around—I believe I changed units twice. My own goals were to just acquire as much knowledge as possible in as many areas as possible. So I was always asking for additional responsibilities. I was one of those go-getter types, I guess. Then, just before my two-year anniversary, I was offered a position of supervisor.

Responsibilities

As a supervisor I am responsible for the claims processors that report to me—currently eight processors and two customer service representatives—and for the way the department is set up. We pay claims for the groups that fall in our zip code zone. I keep tabs on the backlog so I will know when we need to hire temps and things like that.

Also, [I respond] to processing questions, which is a very far-reaching responsibility that draws from my past experience in different areas. I am also asked to make judgment calls on claims-paying practices. Any calls that the customer service representatives are unable to handle are referred to me, so I often deal with irate people.

Why I Like This Company
There have been a number of things that have happened here that confirm that I made the right choice as a company. The fact that I was able to expand in so many different areas even before I was promoted to a supervisor is one. I really appreciated the fact that they were willing and able to let go into those areas and trust my judgment.

Then, once I became a supervisor, the managers that I reported to were very encouraging as far as setting a very good, positive management-style role model. It's basically a positive-reinforcement style. I feel that they have a lot of confidence in me, and they tell me that. At a lot of companies you are left guessing. I've learned that if I am open about how I am feeling about anything, it's a two-way street.

No Politics
We are fairly conservative. We are not the first company in the market to try something new. We generally wait, make sure it's tried-and-true, and then follow suit.

One thing about our company is that we are a mutual company, which translates into job security for the people who are here. And because of that job security, I feel like people are not as concerned with the game playing that a lot of times is played at a stock company where if you don't win favor in someone's eyes, you are released when there is a merger.

The Future
Ten years from now I can easily see myself here. A director position is definitely not out of the question nor is a vice-president position. I am ambitious but I am realistic.

Advice
Researching what you want to do is really important. I can't count the number of people I know who didn't really sit down and research what they wanted to do and got into something that they weren't happy with.

The other thing is the work ethic. I worked 30 hours a week while I was in college and was able to get by on not that much effort. School teaches individuals a sustaining lifestyle. I exemplified that. I did just what needed to get done to get by. But it's where you go above and beyond that that you are rewarded once you get into the working world. Some people are never able to break from that school mentality. That doesn't work here.

BURLINGTON INDUSTRIES, INC.

Corporate Headquarters
3330 West Friendly Ave.
Greensboro, NC 27420
(919) 379-2000

Merchandising Headquarters
1345 Avenue of the Americas
New York, NY 10105
(212) 621-3000

Other Employment Centers
47 manufacturing plants in Virginia, North Carolina, South Carolina, Tennessee, Georgia, Mississippi, Arkansas, and Mexico; sales offices in New York, Chicago, Los Angeles, San Francisco, Dallas, and Atlanta

Products/Services
Textiles

Number of Employees
24,000 worldwide

Job Opportunities
Manufacturing management; merchandising sales

Starting Salary
High 20s to low 30s

Major Pluses
+ Fast-track training (depending on area of work, a variety of training opportunities are available, including in-house training programs, outside seminars and workshops, and special university programs)
+ Employee tuition aid (up to 90 percent of costs)
+ Employee stock ownership plan. Company is majority owned by employees.

Drawbacks
− Many manufacturing locations are in small towns. That may put off those looking for the excitement of a big city (on the other hand, many people who experience living in a small town never want to go back to city life. Recommended viewing: *Doc Hollywood*).

Corporate Philosophy
Hire the best people possible, train them well, and give them a challenging job in the fast-paced and diverse textile industry. Employees are backed by a strong merchandising organization and one of the most modern and productive manufacturing operations in the world.

Atmosphere
Varies according to location and function. Attire at corporate headquarters is businesslike, although there are periodic casual days. Career opportunities are flexible.

Working Conditions
Burlington is a large company but because its many offices are located in small towns, there's not a slick corporate feel to working there.

Tips for Getting a Job
- Show enthusiasm about the industry, even if you don't know much about it. (And don't make the mistake of thinking Burlington is related to the Burlington Coat Factory—there is no relation between the two companies.)
- Demonstrate an industrious attitude. Mention any employment while in school, the financing of your own education, etc.
- Internships and co-op jobs are a plus, especially in a related field.
- Be open to relocation, particularly to small towns.

Profile

Be it denim or draperies, carpets or curtains, chances are you've come into contact with Burlington Industries. One of the world's largest textile manufacturers—with more than $2 billion in sales annually—Burlington produces more than 13 lines of textiles, including fabrics for apparel, decorative home fabrics, and carpets and rugs. Most of its opportunities in manufacturing, technical services, or administration are in the Sunbelt. The majority of the plants and operations are located in medium-sized cities and small towns in the Southeast.

Positions in sales or design are usually in New York City or other major metropolitan areas.

Small-Town Roots
Burlington Industries traces its roots back to 1923 when a group of businessmen in Burlington, North Carolina, built a small cotton textile mill employing about 200 people. The company's first products were flag cloth, bunting, cotton scrims, curtain and dress fabrics, and "bird's-eye" diaper cloth.

Liberal Arts a Plus
Liberal arts backgrounds are looked upon favorably at Burlington. It's a company more concerned about attracting talented people than hiring only individuals with a certain background. If an employee puts in the

time and effort, Burlington will supply him or her with the tools to grow and learn.

Most liberal arts graduates go into manufacturing management or sales. About 30 percent of the firm's yearly hiring needs are in manufacturing. Opportunities are also available in design/styling, plant engineering, research and product development, manufacturing systems engineering, financial management, and management information systems for individuals with appropriate backgrounds.

"One of the advantages of hiring liberal arts graduates is the flexibility they bring to their career and job assignments," says Harold McLeod, director of personnel development. "They are able to go into many areas instead of being highly specialized in one career field." McLeod notes that chairman of the board Frank S. Greenberg is a liberal arts graduate.

Manufacturing Management Careers

Manufacturing management is the bottom line at Burlington. Modern machinery, processing, and management control technology have transformed the textile industry, bringing improvements in quality, productivity, and flexibility. One of a manager's jobs is to help people cope with the tremendous changes new technologies bring.

Management trainees are trained both in the classroom and on the job. The first assignment involves managing a group of production employees, being responsible for planning their work and the overall quality and quantity of production.

As managerial abilities increase, opportunities for advancement are offered. More responsibilities may mean relocation to a larger plant or even to a different division.

Sales Careers

Sales trainees start out in New York. After a three to four week orientation, you'll spend six to 12 months learning the ropes before becoming a full-fledged sales representative with your own accounts. Upon completion of the training, representatives may remain in New York or work in a sales office almost anywhere in the United States.

A sales career is an excellent foundation for future growth and opportunities for a self-motivated person. Superior communications skills as well as a flair for creative problem solving are musts.

As you advance in your career, you can move up to regional sales manager and merchandise manager. If product management is your goal, Burlington offers you the opportunity to manage a product from beginning to end. You'll be involved in everything from the initial concept to the final marketing plan.

The Recruiting Process

Burlington recruits from about 20 schools, primarily in the Southwest, in the fall and spring. Candidates typically go through a first interview on campus. The second round usually takes place on-site and consists of three or four interviews.

Internship Opportunities

Burlington's 13-week summer intern program gives rising college seniors the opportunity to apply their technical, business, and classroom skills to real-life situations. Each intern is assigned a major problem-solving project on the production floor or in a staff support area. Interns determine the parameters of their project, develop strategies, make the necessary decisions, and present their overall recommendations to the management staff.

All summer interns attend a four-day, intensive management development program in which they sharpen their techniques in areas such as communications, rational decision making and problem solving, team building, and participative management.

Interns work closely with managers throughout the summer. At the end of the program they receive feedback on their strengths and weaknesses and find out whether or not they are recommended for employment with Burlington. Exceptional performers may be offered a full-time position after graduation.

Most internships are in manufacturing management. A few positions are available each year in finance, plant engineering, industrial engineering, and other fields.

Report from the Trenches

DIANE ROSE
Position: Account Representative
Age: 24
Earnings: High 30s
School: Union College, Schenectady, N.Y.
Major: Psychology and Modern Language

"You were a psychology and language major—what in the world are you doing in textiles?"

Diane Rose hears that question a lot.

While in college, she decided to get a job in sales, even though she wasn't a business major. In fact, her alma mater, Union College, didn't even offer a business major. Economics was the next closest thing, but she had absolutely no interest in that.

After a stint doing market research for a Spanish television network, Rose landed a job at Burlington. Here's what she had to say about her experience:

Why I Said Yes
I wanted to get into sales because in the long term I was thinking about having my own business. I thought sales would be the best way to understand how a business is run. I hoped being in sales would give me the business background I wanted.

Career Path
I started out as a management trainee. For about three months I went through training in the South, basically learning about textiles. After that I spent a year as a sales representative in the different areas, selling fabric to dress, sportswear, blouse, and intimate apparel manufacturers. After a year I was unofficially promoted to a product manager. By "unofficially" I mean I never received an official letter notifying me about the promotion nor did my title on my business cards change. I became responsible for the entire intimate apparel market, not only in New York, but also for overseeing the out-of-town offices. The next step for me would be a promotion to sales manager.

Corporate Culture
It's very corporate, in terms of a definite structure involved—you know who you report to and who that person reports to. It's also a very high-pressured business. Burlington is a big company, and it has a name to uphold. They want you to do well, but they put a lot of pressure on you to do it.

The environment is team-oriented. We're not on commission, so it's not like we're pitted against each other trying to get money for ourselves. We're working for the company and we're all company people. However, there is a program where you get a base salary, plus incentive pay, which is geared toward our actual sales.

Employee Input
Top management seeks input from lower levels. This is done in sales meetings. We're required to bring fabrics back from the market all the time—so we can say, "This is important," or "We should be doing this," or "These are the colors that are important."

We have formal meetings where everybody comes in from out of town and meets in Greensboro. It used to be every season, which is four or five times a year. Now it's two major seasons with informal meetings the other two or three. Plus, we have a conference call every Monday, which involves everybody across the country so we can tell everybody what's going on in the company.

On Being a Liberal Arts Grad

Don't fret too much about your major because most people don't care. Obviously there are certain industries where it's very important, but I think it's important to really have a good understanding of a variety of things—the whole idea behind a liberal arts education. If you end up not doing what you studied, it's not a big deal.

Whatever your talents are they come out in your work. Even if you get a job right out of college that has nothing to do with what you studied, it doesn't matter. You just get your foot in the door. You get a little bit of experience, which enables you to get a better interview a year or two later toward something that you do want to do.

Looking Back

What I might have done in college is taken more business classes. I was afraid of them, because I'm not a math-oriented person, so I really shied away from them. Now that I'm in business school, I'm having to take them. I think it would have been good to have taken at least a few then.

I don't think I'm any further behind because of my liberal arts background. In fact I'm more open-minded. I was able to travel because I was a language major. In college I went to Japan and Mexico for a term each, so I think, on a certain level, I'm more sophisticated than some people. Even if they know how to do the numbers a little better, I think I have a better handle on life.

Would You Choose Burlington Again?

Absolutely. I've had great training. The benefits are good, but I think the training I got here was phenomenal. You learn the textiles training as you go, but I don't know if I could get this good of a sales training anywhere. I think the best thing in sales is that you have a lot of freedom and spend a lot of time outside, not locked up at a desk.

I feel like I've always been treated well here overall. I know that my management likes me, and to be accepted by a major corporation as somebody who's going to be successful gives you a lot of self-esteem. If I feel that I can be successful here, I feel that I can be successful anywhere.

The biggest surprise to me is probably that I'm in a very independent, self-starting position for someone my age.

LEO BURNETT, INC.

35 West Wacker Dr.
Chicago, IL 60601
(312) 220-5959

Products/Services
Advertising

Number of Employees
2,000 plus in its Chicago headquarters; another 3,000 in 49 offices in 42 countries

Job Opportunities
Entry-level positions in client services, creative, research, and media buying

Starting Salary
Low 20s

Major Pluses
+ Salaries tend to be above industry average.
+ Generous year-end bonuses
+ Two months' paid maternity leave with longer periods negotiable
+ Free, state-of-the-art fitness center at Chicago headquarters
+ Employee tuition program allows for continued studies in the liberal arts.

Drawbacks
− For those hoping to land a job on the cutting edge of advertising, then O'Hare Airport should be a stopover on the way to New York or Los Angeles rather than a final destination.
− Competition among employees is fierce. The concept of Leo Burnett as one big family only goes so far. Not recommended for those who don't enjoy the kill as much as the catch.

Corporate Philosophy
Company motto: "When you reach for the stars you may not quite get one, but you won't come up with a handful of mud, either." Likewise, company's logo is a hand reaching for stars.

Atmosphere
Folksy wisdom of founder Leo Burnett pervades agency, even though he died two decades ago. Company has a reputation of being a kinder, gentler version of the typical Top 10 ad agency, but also a bit stodgier and less creative. Team spirit, rather than individual achievement, is valued.

Working Conditions
New 50-story corporate headquarters located in downtown Chicago's Miracle Mile

Tips for Getting a Job
• Do your research. Before interviewing, make sure you know the history of company, its current client roster, and its competition. Be able to articulate why you want to work for Leo Burnett rather than another agency.

- Demonstrate media savvy. Brush up on the hottest magazines, films, and, above all, television shows, since the company buys more TV time than any other agency.
- Emphasize your individuality. As a self-proclaimed iconoclast in the advertising agency, Leo Burnett looks for like-minded employees. The company values people who have had unique experiences and hobbies. (If you've traveled Asia by bicycle, practiced sky-diving, or owned your own business, let it be known.)
- Project your personality. Advertising is a people-oriented business. Be aggressively confident, personable, positive—even a little bubbly during interviews.
- Demonstrate your creativity. This is the advertising industry, where creativity reigns supreme. Don't be afraid to be a little crazy. Perhaps it's a unique resume (all pictorial) or an invention of yours that you bring to the interview. Or dress up as an apple.

Profile

There's one advantage to Leo Burnett as a potential employer that outshines all the rest. While the recession has ravaged the advertising industry as a whole, this agency is prospering and plans to hire at least 50 new college grads this year.

Bucking Trends

Now ranked second among U.S. agencies based on billings ($3 billion plus in 1991), the story of Leo Burnett's success is one of the tortoise and the hare. While its flashier counterparts like Saatchi & Saatchi and Chiat/Day/Mojo grew by leaps and bounds in the 1980s by rapidly increasing their business and operations, Leo Burnett stuck with its tried-and-true philosophy of limiting its client roster to around 30.

By keeping its costs down, the company emerged from the advertising industry boomtown days of the last decade healthy and wealthy. According to a recent Louis Harris survey of advertising executives, Leo Burnett was the most admired agency in the industry.

Bucking trends is nothing new for the Chicago-based agency, its location being another example. All other U.S.–based Top 10 agencies are located in the media meccas of L.A. or New York. The fact that it is privately owned also makes it unique among the top agencies.

Making middle America its home has influenced the agency's creative output, both to its benefit and detriment, say industry observers. Admirers point to the "big, enduring" quality of Leo Burnett concepts, the Marlboro Man and United Airlines' "Friendly Skies" being prime examples. Critics disparagingly refer to Leo Burnett as the "critter agency," responsible for some of advertising's most enduring cliches: Charlie the Tuna, Tony the Tiger, The Green Giant, Morris the Cat, and the Pillsbury Doughboy.

Within the last three years, however, led by a new management team, Leo Burnett has begun to shed its stodgy image. In 1990 it won fistfuls of major international advertising awards for several trendsetting campaigns, including the "This Is Not Your Father's Oldsmobile," which featured celebrities and their siblings.

In any case, the agency's client base of blue-chip corporations remains extraordinarily loyal. In an industry where it is not uncommon for clients to change agencies every couple of years, half of Leo Burnett's clients have been with it for more than 15 years, 11 for more than 30 years!

Leo's Legacy

More than any other agency, Leo Burnett has been influenced by the philosophy of its namesake and founder. When he began the agency in 1935, at the height of the Depression, Burnett used a couple of converted hotel rooms as his offices. When a local newspaper columnist discovered the agency was dispensing apples to visitors as a means of establishing an identity, he quipped that "it would not be long before Mr. Burnett would be handing out apples from a box on the streets."

Fifty-seven years later, the company continues to give away apples to visitors (more than a thousand each day) at its gleaming new 50-story, glass-and-steel headquarters.

Employees are reminded daily of Burnett's legacy through other traditions as well. Big, fat black pencils, like the ones Leo used, are the *de rigueur* writing instruments of "Burnetters," which is how staffers refer to themselves. They also favor big, black portfolio bags, like—who else?— Leo used to carry. And all incoming employees are shown a film of Leo expounding on the agency's homespun philosophy and given a little book, "100 Leo's," featuring excerpts of his wit and wisdom.

Low Turnover

If all this sounds a little cultist, staff members say the atmosphere can be stifling and monolithic at times. Nor does the concept of one big happy family allow for the personal aggrandizement that counterparts at other agencies enjoy. But the company's low employee turnover—the lowest in the industry—speaks for itself.

The agency prides itself on the accessibility of its top management. To drive the point home, every December the "Burnett Breakfast" is held, during which skits poking fun of the executives are shown on videos. To further demonstrate their humility, executives must perform before their gathered legions. For example, in a recent year's event with a magic theme, members of management had to perform a magic trick of their choice. The generous year-end bonuses also are distributed to each employee at this function.

Employee Recruitment

Employees at virtually every level of the agency, from Hall "Caps" Adams, Jr., chairman and CEO, to Ted Bell, president and director of creative services, have liberal arts degrees. Undoubtedly, this is one of the reasons the company has such an aggressive liberal arts recruitment program.

Recruitment includes on-campus visits to 25 or so colleges. Burnett professionals even teach marketing and advertising classes at various campuses to see candidates outside the interviewing environment.

For each of Leo Burnett's four main departments—client services, creative, research, and media—there's an active recruiting staff comprised of experts in that advertising specialty. Beyond this, management personnel from each department, from executive vice presidents to junior marketing executives, have a role in the recruiting procedure.

Prospective job candidates are given a series of seven interviews on campus, finalized in a luncheon attended by a recent hire. If both sides are still interested, candidates are flown to Chicago, put up for the night, and introduced to the company itself.

Approximately 85 percent of new hires are found on college campuses. The remaining 15 percent are walk-ins or referrals.

Career Path

New employees begin in a department different from the one for which they are hired. For example, new hires to client services would work for the first year or so in the media or integrated communications departments, as a client service assistant, a media buyer, or as a media assistant. There they might be given responsibility for a client's media space or setting up promotional packages. For the first year, they would be assigned to only one brand or product.

The first promotion for a client services employee would be as an assistant account executive, followed by a promotion to account executive and finally account supervisor. After 10 to 12 years of steady promotion, the employee would be elevated to account director (the highest account position possible) beyond which are corporate management positions.

Evaluations are held along the career path, with your subordinates' performances measured as part of yours.

The Industry

Little wonder that advertising and liberal arts have a strong affinity for one another. The kind of broad-based knowledge nurtured by a liberal arts degree is ideal for a business that dispenses ideas about all other industries. On the other hand, there are real limitations to creativity at an agency.

According to one former Burnett staffer, "the client rules at an agency, especially at Leo Burnett, whose client relationships often go back decades. In a disagreement as to whether your idea is brilliant or fruitcake, guess who wins?"

Report from the Trenches

JENNIFER ROWE

Age: 23
Position: Assistant Account Executive
Earnings: Low 30s (est.)
School: University of Michigan, Ann Arbor, Mich.
Major: General Studies

Jennifer knew she wanted to go into advertising by her junior year. She learned about the field through internships in marketing, advertising, and journalism and by reading trade publications, such as *Adweek* and *Advertising Age*. She also learned communications skills through her work on her university newspaper and campus radio station. By the time Leo Burnett began recruiting on campus during her senior year, she was prepared.

Two years after being hired, Jennifer was working in the agency's Chicago headquarters as an assistant account executive in the client services department for the Nintendo account. Here's her report:

Why She Was Hired

They were looking for someone who knew what Leo Burnett was about—both in terms of corporate culture and clients. I think I offered them some experience, talent, marketing know-how, and a competitive spirit. They also told me later that they perceived me as an "idea generator."

The Pit

I was first assigned to "The Pit." That's what they nickname the Persons In Training section, where all new hires get their feet wet in the company. You get to know the personalities in the company and the resources available to them. Really, this is just a holding tank of sorts, until you are assigned elsewhere.

I eventually went to an area of the media department as a media buyer/planner on the Allstate Insurance account. I was there a little over a year, buying media space for Allstate ads and generally learning how to spend money effectively.

The Daily Routine
After one year, I was promoted to assistant account executive in client services. I serve as a liaison between Leo Burnett and clients at Nintendo.

A typical day includes interacting with many departments involved with the account, including creative, research, legal, and production. I work with all of them as an internal advisor, making sure everyone knows what needs to be done. I serve as the strategic guidance, gathering common ideas, or problems, to communicate with the client.

Corporate Culture
There's a healthy competitiveness to get the best product out there. It's exciting both professionally and personally. I look forward to coming to work because exciting things are always happening.

Doing It Over
After two years working here, I would do it again. I think I'll stay, too, because I like the fact that Burnett "grows its own." In other words, it's not like other agencies where your advancement can be derailed by a new, more experienced hire from another agency. They nurture your professional growth here rather than exploit it. There's a sense of assured happiness and success.

Drawback
The worst thing about working here is that there are so many top-notch people willing to work hard and do their best. It can be very competitive at times— you need to rise to the challenge many times to maintain your pride and success. I feel like I need to do my best every day, consistently.

CARTER HAWLEY HALE STORES, INC.
444 South Flower St.
Los Angeles, CA 90071
(213) 620-0150

Other Employment Centers
Phoenix, San Francisco, Richmond, Sacramento, New York, Anaheim

Products/Services
Department stores

Number of Employees
37,000

Starting Salary
Mid to Low 20s

Major Pluses
+ Training (operates a Center for Education, free and exclusively for employees, with course work in all aspects of retail fashion, including market analysis, buying negotiating, advertising, and merchandising as well as personal management courses in leadership, motivation, team-building, and the like)
+ Profit-sharing plan is generous; company is employee-owned, although lately there's been little profit to share.
+ Discount privileges on all merchandise

Drawbacks
− Company is still technically in bankruptcy, but then again so is half the retail industry
− Salary is good but not outstanding
− You have to be willing to put up with the vagaries and superficiality of the retail fashion trade. (Lapel size, not high finance, is the conversation in the employee lunchroom.)

Corporate Philosophy
Refreshingly employee-oriented; also, since it depends on consumer sales, the company makes great effort to maintain good community relations

Atmosphere
Dress is professional with an eye toward being stylish. (You don't have to be a clotheshorse, but it wouldn't hurt.) Since everyone owns a piece of the rock, there is little of the backbiting usually associated with corporate politics. Management, above all, values employee longevity; almost all promotion is from within.

Working Conditions
Employee-oriented with day care, parental leave, and preventive health care programs available

Tips for Getting a Job
• Dress fashionably.
• Emphasize your ability to handle many different tasks simultaneously.
• Try to have at least one summer job in the retail sector on your resume.
• Stress how you thrive in a fast-paced, people-oriented job.
• Desirable elective: public speaking
• Desirable extracurricular activity: anything that demonstrates a leadership role

Profile

There's a reason employees of Carter Hawley Hale tend to be unusually enthusiastic about their place of work: They own it. The company is the only publicly-held retail firm traded on the New York Stock Exchange that is predominantly employee-owned (nearly 60 percent).

Carter Hawley Hale is one of the largest fashion retail conglomerates in the United States. If you live in the West or Mid-Atlantic, there's a good chance you've shopped at one of their 113 department stores: Broadway in Southern California; Broadway Southwest in Arizona, Nevada, Colorado, and New Mexico; Emporium Capwell in San Francisco; Weinstock's in Northern California, Utah, and Nevada; and Thalhimers in Virginia, the Carolinas, and Tennessee. (Until 1987, Neiman Marcus, Bergdorf Goodman, and Contempo Casuals were also part of the company.)

Unfortunately, you've also probably read about Carter Hawley Hale's ongoing financial difficulties. In an attempt to fend off an unfriendly acquisition, the comapny incurred massive debt. When California's robust economy suddenly took a sharp decline in the 1990s, the company, the majority of whose stores are located there, was forced into bankruptcy.

The good news is that the company reported profit in February 1992, only one year after declaring Chapter 11. Company officials are optimistic that by the end of 1992 the company will emerge from bankruptcy. In the meantime, hiring levels continue as normal.

With sales approaching $3 billion in 1989, there's no doubt that Carter Hawley Hale is big business. But you would be hard-pressed to find a company more oriented toward its employees—no matter what the size. Here's the man himself, co-founder Phillip M. Hawley, chair and chief executive officer, on the value of associates (read employees), as stated in the company's latest annual report to stockholders:

> *Employee ownership links shareholder interest with employee interest in the best possible manner. This is an important quality of Carter Hawley Hale that has deep historical roots. Our profit-sharing plan was begun in 1953 with this in mind. . . . The employee ownership base gives us the stability to manage our business for the long-term.*

Favors Liberal Arts Grads

The company has a reputation among recruiters of hiring liberal arts grads and also actively supporting the concept of liberal arts. Carter Hawley Hale was one of 16 corporations to fund landmark 1989 study on liberal arts majors in the corporate sector, sponsored by the Corporate Council on the Liberal Arts in association with the President's Council on the Humanities.

Not all of that is entirely altruistic; the company supports liberal arts grads because it believes these grads bring unique talents to retail: "We are very interested in liberal arts graduates for our management training program, and we look at all kinds of majors. Just because you have a history degree, doesn't mean you can't make it in the retail industry. In fact, we prefer someone with a general knowledge," says Joyce Swenson, who heads up the company's executive recruitment department. "That's what retailing is all about. It's different every day, whether it's sales or buying."

The company hired approximately 150 new college graduates in 1991, recruited from 60 college campuses. About 75 percent of the total were liberal arts graduates, with the other 25 percent mainly computer science and accounting majors hired to fill vacancies in the Information Services Division.

Employees other than the company's recruitment professionals get involved in the recruiting process. Store managers and buyers visit campuses to convey the real-life experience of working in the fashion retail industry.

Qualifications

What does Carter Hawley Hale look for in its management trainees? You'll need skills and characteristics for retailing that are perhaps more diverse than those in other industries, according to a recruitment brochure:

> *Flexibility is important in managing and motivating people while focusing on customer needs. . . . Another key characteristic is the ability to clarify the core of issues and resolve them creatively, using foresight in setting goals, ranking priorities and delegating effectively.*

You've already mastered these skills, of course, by completing a liberal arts degree—now you can put them to use.

Step into Management

Most recently hired liberal arts grads step directly into a sales managerial role. After one month of intensive indoctrination in the basics of the fashion retail industry at the company's Los Angeles-based Center for Education, management trainees immediately begin supervising a department with a staff of 10 to 15 employees and some $3 to $5 million in merchandise. "It's a demanding program, and not everybody wants this kind of challenge," says Swenson.

Typically, the first major opportunity for promotion occurs two years after being hired. At that time, the management trainee can stick with store management or opt to become a buyer, who supplies the managers with merchandise. Buyers have an opportunity to earn more, but their job is less people-oriented and requires considerable travel. Buyers don't have the satisfaction of overseeing a department that's all their own.

Finding Bliss in Retail Fashion

Can a liberal arts grad really find happiness in the glitzy world of retail fashion? "Absolutely," says Swenson. "Fashion retailing is a very creative business. It's quite complex and constantly changing. I can promise you, you'd never be bored. The next season's style, colors . . . you have to know a little about advertising, how to manage people, what appeals to the consumer . . . there's so much you have to keep aware of.

"In fact, I think the opportunities in fashion retail are among the best in any industry for liberal arts grads."

Report from the Trenches

JOHN EMILIO
Position: Sales Manager
Age: 22
Earnings: Mid 30s
School: Furman University, Greenville, S.C.
Major: 20th Century History/Political Science

Like many liberal arts grads, John Emilio wasn't sure what he wanted to do with his degree upon graduation. But the South Carolina native would have never guessed that his history/poli-sci degrees could help him get a managerial position in a big city department store.

One year after graduation, Emilio finds himself in charge of directing a 15-member staff in the merchandising of more than $3 million in inventory. As a Carter Hawley Hale area sales manager at a Broadway department store in Los Angeles, he's responsible for every aspect of his department—from the way merchandise is visually presented to the customer to keeping track of inventory. Here's his report:

High Achiever

I guess you could say I was a high-achiever in college. I graduated in three years with two liberal arts degrees from Furman University, a small but very academically demanding private college.

When I began interviewing for jobs after college, I knew that I would become bored with most of them very quickly. There was no challenge to them.

The position offered to me at The Broadway was different. I thought there was definitely the potential for a career here, rather than just a job.

Interviewed with Competitors

Once I accepted the notion that I might make a career in retail fashion, I interviewed with several competitors. But I went with The Broadway because they offered the most training. It's actually geared to not just making you into a good employee but developing you as a manager. I also got the sense that top management sincerely cares about their 'associates.' (That's what we call employees here.)

Chain of Command

There really is a family atmosphere here. For example, yesterday Mr. Hecht [H. Michael Hecht, chair and CEO of The Broadway–Southern California division of CHH] walked through the store and made a point of stopping to talk with each of the sales managers.

That same kind of approach extends through the ranks. I have no compunction about talking, for instance, with buyers, which I understand at other department stores is strictly forbidden. That may seem trivial, but it's a policy that allows me to do my job more professionally. It gives me more control over my department.

The communication lines are open—up and down—in the chain of command, here.

Previous Experience

I really didn't have any previous retail experience. That didn't seem to matter much. They never came out and said it, but I got the feeling that the recruiting department personnel actually valued my educational background. Later, I learned from one of the recruiters who had reviewed my resume that he knew about my college. That impressed me. It told me they knew about liberal arts graduates.

The Future

The biggest challenge of my job is the tremendous responsibility I have. It's like running your own $3 million-a-year business. Fortunately, they give you all the tools you need in terms of education and training. The sales leadership development courses have been particularly helpful.

After one year, I already have turn-key responsibility, which means I have the keys and authority to open and close up the entire store.

I never would have thought that I would like retail fashion, but I do. It's utterly amazing. In a year or so, I will be able to decide whether to remain as a department manager or go into buying. I'm leaning toward buying, but I'll miss the stores.

CHUBB GROUP OF INSURANCE COMPANIES

15 Mountain View Rd.
Warren, NJ 07059
(908) 580-2219

Other Employment Centers
65 branches in North America and 19 international branches for foreign nationals

Products/Services
A group of insurance companies in America and throughout the world

Number of Employees
8,500

Job Opportunities
Management trainees for a variety of insurance disciplines

Starting Salary
Between $26,000 and $28,000

Major Pluses
+ Financially, one of the healthiest insurance companies in the world
+ Opportunity to move up the ranks quickly

Drawbacks
− Formal, suit-and-tie atmosphere
− High chance of relocation during career

Corporate Philosophy
Chubb takes the creed that an insurance policy is a legal contract to heart, which reflects its ethical and moral standards.

Atmosphere
Professional to a T. Even the water coolers wear suits. Despite the outward appearance, Chubb emphasizes openness, professionalism, and new ideas.

Working Conditions
Mingling among top-management and staff gives anyone who wants it high visibility.

Tips for Getting a Job
- Dress professionally.
- Know as much about Chubb as possible.
- Demonstrate excellent writing skills.
- In interviews, give specific and complete answers. Vague and theoretical responses give the wrong impression.
- Present yourself as a team player.
- Be honest, natural, and trustworthy.

Profile

Those in the know—investors and industry pundits—consider Chubb to be one of the strongest insurance groups in the world. And with sales and assets of almost $4 billion, things are only expected to get a lot better.

What They Want

"Basically, we're looking to hire someone with good people, marketing, and negotiating skills," stated Lisa Durant of Chubb's human resources department. "We want a person who can analyze problems and is committed to being a team person." A strong sense of commitment and ethics is also beneficial, and writing skills are especially prized.

The Hiring Process

After a screening interview, usually held on campus, candidates are invited back for second interviews with line managers of several departments.

Then you have lunch. "People have lunch with previous trainees who are now working," Durant noted. "This gives the applicant a chance to see the people he or she may be working with, and a chance to ask questions about the training process." After lunch, candidates are asked to do a case study.

Training

A comprehensive training process begins with a one-week branch orientation. Next comes three weeks at The Chubb School of Insurance at its Warren headquarters, where basic insurance concepts and product education is taught by the company's senior executives.

Next, employees spend three to six weeks at a speciality school in their division. There, trainees take on their first job responsibilities. Three years into the job, employees attend Chubb Business School for two weeks, which emphasizes the development and refinement of business skills and explores current business trends.

Career Path

Trainees can go into any of these areas: underwriting, loss control, claim and loss, and operation services. "The career path is based on performance, ability, and interest," Durant said. "There isn't a definite road that employees follow, but if someone shows a strong effort in doing things with the company in mind, it will be noticed. There's merit pay based on contribution."

Report from the Trenches

LEE ADOURIAN
Position: Supervisor, Department of Financial Institutions
Age: 25
Earnings: Mid 40s

School: Connecticut College, New London, Conn.
Major: Government

When the stock market crash soured his dreams of being an investment banker, Lee Adourian set his sights on the insurance business. He was pleasantly surprised to find that on top of the good pay, Chubb offered a well-rounded environment and the opportunity for mobility. Here's his story:

The Training Program
I was hired in New Haven as an underwriter trainee. One great thing about Chubb is that they put a lot of time and money into training. Our comprehensive training program is the envy of the industry.

After a week or two in the New Haven branch, the three-tier program took me to a regional, week-long session. I was sent to the branch for a month, then returned to the home office for two months, where all the U.S. and international trainees are in one group. Besides learning about insurance, you also get a lot of free time to mingle with the other trainees.

The whole training process lasts six to nine months, then you are evaluated. I went into the Department of Financial Institutions (DFI). I was given my "book of business," a list of independent agents who sell our insurance. They brought in business for us to bid on. We assessed and underwrote the risk and figured out the premium. After a couple of months at that, I was promoted from the initial trainee grade up a level. I got a merit increase and a promotional increase.

Career Progress
I stayed in New Haven for a year and a half, then I was promoted to their Murray Hill, New Jersey, office. Chubb likes to challenge their people to move up the ladder. In less than two years at Murray Hill, I was upped to a senior underwriter position in New Haven. Now, I'm supervisor of underwriters.

A Typical Day
We're not just underwriters; we're also marketers. I go out and meet with the clients and agents. A lot of our risk evaluation comes from sitting down with the independent rep, CEO and the bank's chief financial officer, when I ask them questions.

Other times, I'm in the office all day. The rest of the time I'm looking at property values, liability, and fidelity bonds and poring through financial statements. You wear many hats here.

Work Environment
I've been surprised with the amount of visibility I've had with the top management—the CEO and president, for instance. They come around a lot; you mingle with them at cocktail parties, during the work day, and in training.

Best and Worst
The best things have been the training program, the fact that you can move up the ladder at a young age, the wide variety of people in the work place, and the ability to rub elbows with top management.

I don't know what's the worst part of the job. Each job is what you make it.

The Future
My next step is becoming a manager in one of the DFI departments in an eastern zone branch within the next nine to 15 months. After that comes a DFI zone manager position, where I'd be on the road meeting with the different branches.

Tips
Read up on the company to get a good idea of what you're interviewing for. Practice interviewing, even for jobs you may not want.

Relax and be yourself, be smart and funny, but not silly and immature.

First impressions are the key, not just during the first day or week, but the first six to 12 months. That's when you build your work ethic into the corporation's mind. It's hard to break that first mind-set. Working hard the first 13 months and putting some flesh and blood into this really gets the ball rolling quickly.

Be willing to move because the more you move, the more experience you get, and the more it helps you move up.

CIGNA COMPANIES
Two Liberty Place
1601 Chestnut Street, TLP-16
Philadelphia, PA 19192-2162

Other Employment Center
Connecticut General Life Insurance Co.
900 Cottage Grove Road, A-1222
Bloomfield, CT 06002

Products/Services
Insurance and financial services

Number of Employees
50,000 employees in offices in 69 countries

Starting Salary
$22,000–$26,000

Major Pluses
+ Paid tuition for advanced degree (MBA or JD)
+ Free employee assistance program (confidential counseling services)
+ Free state-of-the-art fitness center at Philadelphia headquarters

+ Free country club membership

Drawbacks

− BIG! If the prospect of being one of 50,000 other employees conjures up images of ant hills, you have seen your future and it's not here.

Corporate Philosophy

Focused on achieving business goals through superior service to its business clients

Atmosphere

Recently reorganized management structure emphasizes team-oriented and holistic approach to work. Environment is strictly coat-and-tie, but not at the cost of individual employee dignity.

Working Conditions

Very corporate, right down to the individual work modules

Tips for Getting a Job

- Emphasize analytical and organizational skills. Ability to handle multiple tasks and dissect problems is highly valued. Talk about how you successfully managed your time between class projects and extracurricular activities.
- Project "team player." This is a big deal under the company's new management restructuring. Tactic: research the quality circle concept and throw in some of its New Ageian business jargon during your interview.

Profile

By any measure, CIGNA is very large. It is the second largest U.S.–based insurance provider (behind Aetna), with assets in excess of $65 billion. While it is frequently referred to as an insurance company, CIGNA also manages investment portfolios for pension funds and individuals, runs employee health-care programs, manages real estate investments, lends money, and supervises medical and vocational rehabilitation.

The company is one of the oldest continuously operating businesses in America, founded in Philadelphia in 1792 as the Insurance Company of North America. In 1982 it merged with Connecticut General, which specialized in health insurance, to form the present-day corporation. With CIGNA's purchase of EQUICOR, a $2.5 billion corporation, the company also became a leader in managed health care services.

Comprehensive Training

In 1990 CIGNA hired 170 liberal arts undergraduates and taught them everything they needed to know about the insurance and financial products it offers. Each of the company's divisions has its own training program, in which every new employee is assigned a "sponsor," a person who serves as a mentor and guide for the first nine to 12 months.

Initial training consists of six weeks of classroom instruction, which is followed by a series of written tests. After that, performance is measured on the job.

Most incoming college grads begin as underwriter trainees in one of the various divisions, such as municipal, employee benefits, or property casualty. Underwriting essentially means determining a client's insurability. Trainees analyze the inherent risks in providing coverage either to an individual or to a business or governmental entity and determine the cost accordingly.

After the initial underwriting training, employees can transfer to one of the company's internal support services divisions, such as human resources, legal, marketing, or public affairs.

Creativity Emphasized

Can insurance be a creative field? Certainly not in the artistic sense. But in terms of creative decision making, "Most definitely," says Cathy Grimes, CIGNA's director of university relations. "Underwriting constantly requires devising creative solutions to problems. It's a dynamic process."

A new team-oriented management system was introduced two years ago to give employees a "sense of empowerment," she says. "The shared leadership approach allows employees to do a variety of tasks rather than be pigeonholed. It forces employees to see the full circle and to identify problems in the loop and quickly harness resources to solve them."

Creative solutions to clients' needs are highly valued under the new system. "Our new motto is, if it's not broken, fix it. In other words, don't settle for the status quo. Look at the bigger picture and make it better."

The new system also exposes employees to senior personnel on a daily basis. Under the open-door policy, each team of five to 10 people is headed by a manager, who communicates daily with his or her team members.

Career Path

After the initial year as an underwriter trainee, you will be promoted to associate underwriter. After approximately one more year, you will be eligible to become a senior underwriter and then a master underwriter—a process that takes, on the average, six to eight years. Beyond these management positions lie underwriting manager and underwriting VP.

Report from the Trenches

CLARE RYAN

Position: Product Specialist, Municipal Insurance Segment, Underwriting Division

Age: 22
Earnings: High 20s
School: Catholic University of America, Washington, D.C.
Major: American Government

Like many college students, Clare Ryan did not seriously begin pursuing a job until her senior year when friends told her about job opportunities at CIGNA. At first glance, there seemed little opportunity for her to directly apply her major area of undergraduate studies, American government. However, then she learned of CIGNA's municipal insurance segment, where her knowledge of how government works comes in handy every day. Here's her report after one year on the job:

Work Load

It begins at 8 A.M. and officially ends at 4:15 P.M., but I usually stay until 5. Long hours are not encouraged per se, but you're assigned a certain workload and expected to get it done.

The work in our division is very cyclical, since most municipalities operate according to a calendar year. So we begin preparing in September for January 1, when everything is due. Sometimes during this period you have to work weekends.

After the January 1 deadline, we review our work and then begin marketing. In other words we start working with new accounts—evaluating risks on clients requesting policies and looking over new business submissions.

Team Orientation

Work is distributed among teams. The company has been very team-oriented since its reorganization a couple of years ago. We have a very tightly knit group, which consists of two other underwriters, a manager, and two underwriting assistants.

Beyond our group we have daily access to vice president-level personnel. It's necessary because much of my work involves big premium dollars, and some decisions lie outside of my limited authority. I might meet with my manager two or three times daily.

It's a very open-door management policy, and I feel my opinion is valued. Every time I bring in a new account, my opinion is solicited. That's my job. It's good to have that kind of interaction because it lets you know where you stand.

Insurance Underwriting

After a year, I would have to say I like my job because on a daily basis I have to be very creative and very organized. I am constantly working on a lot of different things all at once. It forces you to be innovative. It requires strong analytical skills and decision making skills to recommend what type of insurance is right for the client.

My work is very self-paced. It's not like the jobs that a lot of my friends have, in which they don't have a strong sense of responsibility. On the other hand, there's always someone on my team who's more experienced whom I can ask if I have a question. I think a lot of people are thrown into a new job and it's a sink-or-swim situation. That's never the case here. I could never say I didn't have enough training to prepare for the job I'm doing.

Liberal Arts Background
As a liberal arts major at Catholic University, I was required to take a wide variety of courses. I think that helped me to hone my analytical and organizational skills. As a government major, I understand how politics work, which is useful in determining the insurance needs of a municipality.

The Future
Right now, I plan to stay in underwriting. But eventually I might be interested in a position with the marketing or public affairs staff. Because it's a very large company, there are lots of different job opportunities.

Things have turned out better than I expected. I got my first raise already, which was a big surprise. Initially, the transition from school to work was really difficult. School is a very structured environment. Here, you never know what's coming at you. You may be working on one thing and suddenly have to take a call about something entirely different.

People here are really excited about what they are doing. Everyone is really focused on service and quality. In 10 years I hope to still be with CIGNA and aspire to be in an executive-level position.

CONTINENTAL INSURANCE
180 Maiden Lane
New York, NY 10038
(212) 440-7947

Other Employment Centers
12 regional offices, two automated business centers, one data processing center, and one home office

Products/Services
Property and casualty insurance for commercial businesses

Number of Employees
Approximately 15,000

Job Opportunities
Management training

Starting Salary
Mid to upper 20s, although the more experience and/or higher the GPA, the higher the base pay

Major Pluses
+ Don't have to be a math whiz to do well here
+ Excellent benefits
+ Good job security in an insecure economic climate
+ Rarely have to work overtime

Drawbacks
− Expect to relocate to get a higher position.

Corporate Philosophy
Continental emphasizes service, employee development, and learning how to think independently but act corporately and encourages employees to be active in local community and charitable affairs.

Atmosphere
Professional white collar, but a short sleeves mentality (company strives to work under a first-name basis and rebut its stuffy, starchy stereotype)

Working Conditions
Typical 9-to-5 office environment

Tips for Getting a Job
- Show interest in the field and in the company.
- Exhibit communication and organizational skills.
- Be outgoing, confident, and have a good sense of humor.
- Don't overinflate your accomplishments on your resume, but any extracurricular activities you participated in during college shows off your time-management skills.

Profile

One of the biggest and strongest insurance carriers in this country, Continental has more than $13 billion in assets and $5 billion in revenues. Not only has it paid out billions in claims, it has been paying dividends to its shareholders for nearly 140 years. The epitome of a solid, dependable company—even during these tough times.

What They Want
"We look at the whole individual and develop a profile," stated Paul Kopack, human resources manager. "We go on campus with a list of skills and criteria that we are looking for."

They call it "the seven necessities": analytical skills, decision making, leadership potential, oral and written communication effectiveness, self-assertiveness, and interpersonal effectiveness. These qualities don't just come from school books. While a good GPA helps, just as important is part-time experience, internships or co-ops, leadership in clubs or fraternities, and community service or athletics. Participation in any of these activities, in addition to school work, shows that the applicant has developed excellent time-management skills.

Training

In a company as diverse as Continental, there are individualized training programs, depending on the particular career path you choose.

The Initial Development Process (IDP) is divided into several phases. First comes six months of intensive training that brings the trainee up to a certain level of technical competence. During the early sessions training consists of alternating periods of class instruction and hands-on assignments. On top of receiving individual instruction in your chosen career path, you are also briefed on other areas to give you a more well-rounded perspective of the company.

"This should make us stronger and more efficient," Kopack said. "In addition, it goes a long way in job enrichment and satisfaction to be able to do a variety of things. It benefits both the individual and the company."

The company also offers 100 hours of time off to study for insurance exams and will pay for graduate school and other business education courses.

Career Path

The various departments you can work in are underwriting, claims, information systems, loss control, and actuarial. Training for the specialties is done at different locations. Generally, liberal arts majors tend to pursue careers in underwriting, claims, and information systems.

Continental also encourages its employees to upgrade and diversify their talents to seize new career opportunities. Hiring from within is the rule, and if your performance is up to snuff, you'll be promoted.

The first pay review comes after the first six months of training, accompanied by a promotion to an associate level. Future promotions depend on personal merit, and if you have mastered the position's duties, you can move to a senior position, then to a supervisory and managerial position, or you can go into more specialized, technical fields.

Report from the Trenches

SUSAN FANNING

Position: Associate Underwriter, Continental Excess and Select
Age: 26
Earnings: Mid 30s (est.)
School: Catholic University of America, Washington, D.C.

Major: History

When Susan Fanning decided to go into insurance, the universal response from her friends was "Why?" Yet she has found a comfortable, interesting place to work and has built a stable career. Here's her story:

Getting Hired
Actually, I didn't go through any campus recruiting. My initial contact with the company was a girlfriend who was already employed there. She told me about the company; I met the head of human resources in October. I then interviewed with a couple of other people in human resources in November, and I also interviewed with the president and vice president in Excess and Select, and two weeks later, I was employed.

Training
I didn't start the training program until June of the next year. During that time, I was able to take a graduate-level insurance and risk-management class and I familiarized myself with the New York office. I had two weeks of pre-training in New York before I went to New Jersey for both hands-on and classroom training. Some of the sessions were held in other regional offices.

Career Progress
Naturally, I started in the same department I was training in. I eventually moved from career trainee to associate underwriter, an automatic promotion. I work in directors and officers liabilities; we insure heads and directors in case of things like litigation and breach of duty.

By the way, the training continues. Next March is phase two, a higher level, which will last for about three years or so.

The Typical Day
I handle renewals and new lines submission that are entered in by brokers. Renewals have the first priority. We look at annual reports, 10Ks, legal proceedings the organization may be involved in, and so on. Then I come up with a premium. With new lines, we do the research to see if we want to be competitive and write the line. We analyze the company to see what kind of shape it's in.

Each day is different; there are always new submissions. I regularly contact brokers regarding their renewal applications, I go over accounts with senior underwriters and VPs, and I'm always reviewing accounts for a variety of businesses.

The Work Environment
I have a moderate to heavy workload, but nothing too intense or overwhelming. People don't breathe down your back here; the upper level wants to hear what you have to say.

It's a team-oriented atmosphere comprised of both goal-oriented, motivated people and those who enjoy doing the same thing for years and years. With three underwriters in this department, if we don't work together, nothing gets done.

Best and Worst
The best thing about this company is the support I get from my coworkers, who give me constructive criticism and the leverage to do what I want to do. It's up to you to take advantage of what's been offered to further yourself.

The worst thing is that there's sometimes a lack of communication between upper and middle management.

The Future
My next position will be senior underwriter, and down the road, I hope to make assistant vice president and then vice president, and then, who knows? All future promotions are entirely merit-based.

Tips
Really research and try to figure out what career path you want to take. Don't be afraid to go into a training program you don't know much about; that's what they're there for. It's important to get into a company that gives you a lot to learn.

COOPERS & LYBRAND
280 Trumbull St.
Hartford, CT 06103
(203) 722-1900

Products/Services
Accounting and auditing; tax services; management consultation

Number of Employees
61,000 in 640 offices in 107 countries

Job Opportunities
New employees begin as "associates," who perform a range of auditing, accounting, and tax-related services for clients.

Starting Salary
$27,000

Major Pluses
+ Clearly-defined career path (for the most part, you can work at your own pace as you progress from associate to senior associate to manager and then to partner)
+ Career-long training (company teaches you everything you need to know to function as an audit/accounting associate)

+ Mentor program (every new employee has an experienced employee as a guide for the first year)

Drawbacks
- Long hours—during tax season, expect to work 10 to 12 hour days.
- As with other large companies, being one of several ten-thousand can be daunting.

Corporate Philosophy
The four-step ladder of career advancement is set up to maximize team effort while rewarding individual performance.

Atmosphere
Very competitive and stressful. According to one branch's human resource director, "It's a very high-pressured environment where you deal with clients who want information yesterday."

Working Conditions
Offices range in size from 1,800 to 40 employees, but all have same standardized operating procedures.

Tips for Getting a Job
- Emphasize ability to meet deadlines while juggling many tasks at once. Show how you balanced school, work, and outside activities.
- Talk about team experience.
- Ask penetrating questions during interview. Display a strong intellectual curiosity. C&L looks for employees who can talk with its clients about a broad range of business and world issues. You might bring up a current news event and relate it to some topic being discussed in the interview.

Profile

One of the Big Six accounting firms, Coopers & Lybrand prides itself on its global operations. It is the largest firm in 10 countries, including the Netherlands, Switzerland, and United Kingdom. It is making forays into newly liberated Eastern Europe and was the first CPA firm to have an official representative in the People's Republic of China.

The company is also a leader in developing accounting and management consulting computer software.

Wide Range of Clientele

As a Coopers & Lybrand associate (auditor/accountant), you have new clients and new team members almost every week. The firm's client range spans almost every industry: amusement and recreation (New York Yankees), banking (International Monetary Fund), communications (AT&T),

education (Harvard University), food (Kraft Inc.), government (District of Columbia), and high technology (3M).

Other areas of clientele include: hotels and restaurants (Hyatt), insurance (Mutual of Omaha), nonprofit organizations (National Wildlife Federation), oil and gas (Unocal), retail trade (Saks Fifth Avenue), securities and commodities (Goldman Sachs & Co.), printing and publishing (*Wall Street Journal*), textiles and apparel (Coach Leatherworks), transportation (Holland America Line), and utilities (Tennessee Valley Authority).

Specialization

After the first couple of years as a public accounting associate, you will begin to specialize in one of the industries the firm services. Your core training will be supplemented with training specific to the industry. In effect, you'll be groomed to become an expert in your chosen specialty, whether it is hotels and restaurants or securities and commodities.

Because the management structure is oriented toward teamwork, assigned mentors help new employees with any problems they might encounter.

What They Want

"As far as job experience or being an accountant is concerned, we really teach everybody everything they need to know when they come in the door," says Suzanne Leone, director of human resources for the firm's corporate headquarters in Hartford.

"We teach them what our audit approach is, how we deal with clients and so on. Sure it's helpful if they have worked in any kind of accounting environment, but it's not a prerequisite. More important, the person we're looking for can demonstrate that he or she can set goals and work as a team member."

The Hiring Process

Candidates are prescreened for a 3.0 grade or above. SATs can be factored in but grades are more important. After one on-campus interview, recruiters may ask an applicant to a second, daylong interview conducted in the nearest office.

C&L looks for employees with "people skills." In order to communicate with clients effectively, C&L professionals "need to have a wide variety of interests and experiences. We look for people who can really talk to our clients beyond the technical side of the business and about world issues. They should have a broad understanding of today's business issues as well," says Leone. That's where a liberal arts education comes in handy.

Report from the Trenches

GINA FALCONE
Position: Audit Associate
Age: 22
Earnings: High 20s
School: Providence College, Providence, R.I.
Major: Mathematics

Gina Falcone was hired by C&L under the assumption that she would go on to earn a master's degree in accounting. She attends the University of Hartford under a special curricula arranged by the Big Six accounting firms, all of whom have offices in Hartford. Under the accelerated program, Gina will have her degree after only 15 months of study.

From April through November, she attends classes during the evenings. December through March is the busiest period for accounting firms because of the annual federal income tax deadline on April 15, so the program goes on hiatus at that time. Here's her report after eight months on the job:

Accounting Career
I had no idea that I would go into accounting. I knew I would go into some type of business, but I really was not aware of what a public accounting firm entailed. I liked numbers, but I wanted some variety.

I thought public accounting was the stereotypical bean counting. You know, mindless and unchallenging. But then I found out that you have to think on your feet all the time. You're constantly interacting with other business people at all levels, from the president of a client company to data processors.

A Typical Day
During the fall I work 8 to 5 and then take three classes at night. It's pretty intense. During the busy tax season I don't take classes but have to work longer hours—a minimum of 10 every day. They're long hours but we do get paid overtime.

During a typical day I would get to work between 7 to 8. I would do audits and have meetings with clients. Most of the time I'm at clients' offices so, depending on the client, I may be working in a regular office, a conference room, or wherever they can find room for me. Most clients are within an hour's drive of our headquarters.

Work Environment
It's definitely a high-pressured job, but people here tend to take it in stride. There's a pretty positive attitude about work. We joke around a lot with each other, and management is very accessible in that way. They don't make you feel like there's a barrier between you and them.

Most of my peers are young—in their early 20s. They're definitely ambitious, but the energy is focused into a team effort. When you're conducting an audit you are definitely part of a team.

Best and Worst
I once had to fill in on an audit for someone who was at a more experienced level than I. It was really difficult and frustrating at first, but I pulled it off. My manager had the confidence in me that I could do it, and he was right. It took me to the next level of work that I hadn't previously explored.

That's what I like best about working here. You never do exactly the same thing twice.

The worst part is the hours. You can never be sure that you are going to leave at five. It's a little frustrating. It doesn't happen year round but all through the tax season, it's a little like being a doctor on call.

So Far So Good
I went into the world of business not knowing what to expect. It's been demanding, but so far I like it.

R.R. DONNELLEY & SONS
2223 Martin Luther King Dr.
Chicago, IL 60616-1471
(312) 326-8000

Other Employment Centers
Arizona, California, Connecticut, Florida, Indiana, Iowa, Kentucky, Massachusetts, Mexico, Nebraska, Nevada, New York, North Carolina, Ohio, Oregon, Pennsylvania, South Carolina, Tennessee, and Virginia. Also Barbados, Canada, England, Hong Kong, Ireland, Japan, and Singapore

Products/Services
Printing

Number of Employees
33,000 worldwide

Job Opportunities
Manufacturing management; sales

Starting Salary
$28,000

Major Pluses
+ Fast-track training (two-year on-the-job programs in sales and manufacturing management; also internships and co-ops for college juniors and seniors)

+ Paid maternity and paternity leave

Drawbacks
- Nine-to-fivers would not be happy here since much overtime is involved. Nor would fashion plates feel at home; the printing business is an unglamorous industry.
- Expect 50-hour work weeks.

Corporate Philosophy
Six commitments: (1) to the customer; (2) to each other; (3) to the shareholder; (4) to profit and growth; (5) to quality and excellence; (6) to others (suppliers)

Atmosphere
Publishing deadlines dictate work scheduled. In printing, as in entertainment, the show must go on. However, atmosphere is warmer than at most corporations its size, a factor the firm attributes to being a largely family-owned concern.

Working Conditions
Hours are long and the work is demanding. But if employees become dissatisfied with their jobs, there is no need to start sending out resumes. Donnelley will transfer people to other positions within the company that are more suited to the employees' desires.

Tips for Getting a Job
- Summer work experience is essential.
- Get jobs that expose you to various aspects of business, such as working on a factory assembly line or being an office clerk.

Profile

Graduates looking for a job in this depressed economy can be a little more optimistic if they interview with R.R. Donnelley. Despite a drop in earnings in 1990 (the first since 1974), Donnelley continues to be the largest commercial printer in the world, printing annually some one *trillion* pages.

With more than 50 percent of its business coming from printing magazines and catalogs, Donnelley has been hurt by a weakening of both markets. It has traditionally done well despite recessions, but in 1991 it also faced the costs of expanding its business.

The company acquired competitor Meredith/Burda in September 1990 and also started up three new plants. According to Value Line Investment Survey, the Meredith/Burda companies have already started making contributions to the bottom line.

Donnelley sales range from $3.5 to $4 billion annually, but the company is always looking to improve its product and profitability.

A Midwestern Company

Chicago has been the home base for this printing company ever since Richard Robert Donnelley started the business in 1864. More than a century later, the heartland is still the lifeline for this international corporation.

"We're a midwestern company," says human resources manager John Dugan. And for that reason, the company looks to Big Ten schools in recruiting college graduates, about 40 percent of whom have liberal arts degrees. The rest are technically oriented graduates, and all tend to have GPAs in the B to B-plus range.

"Chicago is a desirable place to live in their eyes," Dugan says. "They seem to work out better than people from Ivy League schools with affluent backgrounds because this is not a glamorous business."

Liberal Arts Grads Need to Focus

According to Dugan, the drawback in hiring liberal arts graduates is that many of them are not focused on a career. Donnelley tries to help graduates decide what they want to do by offering two-year training programs.

With the manufacturing management program, you will spend several months working in each department on the process and financial side of the business. This can eventually lead to jobs such as a line supervisor that involve overseeing the running of presses and crews and troubleshooting to make sure everything runs smoothly. Two-year programs are also offered in sales training.

Most liberal arts graduates start working for Donnelley in the departments of sales, marketing, customer service, and customer representation. Dugan says that while they don't deliberately try to hire customer-oriented people, recruiters tend to be biased in that direction.

Report from the Trenches

JAMIE BUTCHER
Position: Production Planner
Age: 24
Earnings: Low 40s (est.)
School: Columbia University, New York, N.Y.
Major: Political Science

A Chicago-area native, Jamie Butcher decided that he wanted to return home after graduation. He chanced upon a job with Donnelley when a family friend and Donnelley employee recommended that he consider interviewing with them.

Jamie became interested in the manufacturing management training program, but after completing the two years, he decided he did not want to work in that aspect of the business. Now he works as a production planner, scheduling printings and distributions, deciding which plant is best suited for the job, the best way to handle the situation, and making sure everything gets done. Here's his report:

I had made two conscious decisions that affected my career search. Columbia's golden light for liberal arts graduates is to put them on Wall Street. I watched that go on for a while; I talked to seniors when I was a freshman. And then I decided I wanted to work for someone who made something. That was the first decision.

The second was that I decided I was ready to get out of New York, so I didn't use Columbia's career placement center.

Why He Likes His Job
Every day that I come in to work, I have no real idea what's going to happen. One day I picked up the phone and it was a salesman with an event in December where he had three million inserts and nowhere to put them. We were able to work it out.

It's not a three years and up-or-out sort of deal. I was in a job for a while that I didn't want to do, and they found me something else. Here I can do just about anything.

Donnelley Cares
A lot of major corporations are not set up to be caring, and sometimes you have to be. Donnelley is caring about the way people are treated because it was family-run for so long.

Because of the time constraints of the business, it has to be very congenial. It's stressful because you'll get proofs of supreme court cases, and they want those distributed to the public first thing in the morning. People understand that pressure and work together.

The Downside
At times my life isn't as much mine as I'd like it to be. But given my personal situation—I'm not married, I'm recently graduated—and at the moment, I like the hustle and bustle.

It'd be nice to say on a Friday that I'll just leave that until Monday. But if you have three million of something to go, you have to work until you finish, even if that means working until 10 o'clock at night.

The Company's Future
Our corporate people will be the first to tell people who listen that 50 percent of our business in the year 2000 will be based on technology that hasn't been developed yet.

Catalogs and magazines have long been the lifeblood of Donnelley but are now the most uncertain aspect. That's one of the things I really like. In 10 years, Donnelley will still be in business and in good form. It may not be catalogs. It may be diskettes or something that everyone can use.

Advice to Liberal Arts Graduates
Just because you don't know anything about cars, don't turn down an interview with Chrysler. You can turn to sales or write corporate newsletters.

It's that flexibility you bring to the organization that allows them to change and adapt. Liberal arts majors look at something and see how it can be used in the best way. A lot of the skills you think only apply to a given field are really generic and have a wider application.

If you'd have told me in October of my senior year that I'd work for a printing company in the middle of a corn field in Indiana (where the manufacturing management program was operated), I'd have laughed.

EDS
One Forest Plaza
12200 Park Central Drive, Suite 200
Dallas, TX 75251
(214) 604-6000

Other Employment Centers
Herndon, Va.; Troy, Mich.; Geneva, Switzerland. EDS maintains operations in 28 countries and has customer account locations in all 50 states

Products/Services
EDS (an independent subsidiary of General Motors Corp.) is a leading global supplier of information technology services including consulting, systems development, systems integration, and systems management. Industries: finance, insurance, health care, manufacturing, government, energy, transportation, telecommunications, retail, and distribution

Number of Employees
64,000

Job Opportunities
Programming and systems trainees

Starting Salary
High 20s (est.)

Major Pluses
+ Growing company, many opportunities, good training
+ GM car purchase plan (significant discount is available to eligible employees and select family members)
+ Stock purchase plan—employees can purchase company stock at 85 percent of the fair market value

Drawbacks
− Customer service is No. 1 here; high pressure, long hours, and weekend work when necessary

Corporate Philosophy
Change, especially in the information technology field, is inevitable and unpredictable. What makes a difference is how change is approached. EDS's purpose is to help its customers change through the use of information technology.

Atmosphere
EDS is organized into project-oriented industry groups that strive to share the experiences and perspectives of their customers. Members of each group combine their knowledge and research capabilities to build understanding of their clients' industries. A team spirit is mandatory at all levels. In fact, EDS prides itself on the company's ability to retain employees and keep them happy.

Working Conditions
Work intensity varies with project load, and can be demanding at times. Because employees often work at the customer's site, dress is strictly professional.

Tips for Getting a Job
• Before you even mail your resume, research the business of information technology and EDS in particular.
• Emphasize anything that demonstrates your work ethic, for example, campus involvement and any leadership positions you have assumed.
• Be aware this company was once owned by billionaire H. Ross Perot.

Profile

Employee development programs are designed to teach a new trainee the information technology side of EDS, as well as the customer's side. You will spend your first 13 months as a business associate, where you will be given a foundation in EDS policies, business practices, customer satisfaction, and customer relations.

Next, in the account experience stage, you will provide support in a specific industry, learning the business from the customer's view.

When you advance to the position of technical associate, you will spend your first few months learning basic information technology tools and resources. Then, for 10 to 12 weeks, you will be taught technical skills specific to your industry's needs. The length of your curriculum path is determined by the tools and technologies used by the customers you support.

EDS Likes Liberal Arts Graduates

College graduates do not need a technical education to work for EDS. In fact, the training program described above develops technical aptitude after a new employee joins the company. Prospective employees do not need an advanced degree, either. Most EDS recruiting is geared toward graduates with bachelor's degrees.

Because clients come from many different industries, EDS needs people who can communicate well with them and determine what solutions fit their needs.

"Liberal arts students have this emphasis on communications skills," says Chris Ryan, manager of campus relations. "They're able to think on their feet because they've had a smorgasbord of academic challenges in their classes."

What They Want

EDS looks for a strong academic track record, but also seeks diverse students who have succeeded in athletics, clubs, and other extracurricular activities.

Move Fast

"Looking at our history since 1962, there has been tremendous growth over a sustained period of time," Ryan says. "Few companies have the kind of growth history and bright future that we have. This kind of growth means more opportunity for people who want to succeed. And we really base things on performance. An individual who has come in and gone gangbusters is likely to see a quick promotion."

Report from the Trenches

TREY GANNON

Position: Systems Engineer
Age: 26
Earnings: High 30s (est.)
School: University of Texas, Austin, Tex.

Major: Political Science

Trey Gannon never thought a political science degree would lead to a career in computer programming. In fact, as a senior at the University of Texas, he wasn't sure what it would lead to. But a friend who worked for EDS encouraged him to investigate the company, emphasizing that EDS was interested in students with all types of majors.

Six weeks and three interviews later, Gannon found himself training to be a systems engineer at EDS. "I was really lucky because my friend gave me such good insights," Gannon admits.

The training program paid off for Gannon. Today he is a systems engineer, writing user-friendly programs for microcomputers in the banking industry.

Gannon is a member of the EDS Cycling Team, a group of three national-level, and potentially world-class, bicycle racers. The EDS team, whose members hope to appear someday in the Olympics, competes against full-time cyclists. EDS assists the team by treating time spent racing as time on the job.

I pursued a liberal arts education so I could learn about a lot of different things. I use that education every day. I'm selling, communicating with customers very often, writing up documents. I have the confidence to go out and try absolutely anything.

When you're graduating from school, it's very easy to get scared that you don't have a specific degree. I never would have guessed that I would end up programming computers. I'm just happy that I stuck my neck out and gave it a shot. Liberal arts majors are in an advantageous spot because we can apply for anything—we just have to have the confidence to try it.

No Limits
EDS is a completely performance-driven company. If you do a good job, you will go places with this company. Being young and aggressive, it's neat that my seniority has nothing to do with the positions I should think about or my salary expectations. That's a great feeling.

If I do a bang-up job every time I go out there, I'm going to get paid for it and promoted for it. It makes me think I can be here for a long time and still have challenges in my job.

Open Communication
I've had quite a bit of contact with upper management, and I definitely feel they value my input. One of our senior vice presidents came and talked to my group just recently. He asked for our input and also gave us his views and insights of

where the company was going. He asked us where we thought our industry was going and how we could keep the company moving in the right direction.

Time Off for Racing
The flexibility that EDS allows gives us an incredible advantage. I came here with an ability as a bike racer and didn't have to give that up to go to work. Even though I do spend time away from the job while I'm racing, I'm not in any way made to feel like a special person. I'm still evaluated just on my level of performance at work. And when I quit racing, I'm going to come in Monday morning and keep right on working.

The Future
Ten years from now, I could still see myself working on projects like this, except maybe managing a crew. That would be a heck of a lot of fun.

I'll still be working with a group of fast-paced and aggressive people, like I am now. With the money that EDS has spent educating me, I know they plan to have me around for a long time. And I plan on staying with them for a long time.

ENTERPRISE RENT-A-CAR
8850 Ladue Road
St. Louis, MO 63124
(314) 863-7000

Other Employment Centers
By the end of 1992, Enterprise plans to have offices in 36 states outside of Missouri

Products/Services
Automobile renting/leasing

Number of Employees
8,000

Job Opportunities
Management trainees

Starting Salary
$18,000 to $21,000

Major Pluses
+ Generous profit-sharing plan
+ Good advancement potential
+ Discounts on car leasing

Drawbacks
− Long hours
− Unglamorous side jobs, such as cleaning cars

Corporate Philosophy
The company has torn a page from Horatio Alger; put up with long hours and low pay when you start, because you'll get promoted sooner than later.

Atmosphere
Friendly, team-oriented. Everyone is young, well-dressed, and ambitious. Management is frequently close to the rank-and-file on a personal as well as business level.

Working Conditions
Pace is hectic, with employees expected to finish the tasks their co-workers are too busy to finish

Tips for Getting a Job
- Don't be ashamed of working at McDonald's—the company values that type of experience. In fact, you'll make points if you stress that you worked anywhere to pay for all or part of your college expenses.
- Stress that you thrive in a fast-paced, people-oriented job.
- Highlight extracurricular activities that demonstrate leadership abilities.

Profile

The pay is not great, the hours are not short, but the employees of Enterprise Rent-A-Car are happy because they look to the future. And what they see are promotions.

Virtually any college graduate who gets into Enterprise and sticks with it can expect to be a management assistant within a year. If you can stay on top of things and have a bellyful of ambition, the sky's the limit; the officers of this outfit were all promoted from the trenches.

This optimism in future promotions is well founded. In the eighties, Enterprise grew at a 27 percent rate; by the end of the fiscal year 1992 its revenue is expected to hit $1.3 billion. Not bad for a company that started in 1955 with 17 cars.

According to Craig A. Marr, corporate personnel manager, Enterprise employees can count on these promotions for some time to come. "Because of the growth and expansion, we hired 2,000 grads last year." Liberal arts graduates have an equal chance of getting hired.

Step into Management
Most recently hired liberal arts graduates go directly into the management trainee program. After nine to 12 months of intensive training, most employees can be expected to reach the level of assistant manager. In 12

to 18 months, many new employees become assistant branch managers, and in two to three years, a person can manage a branch office. Of course, with each step up comes a higher base salary as well as an increase in profit sharing. How rapidly one ascends depends on his or her initiative and willingness to work.

Pay (Your Dues) or Die

Enterprise is definitely not for the weak-willed. Working long hours and cleaning cars will be your introduction, but if you persevere, you will be rewarded.

"At an early stage in their careers, most people anticipate that they'll get as much out as they put in, and that's not true, explains Marr. "A paying-your-dues type philosophy is something that most liberal arts grads don't want to accept. If they want something safer, they shouldn't work here. You have to ask how ambitious you are. Do you have what it takes to be successful? For people who want to be with a company that is cash-sound, expanding incredibly rapidly, where they can advance, it's all here for them."

Report from the Trenches

CARLEE CASHIN
Position: Management Trainee
Age: 23
Earnings: Mid 20s
School: Eastern Illinois University, Charleston, Ill.
Major: Speech/Communications

Like many liberal arts grads, Carlee Cashin wanted to go into a field where she could be her own boss. She originally believed this meant going into sales, but soon discovered that sales was not as glamorous as it appeared. Working for Enterprise Rent-A-Car may not be all that glamorous either—unless you consider knocking snow off cars exciting—but she is her own boss and expects to work at Enterprise for the rest of her working days.

A little more than a year after graduation, Carlee is a management trainee and expects to advance to the next level—management assistant—within months.

I wanted to be my own boss in some way. I wanted to make my own decisions. I didn't want anyone hanging over me all of the time. I also wanted to sell, but after some interviews with advertising firms I realized it wasn't as glamorous as I thought. It's a competitive, clobber-each-other kind of job.

[Enterprise] makes you feel like you're in charge of something, like you're really important. It's totally team-oriented. It's all teamwork. It's not just within the office, it's with other offices. It's very much working together, and it's very relaxed in that respect.

Everyone's Equal

Everyone at Enterprise does everything. We don't want to have one person in charge of sales or one person in charge of anything. In one day I can go out on sales calls, rent out cars, and do customer service.

Another reason I like it is that it's customer-oriented. Seventy-five percent of our business is insurance replacement. When they come to us, they are not happy campers, and our job is to make them happy. Sometimes you can get real doozies.

The best thing is that they're young people, outgoing and sales-oriented people. Our area managers are young and fun and you can relate with them. It's a personal and a business relationship.

I plan to stick with Enterprise. I can't wait to be an area manager.

Advice

If they [liberal arts grads] know about the way the world works in the real world, they'll be fine. If they have the realistic expectation that their education is about to begin now that they're out of school, they'll be fine.

ERNST & YOUNG

277 Park Ave.
New York, NY 10017
(212) 773-3000

Other Employment Centers
100 cities in the United States, 600 cities worldwide

Products/Services
Accounting and financial services

Number of Employees
22,000 in the United States, 67,000 worldwide

Job Opportunities
Audit specialist, tax specialist, management consulting

Starting Salary
$25,000 to $30,000

Major Pluses
+ Training (Ernst & Young has a core curriculum of 250 continuing education courses each year. The firm also helps liberal arts graduates get into graduate programs in accounting, etc., sometimes partially or completely sponsoring these employees)

+ Quick advancement potential (annual promotions are the norm in the first few years with the firm)
+ Taking six weeks off during the summer is possible if you've worked a lot of overtime during the busy season.

Drawbacks
− From November to March, expect your job to take over your life. Don't ever expect to cruise.

Corporate Philosophy
Best summed up in E&Y's mission statement: "We seek to attract, develop, and retain high performance people, and to deliver the highest quality work and value-added services . . ."

Atmosphere
Conservative and professional while striving to be open and encouraging. Teamwork is very important; a group of people are assigned to each client and must work together to get the job done.

Working Conditions
Lots of overtime during the busy season; lots of time off during the off-season

Tips for Getting a Job
- Demonstrate interest or experience in business.
- Know a little about math or economics (a course or two will do).
- Show your ability to be a responsible team player.
- Be assertive, but not overly aggressive.
- Dress conservatively.

Profile

Ernst & Young is the largest of the Big Six accounting firms and offers a variety of professional services to its clients, including giants like Coca-Cola and McDonald's.

You might wonder why accountants would want liberal arts graduates in the first place. First of all, because they do a lot more than just number-crunching. Broad education and well-developed communication skills are important to the company, says spokeswoman Cathy Davies Salvatore.

Because most employees spend almost all of their time at clients' offices, they could be asked to become an expert on almost anything. If you get a job here, you might be asked to work on a computer industry account, then a publishing account. So you will need the ability to quickly absorb specific information about clients' fields and firms.

A liberal arts graduate could end up in any of the company's eight service branches, most likely in the tax department, expatriate tax services for overseas executives, or in the audit department as an assistant.

Other areas a liberal arts grad might enter are the actuarial department (Ernst & Young is the largest business adviser to the insurance industry); national planning areas; and management consulting. Because one could start anywhere in the firm, there is no typical career path, according to Salvatore, assistant director of national recruiting.

Training

In addition to assisting liberal arts graduates in entering accounting and business graduate programs, Ernst & Young also offers a range of classes of its own.

Reviews

In the audit department, the staff is reviewed after every 40-hour engagement. Then all of these reviews are considered in an annual interview with a specific adviser. Generally, this review helps tailor the job so that the employee enjoys it.

Interviewing

After an applicant submits a resume and transcript, he or she will have a half-hour interview, either on campus or at one of the company's offices.

If an applicant is selected for a second interview, he or she would then go to one of the offices for another interview and to meet people at all levels in that office. At this time, the applicant would also fill out the firm's application.

Report from the Trenches

STUART FURMAN
Position: Audit Senior, auditing and accounting division
Age: 25 (est.)
Earnings: Mid 40s (est.)
School: Colgate University, Hamilton, N.Y.
Major: Political Science and Economics

Stuart Furman knew he wanted a challenging and interesting job after graduation. He interviewed with several companies that recruited at Colgate University and took a position with Ernst & Young. Looking back, he says he wouldn't do anything differently.

After spending his first two years in Boston, Stuart decided he wanted a change and transferred to Raleigh.

Now in his third year with the firm, Stuart is no longer performing the technical work of an auditor, but helps coordinate and budget work with clients, overseeing and reviewing people who hold jobs he held a year or two ago. He spends about 90 percent of his time at other companies' offices, though he doesn't do much traveling. Here's what Stuart said about his career so far in the auditing and accounting division:

The Move
I started out in the Boston office in September of 1989 and spent two years there. My wife and I decided that while we'd gotten a lot out of Boston, we wanted to move to a smaller city.

We took a long time, probably six or seven months, to decide where we wanted to go. When I decided on Raleigh, I put in for a transfer, and within a few months, I was down here. I'm really happy the firm was able to help me so rapidly.

Career Progress
During your initial years at any of the Big Six accounting firms you tend to have an annualized promotion period. When I initially joined the firm, I was a Staff-1 accountant. After my first year I became a second-year or Staff-2 accountant. And after that I became an audit senior.

As you move through the firm you acquire very specific skills year to year, and you learn a lot more about whatever services you're providing, whether you're in the audit department, the tax department, or any of the special services or consulting departments. And you take on more responsibilities. There is the opportunity to be promoted early, but usually it's on an annualized basis in the first few years of service with the firm. There are very specific skills you need to learn in order to advance.

Staff Character
The people who sit there and do the ledgers are not just number-crunching automotons. There are a lot of people from all of the best undergraduate and graduate schools in the country, who are very well-rounded and interesting people.

There's also a strong sense of camaraderie. You get very close to people you work with, and we're constantly doing things together. I know a lot of people in the Boston office actually end up living together with various people they work with.

Hours and Time Off
As far as hours go, I think our industry has kind of a bad rap in that we have a reputation for outrageously long hours. I don't necessarily think that's the case, at least it wasn't in the Boston office. We try to structure engagements so that

people are working a normal 40-hour week. Yes, there is a fair amount of overtime, but I don't think it's unreasonable. And you're definitely compensated for it.

The firm is very flexible in what you can do with the time, or the money, depending on which you want to take. So I may work during our busy season—November through March—a few hundred hours of overtime. I have the option of taking that time off when it's slow, over the summer. So I can't think of another job where I could take six weeks off during the following spring and summer on top of vacation time. So I think it balances out.

Education

The firm has a very, very broad-based education program to prepare you as a professional. Just to tell you my own story, I didn't go to work for Ernst & Young right out of Colgate. I went to Northeastern University to complete an M.S. in accounting first, partially sponsored by the firm. I was recruited at Colgate, but again, at least right off the bat, more than any other career, this is a very technically oriented career, you really need to know a lot about accounting or taxes or whatever it is you want to do.

So it's very hard for someone with just a liberal arts degree to step into the job. Then again, I know in the Boston office almost everyone around me had liberal arts degrees. The firm kind of steers you in the right direction in terms of your career there.

The Future

Ten years from now, to be honest I don't know where I want to be, but I could easily see myself staying with Ernst & Young and perhaps becoming a partner.

FERGUSON ENTERPRISES, INC.

618 Bland Boulevard
Newport News, VA 23602-4310
(804) 874-7795

Other Employment Centers
170 locations spread out (Mid-Atlantic, Southeast, Southwest, Northeast, and Midwest)

Products/Services
Wholesale distribution of products for the plumbing and mechanical industries

Number of Employees
2,200

Job Opportunities
Sales, management, purchasing, and accounting

Starting Salary
$22,000

Major Pluses
+ A lot of different job opportunities within the company
+ Performance, and not tenure, determines pay increases
+ Can move up the ranks quickly
+ Strong, profitable company
+ Noncontributory life insurance equal to annual salary

Drawbacks
− Very long hours
− No one method to handle job (must be able to change way of doing business at a moment's notice)

Corporate Philosophy
Despite its wholesale corporate chain nature, each location is run like a small business. Each is very autonomous and entrepreneurial. Emphasis is on a strong work ethic.

Atmosphere
Each location is comprised of a team-oriented staff who succeed by working together to achieve common goals.

Working Conditions
"Work hard, play hard" mentality

Tips for Getting a Job
- Be outgoing and enthusiastic and show plenty of confidence and initiative.
- Expressing confidence in your abilities builds their confidence in your abilities.
- Show a lot of interest in the company during the interview.
- Be sure to spotlight your interests beyond the classroom.

Profile

No matter what the economic climate is in this country, people will always be flushing their toilets several times a day. So it's not surprising that the largest plumbing supply in the county has remained successful; since Ferguson's beginning in 1953, the company has grown from $500,000 in annual sales to $700 million.

What They Want
When company representatives describe the ideal employee, the same phrases keep cropping up: "entrepreneurial spirit," "strong work ethic," "self-starter with initiative", "communication skills," "confident person-

ality." Ferguson wants leaders who will do what it takes to get as much out of their jobs as humanly possible.

"We rely more on personality than specific grades," noted Audrey M. Clegg, manager of recruiting. "There is no cut-and-dried format. If someone had to work and put themselves through school, their grades may be lower."

The Hiring Process

Initial interviews are conducted on campus, but you can also submit resumes directly. If they are interested, the company will set up an interview. All second interviews are conducted at the Newport News, Virginia headquarters (Ferguson pays for your transportation and other expenses for this interview). The second interviews run about a day-and-a-half for a group of 10 to 15 candidates.

Training

Management trainees are exposed to all aspects of the company before moving into sales or management, in par with Ferguson's hands-on perspective. They start with one to three months in a warehouse, learning about products, inventory, shipping, etc. Progress is strictly based on performance, as opposed to a set schedule.

Career Path

After training in a warehouse, you can intern in any number of directions, from inside sales to purchasing, sales management, outside sales, and operations management. Again, it is important to note that your career growth is entirely dependent on your own efforts. The better you do, the faster you'll move up the ladder and the bigger your raises will be.

"Pay increases are always based on merit," Clegg said. "There are formal reviews once a year. Trainees are reviewed every 90 days for the first year and usually receive a pay increase within the first year."

Report from the Trenches

DAVID SHANNON
Position: Inside Sales Development
Age: 25
Earnings: Low 30s (est.)
School: Virginia Polytechnic Institute, Blacksburg, Va.
Major: Liberal Arts and Sciences

If you had told David Shannon when he first entered college that he'd graduate and work at a plumbing parts sales and distribution company, he'd probably have told you you were crazy. Yet he has been pleasantly surprised to discover the diversification of product and responsibility at Ferguson Enterprises. Better yet, his rise through the ranks has been faster than he expected.

The Training Program

I was interviewed in October and was offered a position one month later. I spent two months as a warehouse trainee, where I received, pulled and shipped orders, and did general inventory control. It was hands-on experience that's more blue collar than what I expected. I was impressed with the management training program because I could go through it at my own pace. In two months, I was promoted.

Career Progress

My new position was in inside sales at the Newport News headquarters; I received a pay increase in the form of a bonus. My next salary bump came exactly one year after I was hired. My next move would likely be outside sales or purchasing. That would probably mean relocation, but that's not always true. Management training is an ongoing system here, so not many people stay in inside sales unless they specifically want to.

The Typical Day

I'm usually in the office by 7 A.M. and I generally leave between 6 and 7:30 P.M. I spend my time quoting material prices to branches, ordering, expediting orders, and obtaining technical information and field test reports. When the phones generally stop at around 5 P.M., I can get a lot of work done.

Best and Worst

The best thing about Ferguson is the opportunities to grow and succeed. Hard workers who are willing to go out and get it will go far in this company.

The worst thing is the hours. I average 55 to 60 hours a week. However, I get up the same time as people who work in a metropolitan area like Washington, D.C. While they're stuck in traffic, I'm already at work, getting paid.

Tips

Don't limit yourself to the specific firms you're looking for. Make sure you know and understand the job you're getting into. The more you know about a company, the better your decision will be.

I was guilty of stereotyping firms like Ferguson. For example, I didn't know they had a heating and air conditioning component until after I was hired.

Fortunately, I like the way this company is structured. You're rated on your own performance; it's not three weeks at one job, three weeks at another. You stay until you understand that area of operations, and then move on.

I'm pleasantly surprised with my progression in this company. I've seen people take much slower paths; I've been fortunate to get the opportunity to progress at a rapid rate.

FIRST UNION CORPORATION

1400 One First Union Center
Charlotte, NC 28288-0953
(704) 374-7961

Other Employment Centers
767 domestic banking offices throughout five states

Products/Services
The 16th largest bank holding company in the country, First Union also runs mortgage and home equity corporations throughout the United States and a capital management group.

Number of Employees
More than 20,000

Job Opportunities
Management trainees

Starting Salary
Approximately $20,000

Major Pluses
+ Strong training program gives great preparation for job
+ Offers a 6% Match Savings Plan on top of regular benefits
+ Child and daycare centers for employees

Drawbacks
− Long hours and stressful work could lead to burn-out

Corporate Philosophy
Employees are "empowered" with freedom to try new ideas to help run the company as efficiently as possible.

Atmosphere
Surprisingly relaxed compared with suit-and-tie atmosphere commonly found in banks

Working Conditions
Rigorous, but fun. Employees carry a large workload, but they enjoy the work and their fellow workers.

Tips for Getting a Job
- Acquaint yourself with the nature and current condition of the company and the banking industry.
- Be able to discuss your abilities and goals clearly and intelligently.

- Don't be vague or say you're just looking for a job to tide you over until you decide what you really want to do.

Profile

The banking industry may be suffering, but First Union has built a stable foundation to withstand the weak economy. With assets of more than $40 billion and earnings of $272 million in 1990, First Union plans to play it close to the vest in its business dealings until economic conditions improve, when it undoubtedly will resume aggressive growth and ideally generate a substantial increase in profits.

What They Want

First Union wants, in a word, leaders. Focused leaders who are outgoing, motivated, sincere, and friendly and who want to make a career in banking.

The Hiring Process

It begins with resumes, transcripts, and multiple interviews. The first interview is usually conducted on campus and takes 30 to 45 minutes. Next comes a full day of interviews with five or six different people. After that comes regional interviews, which focus on specific areas of the company and specific positions.

"A person can go into consumer or corporate areas," notes John Fitzhugh, manager of college recruiting. "We find out what the people want and place them accordingly."

Training

You've got your choice. In column A is the Consumer Banking Associate Program, a seven-month program that combines classroom instruction with on-the-job experience. This program allows associates to work closely with branch managers in credit decision making, customer relationships, and personnel management.

In column B is the Corporate Banking Associate Program, a year-long stint that combines classroom training, independent credit analysis assignments, and guided, on-the-job experience. Associates work one-on-one with experienced bankers to develop financial skills and build strong mentor relationships with senior line bankers. After an initial accounting review, associates become involved in the credit underwriting and approval process and also attend seminars on such topics as commercial product training, business law, and investment banking.

Career Path

There isn't one typical career path, but for the sake of examples, Fitzhugh cited one employee who started in the Consumer Associate Program, became assistant manager of a branch, then branch manager, business development officer, area sales manager, and now VP. He accomplished all this in just six years.

"When you finish the training program, you're automatically placed in a higher position," he said. "After a year of service, there is a review, and four months later, there is another review. Promotions are not always title *and* pay. For instance, in being promoted to associate VP, you get made an officer, but you may only get something like an extra week of vacation."

Report from the Trenches

ROGER COBB
Position: Associate Vice President
Age: 26
Earnings: 50s (est.)
School: University of North Carolina, Durham, N.C.
Major: Economics

Roger Cobb didn't have a specific goal or career in mind when he started looking for a job. All he really wanted was a challenge, which he has found at First Union. Roger has been pleasantly surprised to find that, despite a tough business climate for banks, he has been able to move up the corporate ladder a lot faster than he expected. Here's how he did it:

The Training Program

I was in the Management Training Program from July 1988 to February 1989. This consisted of a few weeks downtown and then in an office; I got to practice what I learned in the office.

Career Progress

I became manager of a small branch until I became assistant manager of a larger branch in May 1989. In April 1990, I became branch manager (also known as associate VP).

There is no typical day or week. I'm responsible for managing accountabilities; I hire and fire tellers and customer service representatives. I get deposits; I call customers about their loans and lending. There's a lot of paperwork and reviews.

The Work Environment

It's fairly stressful. There are 15 people usually asking me to do 15 different things. There don't seem to be enough hours in the day. You feel satisfied if, by the end of a day, some progress has been made. Customers are sometimes irrational, and the teller staff can be frustrating.

Best and Worst

Taking the macro view, the best things are the training, working with people, and the fact that I have a job in 1991. It's nice to have a steady income each month. I gain satisfaction from this job on a micro level.

On the down side, I'm beginning to see that the company is stretching people as far as humanly possible; it may lead to burn-out. I can see how it may get there. However, I've yet to have had a really bad experience.

The Future

I have no idea whether I'll be here for the rest of my career. I honestly don't have any specific long-term goals, but I don't have any intention of leaving, either. As long as I'm continually challenged and promoted along with my peers, I can foresee a long stay here. I may want to do something else within this company— perhaps marketing or commercial lending.

Suggestions

Have a diverse background. A 4.0 GPA without anything else doesn't make you look like you've accomplished much. You must communicate a positive outlook and present yourself well. I was in a fraternity and played sports, and I always had a summer job, so I was marketable.

GOLDMAN SACHS & CO.

85 Broad Street
New York, NY 10004
(212) 902-1881

Other Employment Centers
Boston, Chicago, Dallas, Frankfurt, Houston, Hong Kong, London, Los Angeles, Memphis, Madrid, Miami, Montreal, Osaka, Paris, Philadelphia, San Francisco, Seoul, Singapore, St. Louis, Taipei, Tokyo, Toronto, Washington, D.C., and Zurich

Products/Services
International investment banking and brokerage

Number of Employees
More than 6,500

Job Opportunities
Analysts

Starting Salary
Low 30s plus bonuses

Major Pluses
+ Training. Two-year formal and on-the-job program, including preparation for business school
+ Unlimited earnings potential
+ Good advancement potential
+ Prestige
+ Tuition reimbursement
+ Maternity leave

Drawbacks
− Expect 60 to 80-hour work weeks.

Corporate Philosophy
"Our assets are people, capital, and reputation. If any of these are ever lost, the last is the most difficult to regain."

Atmosphere
Cooperative teamwork, intense, high-pressured, buttoned-down, entrepreneurial.

Working Conditions
Hi-tech, high energy, Wall Street

Tips for Getting a Job
- Emphasize your knowledge of or interest in business or finance.
- Demonstrate good character and high ethical standards with reference letters, awards, or other documentation.
- Demonstrate cooperative personality and team-orientation with discussion of activities.
- Demonstrate creative problem-solving abilities.

Profile

Liberal arts graduates lucky enough to land a job with Goldman Sachs won't have to worry about the trappings of a successful job: money, prestige, career growth, or financial security. Plenty of that automatically follows college graduates who get their foot in the door of this preeminent investment banking and brokerage firm.

Goldman Sachs—the last of the big investment banks still privately held—is essentially involved in investing huge amounts of money and financing big projects for such clients as Sears, Ford, Xerox, AT&T, Colgate-Palmolive, and even cities, states, and foreign countries.

To further distinguish Goldman Sachs from its many competitors, it was recently hired by the Russian government to help attract foreign capital to rebuild its economy. According to the *Los Angeles Times*, Goldman Sachs will also advise the Russian government in dealings with the West and help protect Russian interests in negotiations.

Money Junkies

While Goldman Sachs is the *crème de la crème* of investment bankers and enjoys a reputation for integrity and strong business ethics, it's still Wall Street and may not suit the personality of many liberal arts graduates. This is the fast track of all fast tracks, so be sure you have the stomach for it before you jump in. You'll live and breathe business and finance from morning to night, often seven days a week. Consider, too, that because the company's clients are huge entities rather than individuals, you'll never have individual control of a project. The catch word at Goldman Sachs is *teamwork*. There's little chance for stardom here or even in the near-term for control of a department as you might find at, say, a retail company or commercial bank.

Training

Goldman Sachs is known for its outstanding training program for securities and investment analysts. The best opportunities for liberal arts graduates are probably in the investment banking, equities, and fixed income divisions, where all undergraduates start as analysts. This two-year trainee position is usually followed by enrollment in a prestigious business school.

After obtaining an MBA, trainees may apply to come back into the firm as associates, later having the opportunity to become vice presidents and partners. Company officials say that although most professionals at the company eventually earn MBAs, it isn't absolutely necessary. Some liberal arts graduates who come in as analysts decide not to go back to school and became associates anyway.

What is an analyst, and do you have to be a whiz at math to cut it? Analysts provide research and support for the associates, VPs, and partners who are actually working on transactions for clients. Classroom instruction, including preparation for an MBA program, augments on-the-job training.

"Our analysts get very involved with all the important staff in their areas and support the people who are doing the client work," says Jeff Sanderson, an executive in the human resources division.

And no, you don't have to be a math major or even have excelled in math to succeed as an analyst. Accounting expertise is not why Goldman Sachs values liberal arts graduates. Classroom instruction, which augments on-the-job training, provides all the necessary nuts and bolts for doing the job.

The Toughest Competition

When pursuing a position with Goldman Sachs, brace yourself for the toughest of competition. Of the 3,000 applications received annually, only four to five percent are hired. Many of those brought degrees from top colleges propped up with outstanding academic records and a long list of extracurricular and leadership activities.

However, the company appears to be broadening its recruiting scope. "We've hired trainees from 59 different schools," says Sanderson, "including Duke, Georgetown, Spelman, Amherst, Texas A&M, Morehouse, and the University of Michigan."

The Ideal Candidate

Company executives tell us that character and a well-rounded education are most important in the people they recruit. "We look for the breadth of their education," Sanderson explains. "We look for the inquisitive mind, those exceptional people who want to learn a broad range of subjects."

The ideal candidate has high grades, a background that demonstrates success in a number of areas, a team orientation (there's that T-word again), and the right personality.

"The chemistry has to be right," says Sanderson. "The person might have a 4.0 grade point average, be captain of the basketball team, but still be a one-dimensional, narrowly focused individual. We don't want that type of person."

Another quality stressed by Goldman Sachs is personality. The company doesn't want hot-dog, steal-the-show egotistical types often associated with Wall Street overachievers. It wants tireless team players with interests outside themselves. This theme is often carried out by employees outside the company, too.

"We want people who can do a lot of different things well," says Sanderson. "Many of our analysts mentor junior high school students in different parts of the city. It isn't unusual for them to work seven days a week and still contribute to the community."

Recruiting

Screening and recruiting are two of the company's top priorities. "Recruiting is one of the most important things we do on an ongoing basis," says Sanderson. "If you say you want to [get together and] talk about recruiting, a dozen people will show up."

The interview process is not a casual one. It takes months to complete. The candidate goes through at least eight or ten interviews with executives at all levels before being hired or rejected. Recruiting starts in the fall, which is a good time for senior liberal arts students to contact the company.

Team Spirit

The firm's team spirit comes from the top, and everyone is expected to cooperate with, and help, everyone else. "I would characterize this company as a true meritocracy. Everything is based on merit," Sanderson explains.

Proof of this is in the way employees are promoted and compensated. Besides a very good salary, all employees are eligible for what is usually a generous annual bonus, depending on how well the firm performed that year. Although company executives would not discuss specific numbers when it came to compensation, our guess is that after a trainee completes two years of training and earns an MBA, he or she could earn close to $100,000. Some sources say it's not uncommon for partners to earn well over a million dollars a year.

Report from the Trenches

BETH COGAN

Position: Vice President
Age: 32
Earnings: In the six figures
School: Dartmouth College, Hanover, N.H.
Major: Math and Social Science

When Beth Cogan was a senior at Dartmouth College majoring in math and social science, she was sure she would spend her life as the dean of students at some college. Instead, she ended up on the liberal arts fast-track at one of the top investment banking firms in the world.

A summer internship at the Dartmouth Dean of Students Office changed her mind about a career in academia. "Halfway through the summer, I realized it wasn't motivating . . . I had too much energy and realized that college administration wouldn't work for me," explains Cogan.

Now, 11 years later, Cogan is a key member of the firm's Merchant Bank, a group that invests Goldman Sachs's own funds. Her title is vice president, her salary is in the six figures, and her future is assured. Here's what Beth told us:

Why She Said Yes

The recruiter was so excited about Goldman Sachs I decided to go for a second interview. I saw ten people there in one afternoon. All of them were in love with their jobs. When I got the offer, I said, "I don't think I'll do anything in business long-term, but it would be a great way to spend a couple of years."

The Training Program

I had taken only one economics course in college. I came to Goldman Sachs never having looked at a balance sheet, not even knowing what an income statement was.

At that time, there were only a handful coming right out of college. Goldman Sachs was just starting the analyst program. I learned everything on the job by asking questions. Now they teach you and train you. They explain what income statements and balance sheets are all about.

The Goldman Sachs philosophy was, and is, that a recruit must not be afraid of numbers and they must have a willingness to learn. Goldman Sachs will teach you everything else on the job. What is so fascinating and why liberal arts people do so well in this business is they come here and see many different financing and investing activities.

I look at people right now in the training program. The ones who've had more economics in college are more confident. But the training program really levels everybody out. Backgrounds go away. You prove yourself on the job. As long as you do your job, no one cares what your background is.

Mobility

There is no typical career path here. It's very hard to find anyone who's been in the same job for six years, especially in the investment banking side. People do lots of different things.

Career Path

I came as an analyst in 1980 and joined the Mergers and Acquisitions Department. I had never worked so hard in my life and had never been as stimulated by anything I'd ever done. It was a great two-year experience watching many different senior people work, seeing their different styles. That's how I developed my own style.

After two years in the Merger Department, I went to Harvard Business School and spent two years getting my MBA. Then, in 1984, I came back and joined the Private Finance Department—a group that did transactions in the private markets. I spent two years doing leasing and private debt offerings. Then, I joined the leveraged buy-out group, spending most of the time in leveraged buy-outs, high-yield bonds, and workouts (restructurings). I became vice president in 1988. This is relatively standard. Some become vice presidents as soon as four years [after becoming an associate].

Merchant Bank
At the beginning of 1990, they asked me to switch groups again and I now work in the Merchant Bank. They asked two partners to run the Merchant Bank and asked me to help them set it up. I work on the team that runs the Merchant bank on a day-to-day basis and am no longer doing transactions and doing deals. I'm setting up all the systems. I'll probably do it for a year or so and then decide if I want to go back on the deal side.

Intensely Demanding
When you're doing deals, your life is unpredictable. A 40-hour work week is unheard of. You could easily average 70 to 80 hours a week. There are no regular hours. If you walked up to someone and asked what the hours are, they would look at you puzzled. You come in and get the work done and go home. No matter how early I get here in the morning, there are 10 more people ahead of me in the office.

Corporate Culture
It may sound corny but Goldman Sachs is an extended family. It is not a political place. Do your job and do it well and you'll be compensated for it. And don't forget to have a good sense of humor; it helps in a strong team environment.

Advantage of a Liberal Arts Background
A liberal arts background worked for me in helping me be a well-rounded individual. I can talk to a client about any subject. It makes you a broader person so you can think things through and you're not narrow-minded, no matter what the issue.

Why Some People Don't Make It
Poor interpersonal skills. They lose interest in the business. They are too political. Politics kills you here. They aren't that responsible. Don't want to be part of a team. A lot of what people do in college, especially in liberal arts, are group projects, which will help you at Goldman Sachs. It's not easy to deal in a group. You need to know how to work with others. Group experience is very helpful.

Longevity
At my tenth year reunion, I was one of the only ones who had been in the same place since college.

Major Challenge
It's tough to keep a balanced life between my work and Goldman Sachs life. I'm planning to get married soon, and I want to have children. I may decide to stay in the Merchant Bank Division. We don't do deals here so life is more predictable. Goldman Sachs has several programs to make life easier for working mothers, including the alternative of working flexible hours, so women can continue their careers while staying close to their families.

HOSPITALITY FRANCHISE SYSTEMS, INC.

339 Jefferson Rd.
Parsippany, NJ 07054
(201) 428-9700

Other Employment Centers
Phoenix, Oklahoma City

Products/Services
Hotels (parent company of Ramada and Howard Johnson)

Number of Employees
950

Job Opportunities
Marketing, creative marketing, publishing, public relations, human resources

Starting Salary
Mid 20s

Major Pluses
+ Training (outside seminars to enhance job, for example, photography seminars for in-house advertising group)
+ Tuition refund program
+ Bonus program pays employees from the bottom up. (i.e., support staff gets paid before higher management)
+ Discount privileges on rooms at Howard Johnsons and Ramada Inns anywhere in the world

Drawbacks
− Location is in the middle-of-nowhere (west New Jersey, to be exact)

Corporate Philosophy
Since the company's main function is to serve its franchises, it is important that employees maintain a hospitality-service attitude.

Atmosphere
Dress is relaxed, yet professional (definitely not like a bank). There is a focus on equality. HFS places much emphasis on team spirit as opposed to hierarchical attitudes.

Working Conditions
There are no executive privileges; everyone eats in the same dining room and parks in the same lot.

Tips for Getting a Job
• Dress smartly and professionally.
• Emphasize well-roundedness and responsibility by highlighting extracurricular activities or part-time jobs.

Profile

This company operates the second largest hotel chain in the world. You know it by its Ramada Inns and Howard Johnsons. The company is structured as a network of independently owned facilities, or franchises, which are licensed, and to some degree, controlled by the parent company, HFSI.

Though Ramada and Howard Johnson are two of the more established names in the U.S. hotel industry, parent company HFSI is new. The company's chair, Henry R. Silverman, acquired the two hotel chains from Prime Motor Inns in July 1990 for $200 million. Silverman is a partner in the venture capital firm of Blackstone Group LP, which has a war chest of some $850 million.

Big Plans
One of the group's priorities in buying Howard Johnson was to improve the chain's old-fashioned perception in the minds of consumers.

Under Silverman's management the company has already launched Hojo Inns, a new subchain of economy lodges. More than 100 Hojo Inns were expected to be up and running by the end of 1992. In four to five years, the company plans to more than double the number of Howard Johnson properties.

On a Roll
Since Silverman bought out Prime Motor Inns, he has created more than 200 jobs for his new corporation, which is well on its way to becoming the largest hotel franchise in the world with the planned acquisition of Days Inn.

HFSI's aggressive expansion flies in the face of current wisdom about the hotel industry, which holds that there are too many hotels chasing a dwindling number of business travelers.

"I guess it's kind of funny that we would be growing and expanding at this time (country's economic recession)," said Fran Smith, senior vice president of human resources and administrative services. "I'm sure we are one of the few."

Open Arms to Liberal Arts Grads
The company welcomes diversity, and since liberal arts degrees give beginners needed variety, liberal arts grads are abundant throughout headquarters.

Also, since the corporation's function is to provide support services to all of its 1,100 hotels, a wide range of jobs are available at headquarters.

It usually takes two to three years for a liberal arts grad to move from an entry-level position to a franchise manager position. The next steps would be to director, then vice president.

No Campus Recruiting

Because enough graduates apply directly, the company doesn't find it necessary to recruit on college campuses. But you can check with your school's placement center for a listing of HFSI job openings, which are distributed to many college campuses. Better yet, contact the company directly.

Report from the Trenches

JANIS LINO
Position: Human Resource Generalist
Age: 24
Earnings: Low 30s
School: Barnard-Columbia University, New York, N.Y.
Major: European Studies

Janis Lino loved anthropology and Italy, so she majored in European Studies, knowing she would probably never find a related career.

"My advisor told me that I had nothing to worry about, since my interests fell under a liberal arts degree," admits Lino, who interned in a human resources department her last two summers while in college. "I knew it would prepare me for a job."

Right after graduation Lino worked for a year as a legal recruiter at a New York City law firm. But one day in August of 1990, Fran Smith, who was Lino's boss when she was an intern, called her about a possible position in a human resources department she was creating for a brand-new company—Hospitality Franchise Systems, Inc.

"And the rest is history, as they say," Lino said, who took the job as human resource generalist under Smith's management in November 1990. Here's her report:

How She Did It
I worked hard to get myself a job. It was like a full-time job trying to find a job. I devoted a lot of time to my search. Although I didn't quite understand the interviewing process, I sent out many resumes anyway, and as a result I got an interview [with the law firm].

Long Hours
Because I handle all non-exempt (hourly employees), I usually work 60-hour weeks, including most weekends. My day will come and go, and it will seem like I got nothing done, because people call me all day long. Frequently, I skip lunch or gobble down a sandwich at my desk in 20 or 30 minutes.

I have to listen to their stories and oftentimes take care of their problems. But I try to go beyond what my responsibilities are and deal with situations as they come up.

Future

I want to attend business school on a part-time basis, because I want some finance background to round out my experience. I'm also giving some thought to transferring to the Benefits/Compensation Department. Eventually I want to work my way up to senior vice president status, so I think it would be a good move to better understand the workings of the entire company.

I want to stay at HFSI. There are a lot of opportunities. That's one of the reasons I like this company. They give you the freedom to explore different avenues.

NOTE: The following profile departs from all others in this book in that IFEBP is a nonprofit organization that offers internship training and placement with major corporations. We feel this program is a valuable opportunity for liberal arts students. The foundation is the primary training ground for employee benefits specialists. Most interns who participate in the two-year program during college are placed in career positions with corporations in various industries after graduation.

INTERNATIONAL FOUNDATION OF EMPLOYEE BENEFIT PLANS

P.O. Box 69
Brookfield, WI 53008-0069
(414) 786-6700

Internship Locations
Baltimore, Boston, Chicago, Los Angeles, Milwaukee, New York, New Jersey, Philadelphia, Washington, D.C., San Francisco, and Toronto

Products/Services
Nonprofit organization of approximately 7,000 corporations and organizations; Purpose: research, publishing, recruiting, training and placing interns with member employers

Number of Annual Internships
200

Internship Salary
$6 to $12 per hour

Starting Salary for Internship Graduates
$20,000 to $30,000

Major Pluses
+ Training (nine full-day seminars over a two-year program, plus on-the-job training during the summers)
+ Guaranteed summer job for two consecutive summers
+ Probable job offer upon graduation
+ Excellent advancement potential—there aren't enough people in the field

Drawbacks
− Program is designed primarily for sophomores
− Interns must commit to a two-summer internship

Corporate Culture
Varies depending on which company you are placed with

Tips for Getting a Job
• Don't make mistakes on your resume.
• Dress professionally.
• Demonstrate or express your degree of flexibility.
• Demonstrate exceptional communications skills.

Profile

The International Foundation of Employee Benefits Plans is a nonprofit organization of more than 7,000 corporations, trust funds, public employee funds, and professional firms in the United States and Canada.

The foundation houses the world's largest employee benefits library and publishes seven periodicals, as well as books. Its research department conducts periodic employee benefits surveys and about 50 educational conferences and seminar programs every year. It also offers a certification program for certified employee benefits specialists.

The Employee Benefits Field

Employee benefits is a diverse field with few trained people, and job security is good. The internship links a student with a national association that has strong networks and support services. "By the time they graduate they've got on-the-job experience as well as academic experience," says Dean Ossana, senior director of marketing and membership.

"What we've done is prepare them for the field of employee benefits. Most of these students know very little beforehand. They not only get training and education, but 45 percent of our interns are offered jobs at their sponsoring corporations. In tracking our graduates, we find that 73 percent have jobs that are either directly or partially related to employee benefits.

Internships

This is one field apparently hurting for qualified candidates. One important function of this organization is hiring, training, and placing interns
with its member employers for the purpose of eventual full-time employment in the field of employee benefits.

There simply aren't enough people to fill the slots at major corporations, says Ossana. "Our objective is to introduce people to the field of
employee benefits because colleges and universities don't offer many
courses on the subject."

How it Works

The foundation screens hundreds of college students in April of their
sophomore year who will embark on a two-year journey into employee
benefits. The 200 students who successfully complete the application process are guaranteed a summer job for the next two years. Some companies
use interns during the school year. During the two-year program, interns
are required to take a total of nine classes, ranging from health care cost
management, to investments, to labor relations, to legislative trends.

The I.F. Interns program is coordinated by regional directors who identify qualified students in their second academic year at four-year accred-
ited colleges and universities. Students with a B average or better are
screened to determine if their attitudes, strengths, and career goals meet
the program's high standards.

While selecting students, the regional directors also secure commitments for paid internships from sponsoring organizations. Candidates are
matched and then interviewed by prospective sponsors.

As an intern, you will work for two successive summers in an employee
benefits atmosphere. In addition to your work experience, you will learn
the basics of employee benefits through educational seminars. Over a two-
year period, you will attend nine full-day sessions sponsored by the foundation. Regional directors carefully monitor each intern's progress.

Liberal Arts Valued

Liberal arts students are prime candidates for the internship program.
But the most important feature of the program is that it matches a student's interests with a company's product or service. "We really don't
look for anything specific," Ossana says. "What we're really looking for
are talented students who have a good work ethic. We're also looking for
people who are mature enough to enter a business right away. Those are
the most important qualities."

"Different sponsors want different traits. Some want communications
skills and some want number crunchers. There is such a wide diversity

of jobs out there that what we do is try to match the needs of the company with the student."

Resumes
Resumes are an important tool for getting a job here. They must be professional in every way, says Ossana. "If someone has a misspelled word we notice it. If it's not easy to read we notice it. Someone should be able to explain themselves in a concise manner without rambling."

The Application Process
This is a very competitive program. Regional directors screen students at more than 90 colleges and universities in six regions across the United States. The program recruits students with 3.0 GPA or better.

"We have a lot more people applying for the internships than we have room for. We interview a number of students just for one position," Ossana says. "If they don't come across professionally, seem immature, or they don't dress in a professional manner, they might not be accepted. It's the image they create and how they present themselves."

After applications are accepted, the foundation screens potential interns to select students for a final interview process that is held at each sponsoring company.

Report from the Trenches

ANDREA CASEY
Position: Administrative Analyst
Age: 24
Earnings: High 20s (est.)
School: Brown University, Providence, R.I.
Major: Psychology

Employer: Martin E. Segal Company
1920 N. Street, N.W., Suite 500
Washington, D.C. 20036
(202) 833-6400

I.F. Internship Sponsor: Brown University Personnel Office
I.F. Internship Position: Benefits Assistant

Andrea Casey, a recent Interns graduate, gives two main pieces of advice to young liberal arts students. First, don't confuse the relaxed academic setting with the workplace. Second, don't get discouraged when you begin working without experience in a specialized field.

Getting the Job

I saw an ad in the classified section of the Washington Post. *I didn't know at the time the job was offered through an employment agency. I sent a resume through the agency and was granted an interview at Segal. I actually had two interviews with a total of five people.*

I think I was really lucky. Most of the jobs available through agencies are clerical. I did not go to an agency seeking a job, but I think looking through a paper is a good idea. I'm not from this area. I came here and stayed with a relative and found two jobs in a couple of weeks and it's a full-time job, looking for a job. It takes a lot of time and effort.

Transition from Academics to Business

In dealing with clients I've learned you really have to watch what you say. It's not like school where you can't always say what you feel. It's nice to be honest, but you can't say everything you think. Clients remember. What you say can come back to haunt you. That goes for the workplace, too. You can't just tell everyone what's on your mind. I used to talk about it at first, but now I don't let it bother me. Some things you just have to accept—that's how it is.

I also think that I've encountered some hostility from the secretarial staff that's older than I am. Jealousy and things like that. Those people can make it difficult to get work done. Childish things still go on after school.

The Business of Benefits

What we do here is develop benefits packages for other companies. Each person takes one part of what needs to be done and goes off and does it. Then we come back and talk about it. It's not cutthroat because everyone around here wants to help everyone else. We want a project that looks good for the company, so we work as a team.

I work pretty much on a 9 A.M. to 5 P.M. schedule, except under certain circumstances I'll work until 8 P.M. or so. I haven't been promoted because there's no place to be promoted to, but my first year here my responsibilities have increased. I have a lot to learn, but I've learned a lot since I've been here. Everyone has the same title, so you basically gain more experience. We do more writing of plans for other companies than anything, and we're behind the scenes. A human resource person will take what we've done and present it to other employees.

I'm the one here with the least amount of experience, and it's pretty demanding. There are days when it's not, but most of the time it is. The clients really look to you for advice. I enjoy when they send me things to check over; to be able to help them gives me a good feeling. I get lots of calls from a pension fund we work with. They don't have a plan administrator and we get calls from them all the time. No one ever says, "You did a good job," but I know I help a lot.

Plans
This is a good position for a first job, but ten years from now I think I'd like to work in the type of position I had when I was an intern. That was actually working in a personnel office as a benefits assistant at Brown University. I'd like to be a benefits manager for some company.

Advice for Liberal Arts Graduates
Don't get discouraged when you don't really have a specialized background and you're working with people who do. As long as you learn quickly and keep in mind who you are and what you know, you'll do okay. Be confident that you don't have to know everything right away—it will come in time.

J.C. PENNEY CO.
P.O. Box 65900
Dallas, TX 75265-9000
(214) 591-2316

Other Employment Centers
Regional offices in Atlanta, Chicago, Pittsburgh, and Buena Park, Calif.
1,400 stores in the United States and Puerto Rico

Products/Services
Retail department stores

Number of Employees
190,000

Job Opportunities
Management training (stores or systems)

Starting Salary
Mid 20s (est.)

Major Pluses
+ One of the best benefits packages in the retail industry
+ Security (company is known to treat employees as family)
+ Company-paid pension plan
+ Profit-sharing (after one year, employees can contribute up to 16% of their salaries; company will match up to 6%)
+ Excellent training programs
+ Advancement opportunities
+ Generous relocation package

Drawbacks
− Career advancement can be slow, compared to other retailers.

Corporate Philosophy
Treat customers *and* employees according to the *Golden Rule*.

Atmosphere
Friendly, conservative, tradition-bound
Working Conditions
Most stores are old-fashioned; some have been modernized. Retail hours can be demanding, but some employees do work 40-hour weeks.
Tips for Getting a Job
  • Think of the interview as your final exam; research and study the company as you would for any other topic.
  • On your resume, state your objective and tailor it to the job you want with J.C. Penney.

Profile

If your image of J.C. Penney is that of a folksy, old-fashioned, corny department store, it's half true. The way the company treats its employees and customers hasn't changed since James Cash Penney opened his first store in Kemmerer, Wyoming, in 1902. The company still aspires to treat its employees like family and its customers fairly and justly.

With one of the best benefits packages in the retail industry, the company also encourages employees to bring their relatives on board. Many married couples are employed there, as are two or three generations of some families.

But old-fashioned values doesn't hold back business. In fact, some say it promotes it. With 1,400 stores and more than $15 billion in annual revenues, Penney's is one of the largest general-merchandise retailers in the country. It ranks sixth in the *Fortune 50 Retailing Companies*.

Management-Training Opportunities
In a normal year, the company hires about 1,400 management trainees. Liberal arts graduates are sought after. Approximately 1,200 of them go into the store management training; about 200 go into the systems side, which includes catalog, accounting, and information systems.

The store management training is a very structured 12-month program (someone who has completed the internship program can cut it down to six or seven months). This program will train you in all phases of store operations. The first 20 weeks are spent in a store with a training book under the supervision of the store manager. One week of this period is at the Dallas headquarters. The rest is on-the-job in the store.

The catalog training program is held for six weeks at the Dallas headquarters and includes intensive training in computers and forecasting. Upon completion, trainees are placed in the catalog division in one of many locations across the country.

Upon completion of either program, trainees are immediately promoted in both title and salary.

Typical Career Path

According to Roy Chapman, college relations manager, the path of advancement can be a little slow.

After training in store management, you become a merchandiser and get a small department. In a couple of years you will supervise an area encompassing several departments. Within five years, you will be ready for the corporate offices or second-level management, which includes areas such as operations or personnel manager.

At this second stage, the corporate division begins to pull aboard the best and brightest people in. Everyone must start from the trainee level and work in the trenches to be able to work at corporate. There is no external hiring beyond the trainee level.

The Ideal Candidate

Penney's wants team players. "An I'll-go-it-alone type will not make it here." says Chapman. As a manager, you must have good communication skills to motivate the people under you. The store is open for 69 hours a week, but you're only there for 40. So you must be sure things run smoothly and according to plan when you're not there.

Report from the Trenches

MICHELE MORROW

Position: Catalog Inventory Control Specialist
Age: 25
Earnings: High 20s (est.)
School: University of Texas, Austin, Tex.
Major: Government

When Michelle woke up sick on the day of her on-campus interview with J.C. Penney, she was very upset, because she already knew she wanted to work for this company. But she didn't let this small setback deter her. Back on her feet, she immediately sent to the personnel manager a resume along with a personal letter apologizing for missing the interview. It got her in. Her subsequent interviews at corporate headquarters were very interesting.

The first interview was with Paul Denton, the personnel manager. We talked for about an hour, informally. The second interview was more structured. There were four candidates at the time, and each of us had to meet with two different managers. Then we had 10 questions each with each manager.

A lot of the questions were strange, like: "Tell me about a situation where you weren't the leader in a group but the leader somehow had to leave or wasn't doing the job and you stepped in and. . ." I had to give examples from my past to fit that type of situation. They asked questions about my most embarrassing moment and how I handled it; a lot of leadership questions, things like that.

Training
The training program for this job is six weeks and my training class had 12 people in it. It's classroom-based with an instructor, and they bring in different people in the company to make presentations. You do a lot of practice work— classroom and lecture.

We had to learn all the different systems. Our job is estimating. We work with the catalog, and we have to buy all the inventory that we expect to sell out of the catalog for all the different regions in the United States.

First Assignment
After training, we were assigned our positions in the company. From there it varied; some people were assigned to a mentor and they sat with them. I was one of the people who was put into a department where they really needed me. I was kind of thrown into it. I was in Men's Dress Shoes for about a year-and-a-half. I've been in Men's Outerwear for about six months.

Responsibilities
The two basic responsibilities of the job are estimating and inventory control. The buyer chooses one item and then we look at that and we look at history and other items in the past that were similar. Then we decide how many of that item we're going to sell. If there's no history, we all just put our heads together and guess.

My second responsibility is inventory control. We look at estimates, how the demand is coming in, and then decide if we need to get more goods or cut back our orders. We want to keep, of course, enough merchandise in our distribution centers to service the demand, but we don't want to keep too much because of the cost of the warehousing. So we're constantly trying to keep enough merchandise to service what demand we think is going to come in.

Next Steps
My next step would be to senior control buyer, which is the head control buyer, kind of like an assistant manager, one step below manager. Senior control buyers really don't have a workload; they just help all the other control buyers. They're normally in charge of a department which could be between four or 12 control buyers.

Next step would probably be manager, although I think a lot of people start going into different areas before that. You can either get into systems or other areas. The feeling from most people is that it's hard to get out of inventory control, but I know people who have done it.

They Leave and Come Back
We have a pretty high turnover rate [with control buyers], mostly because with the move of Penney's headquarters from New York to Dallas, they lost a lot of their control buyers. The average length of stay of a control buyer in New York was around 13 years, and they lost so many people with the move, that most of us now are straight out of college.

I think that causes a lot of people to quit because it's their first job. A lot of people I've seen have quit and come back. So that says something to me. Normally they'll get a job with a supplier. That's pretty common. But even at other positions and other levels, I know of people who have left and come back to Penney's.

Pay Raises
The pay raises are very good at Penney's. I was surprised by that. The frequency depends on what your rating is. Ratings are 1 to 5, with 1 being the best. They're determined through evaluations. If you're rated higher, you can get your appraisals more often. If you are at the top of the ratings, you can get nice raises.

Don't Limit Yourself
If I had to go out and search for a job right now, I really would not limit myself. I kind of turned around what some people might see as a disadvantage to a liberal arts degree. I turned it around to make it an advantage. Part of that was pride for the degree itself.

In interviews, I stressed that with all the different types of courses I took, the main thing I learned about myself was that I could learn anything. I said, "If you try to teach me something, I can learn it and I can adapt to it."

JEWEL FOOD STORES
1955 W. North Ave.
Melrose Park, IL 60160
(708) 531-6000

Other Employment Centers
Over 200 supermarkets throughout the Midwest

Products/Services
Large retail supermarket chain

Number of Employees
32,000

Job Opportunities
Management trainee

Starting Salary
$24,000 to $26,000

Major Pluses
+ Decent profit-sharing plan goes toward retirement fund, and can retire with full benefits at 57
+ A people person will like this kind of career
+ Flexibility offers employees chance to change career path as it suits them through job opportunities program

Drawbacks
− Not the place to start a career if you're not a people person.
− You'll be hearing Christmas Muzak eight or more hours a day from Halloween through New Year's.

Corporate Philosophy
"Our philosophy is influenced by what we sell," noted Ed Buron, vice president of human resources. "We meet a basic need in society, and our employees come from the community."

Atmosphere
Very family- and team-oriented. Each management trainee is assigned to a manager, who will serve as a mentor. This, along with the common goal of being responsive to the customer, makes the Jewel family a very close-knit one.

Working Conditions
To convey the wholesomeness of their products, clerks wear white shirts and ties. Dress should convey a good image to the public.

Tips for Getting a Job
• Show ability to lead and manage people. Be active in organized activities such as clubs or athletics.
• Experience in working as part of a team also beneficial.
• Be focused on a career goal.
• Think more in terms of contributing to the company, not what the company can give you.

Profile

If you live in the Midwest, chances are you've shopped at a Jewel supermarket. The subsidiary of American Stores of Salt Lake City boasts more than 200 locations in Illinois, Indiana, Iowa, and Michigan. With its headquarters in a Chicago suburb, Jewel perfectly represents its cross-section of customers with blue-collar ethics that brought in $3 *billion* in sales in 1991.

What They Want

Jewel looks for physical stamina, leadership potential, initiative, and accomplishments. "We also look for a self-starter who can work independently," says Ed Buron, vice president of human resources. "They need to function well as individuals and in groups." Liberal arts majors are perfect candidates for management training because they have been encouraged to think independently. Their only drawback is their lack of focus on a specific career goal. "They should get into the work force having thought, 'What can I do for my future employer?' instead of 'What can this do for *me*?' "

The Hiring Process

After sending a resume to the manager of employee recruiting, the prospective trainee goes through three interviews, talking with a personnel rep, a personnel manager, and a district manager before a selection is made.

Training

On-the-job training starts with an assignment as a clerk in a variety of departments. Clerks are also assigned to managers, who will serve as their mentors. "The manager helps employees in their jobs because he knows he can be most productive in that capacity," Buron said.

Career Path

After being recruited as a management trainee and working in all parts of the store for six months to a year, a grad can be expected to become a manager of the produce, deli, or other department. Assuming the employee has done a good job, he or she will most likely become a candidate for assistant store manager in another six months to a year. From there, a move up to co-manager and then store manager is probable.

Report from the Trenches

JEFF KING
Position: Promotional Products Coordinator
Age: 26
Earnings: Low 30s (est.)
School: Eastern Illinois University, Charleston, Ill.
Major: Economics

The last thing Jeff King expected to do as a career was work in retail. Yet he is well on the way to becoming a store manager. And guess what: he has actually enjoyed his career path. Here's how it all happened:

Getting the Job

I originally got my job through a store manager whom a friend of mine knew. Two weeks after I met with him, I was contacted by Jewel's personnel office to come in for an interview. After that interview, it was two weeks before I was called in for a second interview, this time with a district manager. Two weeks after that interview, I received a letter in the mail offering me a position.

The Training Program

My initial position was as manager trainee. It's one of those positions where they bounce you around through every department in the store, teaching everything that there is to know in the time frame that you're there. The first phase of working nights lasted eight months, then I was transferred to days in the front end as a checker and at the service desk. I did that for another six to eight months. From there, I worked in frozen or dairy, then I moved back to nights as a manager of the overnight crew. Then I was promoted to assistant, managing the store from 3 P.M. to midnight.

Career Progress

At that point, I was promoted to my current position, where I leave the actual store setting. In all, it took two years to get to this point, which is pretty much the norm. With [Jewel's] promote-from-within policy, most of the corporate people come from the stores. So when a position opens up in the office, they'll interview store employees.

The Typical Day

My current job is similar to an inventory analyst. I go over whatever programs we happen to be running. Right now, we're running an Olympic pin program in pots and pans, so I'll go through all my inventories, review what I have, and what each store has and determine how much I need. I usually do that daily. I coordinate and put a lot of correspondence together, communicating to stores about changes or upcoming events that we might run, whether it be TV, print, or radio. I proof all that and help organize and put it together, then the actual artist will lay it out. We'll then determine what we want and don't want as far as signing. I'm the only person with this responsibility, but I have two part-time assistants.

The Work Environment

You get a lot of assistance here; you want something, your warehouse people or whoever will do whatever they can for you. Most of their responses are, "Whatever we need to do to get it to the customer." It's nice to work with people like that.

Best and Worst
Probably the best thing is the people I work with. The worst thing is if you feel that the things you do during training are below you. You feel like you really shouldn't have to go through it to get to what you're doing now. But once you get there, the experience proves very valuable in helping you make the decisions that need to be made.

Tips
It's great to have expectations about what you want to do, but keep your eye out for the unexpected. Like me ending up in retail. That's the last place I thought I'd ever be. I really had no inclination to do any such thing, but I basically ended up here, and now I want to grow and enjoy it. It's good to have expectations, but be ready to change when the environment changes.

KAY-BEE TOY & HOBBY SHOPS, INC.
100 West St.
Pittsfield, MA
(413) 499-0086

Other Employment Centers
1,200 stores throughout the United States and Puerto Rico; distribution centers in Phoenix, Indianapolis, and Danville, Ky.

Products/Services
Retail toys

Number of Employees
8,000 to 15,000

Job Opportunities
Assistant manager, executive development program trainees

Starting Salary
Low 20s (est.)

Major Pluses
+ Lots of play on the job, advancement potential

Drawbacks
− Mall hours—nights and weekends, long hours during Christmas season

Corporate Philosophy
Mission statement: Our primary purpose is to satisfy our customers by providing service, quality, and value in all of our stores.

Atmosphere
Fun; must like kids, selling

Working Conditions
Malls, malls, malls

Tips for Getting a Job
- Demonstrate communication skills.
- Familiarize yourself with the concepts of balance sheets and profit margins.
- Ask questions about the day-to-day operations.

Profile

Kay-Bee employees are expected to play on the job. Even the CEO takes breaks with the toys he keeps in his office. But life in the retail toy business is not all fun and games. Competition is stiff between Kay-Bee and the toy industry's leading chain, Toys R Us.

Kay-Bee has become the second largest U.S. toy chain by finding its niche as a mall toy store, designed to appeal to impulsive shoppers. Run under the names Kay-Bee Toy Stores, Toy Works, Circus World Toys, and K&K Toys, the stores generate close to a billion dollars in sales each year.

The toy company is a subsidiary of Melville Corporation, a multibillion dollar company that also owns such specialty retail stores as Chess King, Thom McAnn, This End Up, and Marshall's.

Customer Service First

Kay-Bee believes that the difference between its small, enclosed stores and the warehouse-type Toys R Us lies in customer service and visual presentation. Every Kay-Bee employee, from sales associates to regional managers, must enjoy working with the public and be willing to give customers individual attention. That's where liberal arts graduates fit into the company's game plan. Graduates who have a balanced education and interact easily with people are valued at Kay-Bee. But in the competitive world of retail, business sense is also a necessity. Employees need to be organized and goal-oriented because the company likes to give its managers authority over their own stores. A Kay-Bee employee also has to understand balance sheets and profit margins so that the numbers stay in the black.

The Training Process

Kay-Bee recently started a week-long manager training course at its corporate headquarters. It is a hands-on program in which managers participate in activities similar those they encounter at their jobs. Emphasis is placed on learning visual presentation, financial management, and supervisory skills.

Moving Up

Most liberal arts graduates start as assistant store managers, although graduates with strong retail backgrounds have been hired as store managers. From there, they can become district sales managers, overseeing a number of stores, and regional sales managers, or they can move to positions at the corporate office.

"It's easy to move up the ranks at Kay-Bee," says Beth Erickson, director of training and development. "You just need to communicate, perform, and show potential."

But Erickson cautions that employees shouldn't expect a promotion until they have spent enough time learning the basics of the business, which usually takes more than a year. Getting through at least one holiday season is mandatory training for every management aspirant. During November and December, when Kay-Bee does about 50 percent of its business, you will be expected to work long hours, including nights and weekends.

Mobility Helps

Kay-Bee doesn't require its employees to relocate in order to be considered for promotion, but flexible employees may get more opportunities than those who are tied to one location.

Report from the Trenches

BRIAN LENHART

Position: District Manager
Age: 31 (est.)
Earnings: High 30s (est.)
School: Slippery Rock State University, Slippery Rock, Penn.
Major: History, Geography, Education

Brian Lenhart was looking for a temporary position between teaching jobs when he applied to be an assistant manager for a Kay-Bee store in Montana in 1983. But he soon recognized the potential for advancement at the company and decided to stay.

His stint with Kay-Bee has taken him to several states, including a memorable period opening Kay-Bee's first Alaska store in Anchorage. Lenhart currently works as a district sales manager, overseeing the operations of eight stores in central Texas.

I started with Kay-Bee with no long-term plan for a career. I was looking for a teaching job in Montana, but wasn't certified to teach there. I needed a few more classes. I felt kind of desperate. When I interviewed with the manager and district manager, I was very forceful. I needed the job and really did feel that I was the best person for the job.

I started as an assistant manager. I saw a lot of opportunity, a lot of young people in positions of authority. I was an assistant manager for a little over a year and my plans to teach evaporated.

I went on to manage stores in several different states. It seemed at the time that if you wanted to advance, it was best to be fairly mobile. I had been a geography and history teacher so when the opportunity came up for me to move with Kay-Bee, I jumped on it. Each one of my moves showed me I could better myself.

In the past two years, the company has been turning more to bringing in new blood. There are a lot of fresh new ideas coming in. The opportunity is still here for advancement within the organization.

District Manager

Now I'm responsible for eight stores in central Texas. I cover a large territory and drive a lot. I'm in a different store every day. I deal with a lot of personalities. There's a lot of variety. Little things always come up.

I'm responsible for the operation of those stores. I walk down the aisles, looking at the general condition. I also have to verify the paperwork that is done—review the payroll, memos from the home office, bank deposits, and schedules.

At Christmas time the work load triples. Toys are coming in faster, and things get crazy. I work with the managers, dealing with any problems they might be having.

Our managers have more flexibility than ever. One of the new words at Kay-Bee is decentralization. *We put a lot more power in the hands of our district managers and store managers. We have an opportunity to be a lot more creative with what we are doing.*

Most Fun I've Ever Had

I consider this the most fun I've ever had. I was trained to be a teacher, and I thank goodness that I have the education behind me. I think it was very helpful.

This is the best atmosphere to work in. If you're going to work in the retail business, I can't imagine anything more fun than toys. Working in a shoe store or a jewelry store sounds boring to me. The best thing is dealing with the merchandise. I learn all the ins and outs about toys. Maybe I haven't gotten out of my first childhood.

The Future

In 10 years, I will still be with Kay-Bee. I will probably be in some higher area of authority. I think I will be in charge of a number of stores and possibly a number of district managers. Or maybe I will be acting as an advisory person.

I feel I have had so many experiences with Kay-Bee, maybe I will be called upon to share that knowledge.

LAZARUS DEPARTMENT STORES

699 Race St.
Cincinnati, Ohio 45202
(513) 369-6468

Other Employment Centers
40 stores throughout Ohio and Indiana

Products/Services
Retail department store chain

Number of Employees
12,500

Job Opportunities
Merchandising, sales management, distribution/operations, store management, financial services, visual presentation, advertising, and human resources

Starting Salary
Mid 20s

Major Pluses
+ Paid 12-week internship program in sales management or buying, depending on employee's career track
+ Comprehensive benefits package
+ Discount on merchandise

Drawbacks
− High pressure
− Recent financial problems

Corporate Philosophy
Hard-driving risk-takers. Open to trying new ideas. A climate that balances the creative spirit with a disciplined operation.

Atmosphere
Competitive, yet still open and friendly. The company still has that family-owned feeling.

Working Conditions
A predominantly under-40 staff is flexible both in dress and attitude. Long hours are not required. What counts are results, not time spent on the job.

Tips for Getting a Job
- Highlight extracurricular activities demanding strong communication and interpersonal skills.
- Research the different functions performed within a retail department store. Be prepared to explain how your interests and skills would best fit a particular area.
- Show how your coursework and previous job experience has developed creative problem-solving abilities and a comfort with numbers.

Profile

Founded in 1830, Lazarus has grown to become the 12th largest full-scale retail department store in the country with an annual sales volume of more than $1 billion. The store's history is dotted with "firsts." Lazarus was the first to sell ready-to-wear for men and women, the first to institute a one-price policy to eliminate bartering, and even the first to have an escalator!

The Midwest chain is part of a still larger chain, Federated, the retail giant that owns 200-plus department stores in 26 states including Bloomingdale's, Abraham & Strauss, Bon Marche, Jordan Marsh, and Rich's. Federated, which registered $7 billion in sales in 1991, is one of the few retail success stories of the early 1990s, having emerged successfully from bankrupcty in March 1992.

Lazarus management shrewdly used the bankruptcy shield to its advantage, closing antiquated stores while opening new ones. As a result, the revamped company is stronger than ever.

Liberal Arts Graduates Hired
Half of the approximately 100 college grads Lazarus hired in 1990 were liberal arts graduates. "Problem-solving and excellent communication skills are typical of liberal arts graduates," Ann Lazarus, college relations coordinator, explains. "They are taught not to think in terms of black and white, but in terms of gray. And there are a lot of gray problems in retail."

What They Want
"We don't look for a standard person, in terms of grades, work experience, or curriculum," says Lazarus. "Basically, we seek people with leadership ability, who are well-rounded and bright (not necessarily tied to GPA)."

In addition, Lazarus wants to see evidence of a strong numbers or bottom-line understanding. "Initially, this is sometimes hard for liberal arts graduates," says Lazarus. "They must understand the relationship between the task and the final objective."

Who They Avoid at All Cost
"Some applicants tell me they love to shop. That's why they want to work in retail," Lazarus says. "That almost guarantees a rejection letter. Those people don't understand the business of retail."

The Hiring Process
Lazarus conducts heavy on-campus recruiting. Those selected on the basis of the initial interview attend on-site interviews and meetings with senior management, as well as with a recent graduate of the training program. Applicants are then given either a tour of the city or information regarding the city for which they are being considered.

Training Programs
The 12-week employee training programs are divided into two different paths: sales and buying. All are conducted in Cincinnati.

The sales management training program exposes MITs (managers in training) to Lazarus's management and selling philosophies, visual presentation standards, human resource issues, and customer service policies. Trainees are assigned their own selling area with supervisory responsibility so that they can apply what they learn.

After training is completed, graduates may be placed in any region— Indianapolis, Cincinnati, Dayton, or Columbus. Sales managers are responsible for a host of duties—staff motivation and development, team building, visual presentation, and customer service. Through a combination of classroom and on-the-job training, buyer trainees learn computer system operation, stock analysis, advertising and promotion, assortment planning, gross margin, time management, and general management.

Graduates are placed as merchandising assistants, responsible for making sure the buyers' offices run smoothly—working with vendors on shipping, writing ad copy, tracking sales volume, and assisting buyers in strategic planning.

Career Path
A sales manager can advance to group sales manager, and from there on up to director of selling, store manager, regional vice president (there are three), and executive vice president (there is one).

A merchandising assistant may be promoted to planner and distribution analyst. The next steps are associate buyer, buyer, division merchandise manager (there are 15), and general merchandise manager (there are four).

However, employees need not stick with their original career path. There are opportunities to move into other divisions, such as advertising, human resources, financial services, or visual presentation.

Internships

The recently revamped internship program is similar in content to the training program. Lasting from 10 to 12 weeks, the paid internships are divided into either sales or buying. The location for the internship depends on where the most talented coaches work and the intern's preference. With a focus on business analysis and office operation, interns in the buying office gather a solid base of knowledge and understanding of retail mathematics, computer systems in buying, and the operation of the buying office.

Sales management interns learn Lazarus's operation procedures, policies, and systems. Through floor experiences, management meetings and some classroom instruction, interns gain exposure to the responsibilities of the sales management team.

Report from the Trenches

KATHY REICHERT
Position: Associate Buyer
Age: 25
Earnings: Low 30s (est.)
School: Bowling Green University, Bowling Green, Ohio
Major: Interpersonal and Public Communications

Right out of college Kathy entered a buyer training program with a retail store. But she soon discovered that all trainees had to work as sales managers before they became buyers. More interested in buying than management, she quit her job after six months and moved to Lazarus, where the sales and buyer trainee programs were completely separate. Here's her report after four years on the job:

Training

There were a group of us in the same boat—either not right out of college or with a little prior experience. So we had a few classes, but most of the three months of training was on-the-job. We came into the buying office, stores, distribution center, and planning organization.

But the training program is much more structured now than when I was in it. You take classes in advertising, retail math, computer (since it's such a big part of our job). Then you take tests after each course. That gives the trainer an opportunity to deal with any problems.

Career Path

Lazarus really tries to pay attention to what you're looking for in your career. We often meet with human resources to see how we can make it happen. They are open to letting you go onto your own career path and will work with you to help you get there. In the next month or two I should be promoted to buyer.

Responsibilities

On Monday I analyze sales per item, plan ads, determine markdowns to be taken. A lot of the job is reacting to your business. If an item sold well, I try to find a new item like it. Every hour of the day I talk to vendors, checking on shipping. A lot of the job is troubleshooting, working with the distribution center when there are problems. Associates and buyers go on buying trips every month. For my area (I buy better blouses) I just travel to New York. Others go to California. Home areas go on overseas buying trips.

Corporate Culture

It's pretty open for a corporation. They are understanding and let you speak your mind. We have a CEO who listens. And people do speak out when they're upset. Management is concerned how you feel. If you're not happy, they want to know why and help you fix it.

Coworkers

My best friends work here. Everyone is open and friendly. People tend to like each other and stay for a long time. In fact, a lot of people leave here and then come back. They see they had it pretty good here.

I would describe my colleagues as personable, analytical, very creative, work-hard-play-hard, open with their success. The atmosphere is friendly, but very competitive. You are happy about the good people who get promoted. People here always try to feed off of others' success. Everyone is willing to share.

Most of your coworkers are your peers. There are a lot of people under 30. In fact, most people are 40 and younger. They are flexible in what they wear and in attitude.

Advantages

Advantages? The people I work with and the 10 percent discount on merchandise—you can't beat that. There's a lot of opportunity. It's hard to narrow down to one thing though.

Drawback

Stress is the biggest negative. This is not a job for the faint of heart. You are under a lot of pressure.

Advice
Sometimes I think college graduates limit themselves too much. They rely too much on recruitment. I hear fewer and fewer students are getting jobs that way. You must be a little more creative in how you search.

Whether it's going through newspapers, sending out resumes, or going through your own resources, you must do different things. I know people in sororities and fraternities who have gone through alumni listings and gotten jobs that way. How you get your foot in the door depends on how creative you are.

LIBERTY MUTUAL INSURANCE GROUP
175 Berkeley St.
Boston, MA 02117
(617) 574-5861

Other Employment Centers
350 offices throughout New England, split into nine divisions or regions

Products/Services
Consumer and commercial insurance carrier

Number of Employees
22,000

Job Opportunities
Management trainees in a wide variety of fields, from financial analyst and claims adjuster to sales rep and underwriter.

Starting Salary
Mid 20s (est.)

Major Pluses
+ Outstanding benefits package, including medical, dental, income protection, group life, and retirement plans
+ Aggressive promote-from-within policy means good chance of rapid movement up the ranks

Drawbacks
− Long hours and stressful work
− *A lot* of relocation
− Many employees are hired at one time, and more than a few wash out

Corporate Philosophy
Employees are challenged to effectively deal with their customers and to better themselves within the company.

Atmosphere
Currently streamlining bureaucracy and decentralizing decision-making process, which challenges employees to find own ways to work. Very people-oriented, with an emphasis on teamwork inside the office.

Working Conditions
Hard work, diverse responsibilities, and opportunities

Tips for Getting a Job
- Be confident in your abilities, and demonstrate how you can use your talents to get results.
- Show interest in the insurance industry, and be familiar with the company.
- Don't come to interview looking for a job; tell them what you can do for Liberty Mutual.

Profile

Liberty Mutual Insurance Group is a $17 million insurance organization with offices from London to Honolulu. The company carries policies on more than two million individuals and 10,000 businesses. And judging by the sheer deluge of material that covers their employee benefits, their belief in a staff possessed with strong minds and bodies is truly laudable.

What They Want
"We look for aptitudes, not personality traits," stated Helen Sayles, vice president and manager of human resources. "We look for experience, education, and self-confidence in how they come across in the interview."

Analytic and communication skills are always important, but your specific skills will determine where they'll place you in the company. "An underwriter deals with salespeople and financial and business data," Sayles noted. "He or she would need versatility. In claims, a person needs to communicate well and think on his or her feet; they often meet and get into adversarial situations."

The Hiring Process
Decentralized into larger, functional areas, hiring is conducted by a combination of people who have skills in recruiting, hiring, and higher management. Besides on-campus interviews, Liberty recruits through employment agencies, newspaper ads, employee referrals, and resumes. There are multiple interviews, transcript and reference checks, and, for some positions, specific tests.

Training
All new employees are given orientation and basic training by their respective departments so they can become familiar with the company and gain specific experience. The length of training depends on the position and work. Claims adjusters, for instance, spend five to six weeks in

classroom and on-the-job training before assignment to an office. Training often continues in advanced training seminars, which provide greater technical knowledge. Bottom line: the more you train and know about your position, the better off you will be, and the higher you'll go in the company.

Report from the Trenches

MICHELE KERRY

Position: Director of Hiring and Training for Claims
Age: 32
Earnings: Low 50s (est.)
School: Regis College, Weston, Mass.
Major: Sociology

Ten years ago, Michele Kerry was just hoping for the best when she submitted her resume to Liberty Mutual Insurance. Now, she spends a good deal of her time evaluating the resumes of potential employees and choosing the best training programs so they can reach theirs—and the company's—potential. Here's how she got this far . . . so far:

After graduating in May 1982, I submitted a resume to be an adjuster or in Memory Writing. I got a response from Claims in a follow-up phone call. There was one quite lengthy interview. I began in July of 1982. The training program was six weeks long, after which I became an adjuster.

Career Progress
In April 1984, I moved to the home office to become a senior adjuster. I handled special policy holders. In June 1985, I was moved to West Roxbury as a claims service coordinator, a liaison between policy holders and the claims department.

In July 1986, I was moved to Chestnut Hill as a claims supervisor. Adjusters reported to me; I reviewed their work, assigned classes and monitored those cases. In 1988, I moved back to West Roxbury to be district supervisor. The job is identical to claims supervisor, but the authorization power is greater. In September of 1989, I became director of hiring and training. I hire and fire entry-level claims appraisers, adjusters, and so on.

The Typical Day
A typical day involves a lot of interruptions. I'm actively involved in the six-week training program. I speak to the trainees. I also receive phone calls from employees, too. There's the budget and hiring to consider. There's a lot of variety in this job, which I find enjoyable.

The Work Environment
It isn't relaxed, but it's not too stressful either. I'm very busy, but I like the workload. I prefer to be busy. We're allowed to be independent, but all departments want to work together. My department is characterized by the team approach. My colleagues and I have a good working relationship. The hours are lengthy and the work keeps me busy, but we do find time to talk on a personal level. A sense of humor helps.

Best and Worst
The people are the best thing about working here. The opportunities are great as well. Everything I want to accomplish is attainable.

The lines of communication didn't used to be very open. Sometimes, I'd make a decision and want to run with it, but I couldn't. Bosses like to discuss things, but the communication from the top down is getting better.

The Future
In 10 years, I'd like to be the assistant division claims manager. There is a promote-from-within policy, which provides a lot of opportunity. You get paid for performance. If you do a good job and work hard, you get where you want to go.

Tips
To be in claims, the more areas you involve yourself in, the better. You have to juggle a lot here. If you have experience dealing with people and other things, that's helpful. When I look at a resume, I ask myself, "Do they have a competitive edge?"

LIZ CLAIBORNE, INC.
One Claiborne Ave.
North Bergen, NJ 07047
(201) 662-6000

Other Employment Centers
Canada, China, Hong Kong, Korea, New York, the Philippines, Singapore, and retail outlets nationwide (most employment opportunities are in New Jersey and New York)

Products/Services
Women's clothing/retail outlets (although in the past few years the company has expanded into men's fashion as well)

Number of Employees
5,200

Job Opportunities
Sales and marketing, design, merchandising, research, production, management information systems

Starting Salary
$22,000

Major Pluses
+ In-house training. Comprehensive six-month management training program. Company always tries to fill positions from within.
+ Bonus program for all employees
+ Continuing education (tuition reimbursement for graduate courses as well as job-related seminars and certification programs)

Drawbacks
− Many positions are based in Liz Claiborne's corporate headquarters in northern New Jersey, not exactly a burgeoning cultural mecca.
− If you are looking for an environment on the cutting edge of fashion, this ain't it. LC did not grow to be the biggest fashion supplier to working women by setting trends.

Corporate Philosophy
"Let's make the best even better." With Liz Claiborne this means not just with product but in the work environment as well, hence the often quirky perks such as "open suggestion systems," "humanitarian awards," "Johnny-on-the-spot awards," an in-house newspaper, and company-wide contests. The company is big on team spirit with "lots of Indians and few chiefs."

Atmosphere
Fast-paced, high-pressured environment. People aren't worried about losing their jobs.

Working Conditions
Headquartered in New Jersey with New York City the center for marketing and design. Good training and advancement potential are within one's area, although employees sometimes feel pigeonholed.

Tips for Getting a Job
• Research the company. Before interviews, familiarize yourself with Liz Claiborne products. Information is mailed twice a year to all campuses where the company recruits and is also available from libraries and the corporate headquarters public relations office.
• Stress work experience. Liz Claiborne believes previous work experience is a good indication of energy level and a willingness to work.
• Highlight abilities as a team player. Recruiters look for enthusiasm, high energy, team spirit, and a sense of humor.

- Emphasize your well-rounded background. Most of the recruiters at Liz Claiborne tend to like students with a diverse background and at least some exposure to business (e.g., introduction to accounting or business classes).
- Emphasize your adaptability. If you can handle only one or two things at a time, or if you need constant praise, don't bother to apply here. The work environment is fast-paced and immediate response to your work may not come.

Profile

Liz Claiborne's fashion-savvy styles appeal to a great cross-section of women and have found a particularly healthy audience in the "young working woman's" arena. Known for high quality and reasonable cost, Claiborne's collections continue to dominate the market share of women's fashion. Claiborne's success is her identification with her customers and vice versa. Representatives from Liz Claiborne, Inc. spend a healthy amount of time each year on the road talking to consumers about what they want, and their model was Claiborne herself, who built a business on finding out what women really want in fashion.

As a result her personal dedication, Claiborne has a large fan club. When she recently made an appearance at New York City's Macy's Department Store, Claiborne was besieged by a crowd of 600 loyal fans who view her not only as a designer, but as an icon for working women.

A Company in Transition

Claiborne founded the company with her husband, Arthur Ortenberg, and two other partners in 1976. Liz and Arthur officially resigned from their top corporate posts (CEO and vice chair) in August of 1990. Naturally, the question on everyone's minds was, "Will her customers continue to identify with the line?" The answer has been a qualified yes. The company's 1991 fall fashions were well received by the fashion world and consumers alike.

That positive response shouldn't come as much of a surprise since Liz's team of 31 house designers has been working on the Claiborne line since 1987, although Claiborne herself still actively reviewed each and every collection.

How You Can Fit In

Liz Claiborne, Inc. is among the largest apparel companies operating in the United States. Throughout the company, you'll find opportunities in sales, marketing, design, production, merchandising, operations, accounting, finance, and human resources.

The company fills most entry-level positions through on-campus recruiting during both semesters. You might find Liz Claiborne job openings posted in your campus career office or at career fairs, but don't look for them in the classifieds, because the company doesn't advertise.

Management-training candidates can expect at least three interviews: one with a corporate recruiter, another with a director or senior level person, and a third one with a corporate level VP.

Training
On-the-job training is provided for most positions. If you get into the Careers in Management program, the training is a little more formalized.

Report from the Trenches

NINA ZOLFAGHARI
Position: Product Manager
Age: 25
Earnings: Mid 30s (est.)
School: University of Delaware, Newark, Del.
Major: English

Nina's hiring at Liz Claiborne was an exception to the rule: she got her job through a headhunter. While we recommend attempting to secure a position first through on-campus interviews or by contacting the corporation directly, Nina's success proves there are no hard-and-fast rules in job hunting. Here's her report after three years, during which she has held several positions:

Finding the Right Niche
I originally interviewed several times in the dress division, but it wasn't right for me. These positions were more administrative than what I wanted. Finally, I interviewed in Missy sportswear where I was hired, and now I work in the Petite sportswear division.

I started in an entry-level position, as a bookings coordinator, and have been promoted twice since, progressing to advertising coordinator and then to product coordinator. Currently, product coordinator is the highest divisional position short of manager.

I am basically in marketing, which is a good area to be in, since the skills can be applied to other divisions.

Training
I had mostly informal training, mainly through the person who had the position prior to me. The department manager also helped. This department tends to move its personnel quickly; the person who had previously held my job had had it only eight months before being promoted.

The Liberal Arts Factor
I'm the only one in my department with a liberal arts degree. Everyone else has a business or marketing background, so sometimes I feel I am lacking the proper education, especially since I'm in such a business oriented position.

On the other hand, my job is so specialized that a business degree would not have been helpful. If anything, my liberal arts degree has given me a broader perspective than I would have had with more specified majors. I've never found anything in my work too difficult to accomplish; I've always been able to adapt.

The Typical Day
A lot of my work day depends on market schedules. I prepare reports for sales people after every market season. There are six market seasons per year. I generate reports based on past sales and future projections. It's more of a numbers-oriented position than I had wished for.

Best Thing
The overall experience of working in the fashion industry has been helpful in helping me decide where I want to go from here. Liz Claiborne gives you plenty of opportunity to gain a broad knowledge of the industry.

Worst Thing
Now that I am in one of the highest positions within the department, it's hard to think about starting at the bottom again in another area. Also, the pay is not very good in comparison to other companies. But Liz Claiborne is a respected and solid company so I feel I should be happy just being part of it.

I still think I want to be involved in the fashion industry; I want to be in something that is more people-oriented. On a day-to-day basis I work only with the people within the company.

Advice to Grads
I didn't look down the road at what would be happening to my career in a year or longer when I took this position. You should go on informational interviews. They may sugar-coat the information, but at least you will have a much better idea of the company and your career path there.

Also, don't take the first job you are offered. Sometimes you become scared that you will never get a job, but you will. It's better to hold out for what you really want to do.

THE MAY DEPARTMENT STORES
611 Olive St.
St. Louis, MO 63101
(314) 342-6300

Other Employment Centers
Meier & Frank (Portland, Ore., May D&F (Denver), Volume Shoe Corp. (Topeka, Kan.), L.S. Ayres (Indianapolis), May Company (Cleveland), Lord & Taylor (New York), Filene's (Boston), May Company (Los Angeles), Robinson's (Los Angeles), Foley's (Houston), Kaufmann's (Pittsburgh), Hecht's (Washington, D.C.), G. Fox (Hartford, Conn.), Thalhimer's (Richmond, Va.)

Products/Services
Department stores and discount shoe retailers

Number of Employees
166,000

Starting Salary
$28,500 ($30,000 in New York City)

Major Pluses
+ Excellent starting pay
+ Management training (10 weeks of both on-the-job training and classroom training)
+ Career support system (formalized feedback and structured support program throughout career path)
+ Merchandise discounts
+ Relocation assistance (recent college graduates are provided one-way transportation expenses to job locations plus temporary living expenses)
+ Profit sharing
+ Location (affiliated stores located in some of the nation's most desirable urban/suburban areas)
+ Stability (company has experienced enviable track record of growth and profitability over the last 15 years)

Drawbacks
− Long hours. Expect to work overtime during holiday season.
− Long-term economic forecast questionable due to changing consumer shopping patterns.

Corporate Philosophy
Thoughtful, proactive concern with employees. "We believe that excellence in retailing can be achieved only by building a premier organization composed of the finest talent in the business. Our success is based on people—the company's most creative and valuable asset."

Atmosphere
Fast-paced and positive, although long hours and deadlines can be stressful. Company is huge but decentralized, which makes it more personable than number of employees would indicate.

Working Conditions
Generally very good. The company has a good record of re-investing in its properties. Many of its affiliated department stores are upscale and among the best in the country.

Tips for Getting a Job
- Show leadership. Company looks for articulate individuals who can demonstrate "flexibility, people-orientation, determination, realism and goal orientation."
- Be alive and extroverted. During an interview be specific in your responses and draw on your past experiences. Be ready to give examples of the success you've had in a variety of areas where you had to compete.
- Analytical skills. Discuss any courses involving accounting, statistics, or quantitative methodology. Good merchants are afraid of numbers.
- Retail experience. It's worth a mention, but not required since company teaches the basics.

Profile

The May Department Stores Company typifies the liberal arts–friendly, progressive corporation discussed in Chapter 1. The Company is aggressive in recruiting liberal arts graduates but not just from a handful of Ivy League schools. A brochure welcoming the class of 1991 new employees revealed liberal arts graduates from dozens of schools nationwide, many of them small liberal arts colleges as well as larger private and state universities.

Top management for May's come from a liberal arts background and actively set a pro-liberal–arts tone for the entire company. The company has a fast-track management program with substantial raises built in along the well-defined career path.

Finally, the work itself is fast-paced, varied, and marketing-oriented, requiring flexibility, communication skills and creativity—an environment where the liberal arts–educated can spread their wings.

One of the Biggest
With sales over $10 billion in 1990, this company is one of the country's largest retailers, with 14 separate department store chains serving market areas of 122 million people nationwide. It currently operates 324 department stores in 31 states. Additionally, it operates Payless ShoeSource, the country's largest chain of self-service family shoe stores.

For the past 16 years ending in 1990, May Department Stores Company could boast of consecutive years of record growth and earnings. The company's five-year capital expenditure plan for 1991 through 1995 totals $3.6 billion. Plans include opening 100 new department stores and 1,200 new Payless ShoeSource stores.

The company, founded in Colorado in 1877 by David May, has been listed on the New York Stock Exchange since 1911.

Changing Shoppers?

One dark cloud in an otherwise bright forecast was 1991's Christmas sales which declined 1 percent from the previous year. The decline might be dismissed as nothing more than a periodic downturn in the volatile retail industry. Some analysts believe, however, that once the dust settles from the consumer spending binge of the 1980s, May could be one of the losers. Along with other upscale department store chains, May could suffer as shoppers increasingly turn to discount chains such as Wal-Mart, Kmart, and Target.

May's management prides itself on its buying processes and merchandising skills and is anticipating a possible change in shopping patterns by expanding its moderately priced goods and upgrading services.

Training

Liberal arts graduates enter the company's 10-week executive training program, which focuses on buying. The program is composed of on-the-job activities and supplemented by weekly classes. Regular feedback is provided through a supervisor and human resources counselor.

Upon completion of the program, the executive trainee works as an assistant buyer for up to two years later placed as an area sales manager in a branch store for 12 to 18 months.

Career Path

After serving as an area sales manager, the employee can follow one of two career paths: merchandise or stores. The merchandise path leads to a position as buyer, then divisional merchandise manager and general merchandise manager (the most important position next to store president).

The buyer, who has a front-line job in retailing, is responsible for achieving sales, gross margin, and profit goals and managing receipts and inventory levels. In addition, the advertising and promotion plans must be developed, budgeted, and implemented. Buyers receive additional management training through the Leadership Through People Skills program.

The stores path is concerned with store management and operations functions such as purchasing, customer service, distribution, traffic and stock control, human resources management, audit, accounts payable, and accounts receivables.

The company adheres to a promotion-from-within policy and has even created a computer software system, known as Executive Track, to spotlight candidates for job openings.

Recruitment Process

There are three on-campus interviews. The first one lasts 30 minutes. From this a selection is made for the second round of interviews the following day. The second interview lasts an hour and is with the line managers.

In the third interview, the candidate is invited to a store. At this point a job offer usually has been made, and the purpose is to acquaint the prospective employee with the work environment. It's usually an all-day affair, consisting of four or five interviews interrupted by meals and panel discussions.

Most new executive trainees are hired through the company's extensive campus recruiting efforts, but not all, as the following report illustrates.

Report from the Trenches

MATTHEW FAIRCHILD
Position: Assistant Buyer
Age: 23
Earnings: High 30s (est.)
School: SUNY Albany, Albany, N.Y.
Major: Psychology

Working for a department store wasn't exactly what Matthew had in mind when he decided to major in psychology. Then again, his educational background has come in handy in his people-oriented work as an assistant buyer for Filene's, the Boston-based department store chain owned by May.

Here's his story after a year on the job:

Getting Hired

I submitted a resume to Filene's personnel office in Boston and then met the college recruiter. Filene's wasn't recruiting from my school so I walked in personally. They gave me a call back, and I went through an all-day interview process; I bypassed the normal process.

I interviewed with several different vice presidents. I interviewed with the recruiter's boss, and he showed me what he did. There was also a short psycho-

logical exam. They must have liked what they saw because at the end of day I was offered a position.

Year One

I immediately started three months of classes and on-the-job training. In September everyone was placed, and I wound up in the shoe division. After three months I was placed in the men's clothing area, where I became a sales manager. After six months I was then brought back into the buying division, where I am now.

There is no typical day. It depends on what's going on. I once even had to do stock work. You never know what you're going to walk into. You rarely have a week under 45 hours with 8 A.M. to 6 P.M. typical hours.

My colleagues were all in my classes with me. Some were very competitive. The way we—there were 30 people in the program with me —were recruited, however, made us close and created a helpful and supportive environment.

Best and Worst

The best thing about working here is the daily challenge. There is always someone smarter than you here. And there are real opportunities to learn. For instance, my boss, a buyer, is not here the whole week, so I have had to learn how to do everything [he does] and do it well.

The worst thing here is the amount of movement and circulation a person has to deal with. There's a lot and it's very tough, especially on a new person. I have had five bosses in two years. You've got to be strong and ambitious to perform well under those conditions.

Doing It Over

If I were right out of college looking for my first job, I would probably take a broader approach than I did. I perhaps was a little too focused. I just started out looking in an industry that sounded interesting. I would look at more companies and do more research.

But, yes, I would work for this company again. I have had a good experience here. I don't envision spending the rest of my life at any one place. But the next step for me here is buyer. After that I would like to be divisional vice president.

METROPOLITAN LIFE INSURANCE CO.

One Madison Ave.
New York, NY 10010
(212) 578-5592

Other Employment Centers
Major facilities in New York City and Bridgewater, N.J.; sales offices in each state and international operations in Canada, Spain, Taiwan, South Korea, and England

Products/Services
Insurance, pensions, investment management, real estate, mortgage banking, managed health care services, and mutual funds

Number of Employees
54,000

Job Opportunities
Trainee positions in management, actuarial development, and information systems; assistant programmer, marketing/group sales representative, financial analyst, and business systems analyst

Starting Salary
Low 30s

Major Pluses
+ Two-year, fast-track management training program
+ Corporate fitness center
+ Full tuition reimbursement
+ Free lunch each day
+ Free van service to train stations
+ Six-month parental leave for mothers *and* fathers
+ Six-month sabbatical available for a variety of reasons, including travel
+ Flexible hours

Drawbacks
− Organization can be bureaucratic

Corporate Philosophy
Business ethics and customer service stressed more than anything else. Commitment to community involvement. Company will match employees to volunteer opportunities.

Atmosphere
Company is often called "Mother Met" because of management's parental attitude toward employees. Strong cooperation between departments. Staff is encouraged to have a we-directed versus me-directed attitude.

Working Conditions
Slick and corporate, physically; noncompetitive and friendly, emotionally.

Tips for Getting a Job
- A 3.2 GPA helps but is not essential.
- Display an interest in developing and growing in the organization and becoming a manager.
- Emphasize leadership abilities developed in previous work experience, courses, student government, or extracurricular activities.
- Be aware of current trends and issues in the business world, especially as they relate to the commercial insurance industry.

Profile

In 1868, MetLife began as a small personal insurance company. Today, it is an enormous family of companies, providing customers with a broad array of financial products and services, everything from real estate (Century 21) and hotels (Doubletree and Compri) to pensions and managed health care services.

In 1989 MetLife surpassed rival Prudential as the largest insurance company in the United States, based on the total value of its policies. Because of its diversity and size ($134 billion in assets under management), MetLife offers numerous career avenues—product development, research and planning, and financial analysis, to name a few.

Liberal Arts Fast Track

Of particular interest to liberal arts graduates is its two-year Management Associate Program (MAP), which offers the chance to try out different disciplines through four six-month hands-on work assignments. As of fall 1990, 86 percent of MAP participants were liberal arts graduates from a wide range of majors, including anthropology, religion, East Asian history, psychobiology, urban studies, French, political science, and English.

"Since our philosophy is to develop generalists with a broad corporate view, the well-rounded liberal arts major is an especially good fit for this program," says Georgann Occhipinti, MetLife college relations consultant.

What They Want

MetLife looks at a number of factors when evaluating applicants—national ranking of school, GPA and demonstrated leadership ability. "Leadership is really a critical factor," says Occhipinti. "This is our only indicator of what type of manager they may become. Often we recruit at schools where students are actively involved with the campus and its governance. Or perhaps an applicant may have camp counselor experience where they have been responsible for 200 12-year-olds over the span of a summer."

In particular, MetLife looks for people who fit their corporate culture. "She or he should be accomplished and intelligent, but also someone who doesn't feel he or she is better than another individual," Occhipinti says. "We are an extremely interactive organization, from technical to marketing. People who are me-directed versus we-directed set up a red flag for us."

The Hiring Process

MetLife uses a number of hiring sources—college campuses, career fairs, advertisements in *Career Insights, Business Today,* and the *College Placement Council Directory,* as well as referrals from current employees. After a successful interview, an applicant is invited to interview at the home office in New York City. Response usually takes two to three weeks.

Advice

"Don't underestimate the value and quality of your liberal arts education," advises Occhipinti. "Look at skills gained in your education, rather than at the list of courses you've taken. The liberally educated are generally quite flexible, open to new ideas, and eager to explore—valuable qualities, since change tends now to be a given in the business world. These graduates also tend to have a broad perspective, an especially useful attribute in today's global marketplace."

Mistakes Applicants Make in the Interview

"They are too anxious to impress," Occhipinti says. "They interrupt or become overbearing. They may not always be listening. They need to realize that they are talking to an interviewer for the first time and must be explicit even if they have done 10 interviews in a week.

"Also applicants sometimes interview for anything, without giving any thought to what they may want." Occhipinti suggests that candidates research different organizations and industries, as well as keep abreast of current business news. "Some students will come in and not be too aware of what's in major publications and on the nightly news concerning the business world in general."

Training

MAP (the management associate program) consists of four six-month work assignments designed to groom college graduates for management responsibility. Every associate's work assignment sequence is unique. For the first stint, previous accomplishments and skills determine placement. However, for the remaining three assignments, trainees have the opportunity to interview with a variety of departments and choose the areas where they'd like to work.

Through their assignments, associates develop an understanding of key functions, such as marketing, customer service, research and planning, product development, and financial analysis. Associates also learn to use computers as a management tool and experience different management styles and work environments.

A distinct advantage of MAP is the opportunity it provides associates to gradually formulate career interests and objectives based on their program experiences and, upon completion of their training, to choose the position that best meets those objectives.

Career Path

After graduating from MAP, employees must apply to the area within the organization which interests them the most. The process is similar to applying for any new job: send a resume and cover letter to the appropriate person within the department.

Report from the Trenches

SHARON KNAUER

Position: Management Associate
Age: 24
Earnings: High 30s
School: Yale University, New Haven, Conn.
Major: English

After graduating from Yale, Sharon began a two-year management training program at Metropolitan Life in New York City. The program allowed her to try out four different departments: Pensions, Managed Care (providing medical management for HMOs), Investments, and Corporate Wellness and Fitness Services. Here's her report three months before she was scheduled to complete her training.

Training Program

At the beginning it was very intense. I worked long hours. In Pensions, I provided phone support with the sales representatives. I really got to write my own ticket and do a wide range of things. I became the expert on new demographic systems, and I got to train high-level people. That was quite exciting.

Since I got to pick my second assignment, I wanted to try something that was really a hot area that had a lot of attention behind it. That was in managed care services. I was involved in getting together a database to provide broad-based credentialing information on doctors. I got to make presentations to high-level people, often talked to group sales people, and analyzed cost benefits. We were working on a contract to hospitals for transplants, and I wrote a brochure for that.

I've been at Met almost two years and I have developed a real sense of what I like and realize that some of the things I thought I liked I no longer think I do. I was very fortunate because the training program gave me the chance to try things risk-free.

Career Path

At Met if you find a spot where your talents are being used and you are making an impact, you often stay forever. A lot of people here find that place. After the Management Associate Program, it's like looking for a new job (within the organ-

ization). Now I'm putting my resume together, writing letters, and so forth. I would like to remain in the health area in a new capacity.

Corporate Culture
Except maybe in investments, Met is very parental. The term "Mother Met" is passed along a lot. The climate is nicer and friendlier than banking. It's not a very competitive place. It's easy to lose ambition because of the lack of competition.

Advantages
The people here and the flexibility to try new things. I never feel like my career is on the line with a letter or a phone call. People are excited here.

Drawbacks
Bureaucracy can be a problem. It's no one's fault and it happens everywhere, but it frustrates me. Often it takes a lot more time to get things done than I expected.

Advice
I would have explored beyond on-campus recruiting. I can't help but wonder, "What if I had gone a different route?" I don't regret it, but I would have been more broad in terms of both occupational areas and geographical locations.

Also, keep an open mind. I would not underestimate the importance of a good income. I have a nice salary. It's nice to be financially comfortable. I wouldn't be afraid of making the wrong career decision. Nothing's permanent. I've had friends go through three or four jobs quite successfully.

Be very aware of what you're getting into. I have a roommate, an investment banker, and per hour I must make three times as much as he does when you consider the amount of time he works.

Biggest Surprise
I never expected to become so involved with my work. Some of my best friends are people I work with. We talk a lot about work. I did not fully understand the importance of having a job I like and the effects it would have on the rest of my life. I thought a job was something you did, but it's something you live.

MOORE CORPORATION
International Corporate Headquarters
1 First Canadian Place
P.O. Box 78
Toronto, Canada M5X1G5
(416) 364-2600

U.S.A. Corporate Headquarters
1205 Milwaukee Ave.
Glenview, IL 60025
(708) 615-6000

Midwest Sales Headquarters
1419 Lake Cook Rd.
Deerfield, IL 60015
(708) 940-8688

Other Employment Centers
All major North American cities; also in 45 countries

Products/Services
Business forms; information and database management services

Number of Employees
26,000

Job Opportunities
Sales

Starting Salary
$24,000 plus commission

Major Pluses
+ Training (year-long program teaches you everything you need to know about selling product)
+ Unlimited income potential—the more you sell, the more you earn
+ Good money. Quotas are established for each sales representative to make. Employees are evaluated periodically for sales and management techniques. The payoffs are lucrative rewards and bonuses.
+ Company car

Drawbacks
- Sales positions only—you either love it or hate it

Corporate Philosophy
Views itself as company at the forefront of innovation, despite its seemingly mundane field of business forms. Here's an excerpt from its corporate statement: "A leader possesses the ability . . . to seize the opportunities inherent in change. That is the mark of a leader, the hallmark of Moore." Hail, Caesar!

Atmosphere
Company encourages friendly in-house competition to improve productivity. As a salesperson, you'll live or die by your own resourcefulness. On the other hand, you're still part of a sales team (toward which you're expected to act civilly).

Working Conditions
Modern, corporate environment. Each employee gets a modular work station (better known as a cubicle) in an open-area floor plan.

Tips for Getting a Job
- Play up your broad range of studies. A liberal arts degree is highly regarded here. "To be successful in sales, you need to be exposed to a broad spectrum of ideas," says company representative.
- Be prepared to explain your penchant for individual initiative while simultaneously being a team player.
- Brush up on those communications skills. You're going to have to sell, rather than just offer, yourself as the right person for this job. You can't be too aggressive in this regard.

Profile

A corporation with operations on every continent, Moore is the largest business forms company in the world and the only one that operates on a global scale. Despite the recession, this company has sustained its steady pattern of growth, in part by expanding into other services, such as direct marketing and database management, which are becoming increasingly important as global marketing is turning to "narrow-casting"—targeting niche audiences to enhance sales.

Moore spends a good deal on research (around $35 million annually) to improve information systems technology. As a result the company is a leader in automatic identification systems (bar-coding) and was chosen by the U.S. government to create and disseminate the 1990 census forms— a $20 million order that was the largest in the company's 107-year history.

Business Outlook
While some people predicted that the computerization of business would be the death knell for the business forms industry, the opposite appears to have happened. Rather, computers have required reams of new forms. Sales of these specialized forms have doubled for Moore in the last two years.

Despite Moore's global operations, its U.S. sales account for 60 percent of its revenues. A deepening domestic recession could end Moore's 12-year pattern of growth. Nevertheless, the company enjoys an excellent reputation for stability, having earned an A++ rating for financial strength from a Value Line Investment Survey in 1991.

Training
Sales positions are the only opportunities for liberal arts grads at Moore. If you know nothing about sales, but think you still might like it, don't worry, says Reid Gimian, sales recruiting manager for the Western region headquarters, in Los Angeles. "Training is extensive."

Your first three weeks will be spent in computer-based product training in the local office. During the fourth week you'll be at Moore's Chicago sales headquarters.

Within a year, Moore sends its new sales representatives through the manufacturing plants and gives them further training in sales and product knowledge. After a year, additional classes in negotiation, time management, sales management, and education are available, as needed.

Career Path

Step 1. Trainee. Step 2. Sales Representative. Everyone gets assignments. You work with customers, both new and old, and begin building relationships. You also start cold-calling prospective clients to see how they can use Moore products. You learn the process of setting up and closing a deal. The initial work is similar to what people do 10 years later.

Step 3. Sales Representative, Level 2. Assignments get much larger.

Getting Hired

Recruiting is conducted through college interviews, phone calls, walk-ins, and referrals from current and former employees. Each office does its own hiring, and each prospective employee goes through three interviews with a regional manager, including one day spent in the field with a sales representative.

Report from the Trenches

SHARON DIEMER

Position: Sales Representative
Age: 27
Earnings: 40s
School: San Diego State University, San Diego, Ca.
Major: Finance

After graduation Sharon worked in retail sales for a few years before she decided to go back to Moore, where she had worked part-time while in college. In college, she was active in student government activities, including "Ambassadors," a group that acts as a liaison between students, parents, alumni, and prospective students. The fact that she was a well-rounded person who could balance her time between work, academics, and activities made her an attractive prospect to Moore.

Since coming to Moore just over two years ago, her sales status and responsibilities have increased steadily. Here's what Sharon told us:

Why She Said Yes
I had narrowed my job search to two companies: Moore and Merrill Lynch. Merrill Lynch was similarly attractive, but it was something I wasn't ready for. I wasn't up for selling securities. I was familiar with Moore from college, so I was pretty comfortable with them right away.

Training Program
I interviewed for three days at Moore in Orange County [a suburban county south of Los Angeles]. One day was split in two. In the morning I went around with a sales representative; in the afternoon, I made routine calls.

For the next three weeks, the training was in-house, and from there I went on assignment. The in-house training is relaxed, but you spend the entire time on disks, taking test after test after test. But there are no time pressures. You can continue until you're done.

Mobility
It's very easy to move around here. After the first couple of years, you see a big change in how you do things. Your assignments get much larger. You give yourself your own raise. Besides the salary [raises], I have gotten into the Moore's Achievement Club [traveling program], the bonus program and the company car program.

Not a Pressure Cooker of a Job
The system is set up so that you can sell for all of your career. Moore is a stable, safe sell. It's the standard in the industry. It's not too aggressive, and it's not 100 percent commission, but there is a continuing demand to do well here.

Liberal Arts a Plus
Moore looks for well-rounded people. It took me five years to go through college, but I worked 25 hours a week and was involved in school activities. On top of that, I took a semester on an exchange program in New Hampshire. Moore likes that.

Ten Years from Now
I prefer to stay in sales. I hope to go on into the national account division, where I'll be dealing with clients nationwide. I just love what I do.

NATIONAL WESTMINSTER BANK, USA
175 Water Street
New York, NY 10038-4924
(212) 602-1000

New Jersey Headquarters
10 Exchange Place
Jersey City, NJ 07302

Other Employment Centers
126 branches in New York, Long Island, and Westminster; 136 branches
in New Jersey

Products/Services
Commercial/consumer banking

Number of Employees
7,500

Job Opportunities
Management trainee in lending, auditing, or consumer banking

Starting Salary
$28,000 to $31,000

Major Pluses
+ Good training
+ Advancement opportunities

Drawbacks
− Banking is banking (if you don't have an interest, it will be boring)
− Locations in Northeast only

Corporate Philosophy
NatWest believes that they can teach you all you need to know about
banking. Their statement of values is to "grow their own talent."

Atmosphere
Open-door management policy. Friendly yet professional and business-
like. Suits are required.

Working Conditions
A bank is a bank.

Tips for Getting a Job
- Show some knowledge of or an interest in commercial banking.
- Emphasize academic achievement but not perfection (they don't
  want bookworms).
- Highlight any customer service work experience.

Profile

Originally chartered in 1905 as the First National Bank of Freeport,
National Westminster is the product of several mergers, having acquired
its current name in 1983 as the result of a purchase by its London-based

company of the same name. Nicknamed NatWest, the bank is well known throughout the New York/New Jersey/Connecticut area. NatWest, a commercial bank that specializes in small- and medium-sized businesses, is among the top 30 bank-holding companies operating in the U.S.

Training

The training, a five-month program of classroom instruction and seminar work, will enable the employee to work anywhere in the corporation. The curriculum includes the foundations of banking and exposes its participants to various groups of the bank. It includes computer training (Lotus, E-mail) macroeconomics, business ethics and law, business writing, credit analysis, financial marketing, introduction to retail, human resources and administration, and advanced accounting.

After the core curriculum is completed, the participants work in specialized areas. They also receive additional classroom and seminar training, sometimes at outside institutions. After three rotations of this, which last 10 to 12 months, the employee is given a permanent position in a particular department.

Career Path

Because there are so many opportunities, there is no typical path for liberal arts graduates. The company's emphasis on personal growth through internal experimentation makes it possible to do as little or as much as your own growth dictates.

However, most liberal arts grads go into lending, consumer banking branches, or auditing departments, starting out as loan officers or lending representatives with the official title "assistant treasurer."

They can then move up to relations officer, assistant vice president, and then vice president. On the average, it takes six to eight years to become a vice president.

Moves can be lateral as well as vertical, because internal postings encourage movement from one department to another and training is ongoing.

Qualifications

NatWest looks for graduates with a 3.0 GPA, although extracurricular activities are just as important. The company looks for team players who are enthusiastic and excited.

This bank usually rejects bookworm candidates with no outside activities and favors those with well-rounded backgrounds. The rationale: very high individual achievers don't work as well within the bank's team concept.

Because the bank's focus is on developing relationships with local business people, recruiters look for people from the Northeast who care about the area and want to settle there.

Interviewing

Pre-recruiting takes place from September through December, and NatWest pre-screens applicants in January and February. Graduates are encouraged to submit resumes by late December or early January.

If you don't attend one of the 19 Northeast campuses at which the company recruits, you can contact the bank directly for an interview. "We want you to let us know when you'll be in the New York area, so we can set up an interview," says human resources officer Jeffrey Robinson.

The preliminary round of screening interviews with human resources is over by early March. The second, more extensive, round will keep you an entire morning. You will be seen by three to five interviewers for a half an hour each, followed by lunch. You will know in April if it's yea or nay.

Report from the Trenches

MONICA AITKEN
Position: Assistant Treasurer/Lending Officer
Age: 26
Earnings: Mid 30s (est.)
School: Montclair State College, Upper Montclair, N.J.
Major: English

While studying English and working for a teaching certificate, Monica Aitken worked part-time at National Westminster. When graduation approached and she was offered a permanent position in the Residential Loan Department, she decided to abandon teaching.

After a stint in Credit and Administration and completing the training program, she is now a lending officer who handles more than 20 customer accounts. In effect, Monica is the main financial advisor to businesses with $15 to 20 million in annual sales. Here's her report:

On Training

The training program was wonderful. They had college professors come in. We did three rotations, working closely with the people on line. What you need to know as far as banking and crunching numbers, they'll teach you. The company has given me lots of skills and opportunities that I didn't know anything about. Training is constant. Just last week I had three full days of training.

The Actual Job
My love of writing and literature is being used. A lot of my work involves writing financial proposals for customers, and I have to communicate effectively in writing as well as verbally with my customers.

As a lending officer, I take care of all their financial needs—monitor their cash, pension, and investment needs. I also coordinate the bank's specialized services with the needs of my customers. I often work with other departments in the bank to offer my customers different services. This way, the customer and the bank receive maximum benefits.

After two and a half years, I do not require a lot of direction. They have given me the skills and let me do my job. I'm very happy.

The Future
Ultimately, I hope to move into a vice presidency. But right now I enjoy the options of moving within the different departments of the company. The more I learn, the more valuable I am to the company and myself.

NATIONWIDE INSURANCE CO.
1 Nationwide Plaza
Columbus, OH 43216
(614) 249-7111

Other Employment Centers
13 regional offices and many other subsidiary offices around the country, including San Antonio, Raleigh, Harrisburg, Penn., Gainesville, Fla., Portland, Ore., Syracuse, Englewood, Colo., and Annapolis, Md.

Products/Services
Life, health, property, and casualty insurance

Number of Employees
17,000

Job Opportunities
Claims, underwriting, management training

Starting Salary
$20,000 to $22,000

Major Pluses
+ Outstanding insurance benefits, including paid maternity leave and group life
+ Credit union
+ Fitness center
+ Job security
+ Plenty of opportunities to relocate and move up

Drawbacks
- Climbing the corporate ladder takes time and patience.
- Lots of competition

Corporate Philosophy
"We believe that by working together people can develop an economy of abundance which will provide a maximum of opportunity, freedom, and security for all."

Atmosphere
Conservative, formal business dress code, but people are down-to-earth and disciplined (no long lunch breaks or late arrivals)

Working Conditions
Modern offices with fitness center and cafeteria

Tips for Getting a Job
- Show initiative and sense of responsibility (previous job experience helps).
- Show courage, reverence, integrity, and a strong work ethic.
- Mention community service work.

Profile

Founded in 1926 as a small automobile insurance company, Nationwide today is a multibillion-dollar international business complex of more than 130 companies that provide insurance and other financial security products and services.

With $9.3 billion in premiums written in 1990 and its ranking as *Fortune* magazine's 23rd largest life insurance company, Nationwide continues to offer security and promise to its policyholders as well as its employees.

Qualifications

Although no clearly defined career path exists for liberal arts graduates, a wide variety of opportunities exist for candidates with a 3.0 or higher GPA. According to employment manager Randall Swecker, the company is mainly concerned with initiative and thus looks for graduates who were employed in college or during summers.

"Some work experience, even an internship, indicates initiative and some basic business skills." Swecker says he is also impressed when a candidate has paid for some or all of his or her college expenses. Contrary to presumptions, the firm does not emphasize math skills, preferring instead personable, well-rounded employees who see the world with a broad perspective.

High Expectations

Swecker says recent graduates' expectations are sometimes too high in terms of pay and promotions. "Expect to be a sponge for a few years," he says. The employment process at Nationwide includes completing an application for a specific job, taking the Job Effective Prediction Series (JEPS) test, possibly interviewing in the placement center, and interviewing with the hiring manager of the specific department. The JEPS test is a basic skills test designed for insurance companies.

Opportunities

Swecker says that Nationwide encourages new employees to work in different areas of the company to get broad-based experience and increase their chances for a promotion to management. Following are some of the career paths that could be open to liberal arts graduates, depending on the needs of the company.

Agents concentrate on either family or business insurance markets, helping their customers evaluate and fulfill their insurance needs. Agents also offer services in mutual funds, group insurance coverages, and retirement plans. Agents must complete a development program at The Nationwide Training Center outside of Columbus and regional training at the employee's base office. Agents earn salaries while in the training program and can qualify for monthly bonuses during training. After two years, agents can become independent contractors and earn extra income from commissions. There are no prior course requirements for agents.

Underwriters evaluate and select the risks Nationwide insures and analyze the company's losses. On-the-job training, industry associations, and training programs educate underwriters to effectively complete their jobs. Nationwide also offers financial help to employees seeking specialized courses for underwriting. No specific courses are required, but candidates should possess an analytical mind and good problem-solving skills. Underwriting is often a steppingstone to higher management jobs.

Claims adjusters investigate customers' claims and negotiate settlements. Training includes working with an experienced adjuster and completing three weeks at Nationwide's basic claims training school. Additional courses may be required for better job proficiency. Employees receive full salaries while in training. A college degree is essential for claims adjusters, but no specific courses are required. Adjusters should be open to relocations.

Training

At certain junctures in their careers, Nationwide employees have opportunities to take part in advanced programs at the Nationwide Training Center near Columbus, a modern complex of classrooms, audiovisual rooms, library, dining rooms, and recreational facilities. The training center employs a staff of experienced insurance professionals to help employees increase their skills and knowledge.

Continuing Education

Through its Educational Assistance program, Nationwide offers between 50 and 100 percent reimbursement to employees who take courses. Many employees have earned masters degrees and professional designations by taking advantage of the program. The company's Personnel Data System contains records of every employee's educational background, abilities, and job experience to assure equal consideration for career advancement.

Report from the Trenches

RANDY ELLIS
Position: Market Planning Intern
Age: 21
Earnings: $6.50/hour
School: Ohio Wesleyan University, Delaware, Oh.
Major: International Business/Spanish

Randy has been a part-time intern at Nationwide for most of his senior year in college. He hopes to be hired full time when he graduates in June 1992. Although he's somewhat removed from the typical career path of a liberal arts graduate, he told about his experiences with the company.

One of our professors had a connection within the [marketing] department here. They were looking for some interns and started looking at Ohio Wesleyan. Through a recommendation from the professor and then through an interview process I got hired. One of the reasons was that I was able to work in the group and pick up ideas and concepts pretty quickly. They were interested in my computer skills, especially my use of the Lotus program. I was interviewed by the person in the department and the manager, not by the recruiting department.

Market Planning Function

We evaluate different areas for agents' locations—new agents or relocating old agents. We analyze different areas to determine their potential for agency or regional managers. We share a lot of demographic and industry data with agency managers.

What I Do

When I was hired last May I would produce Local Area Market Plans ... LAMPS, a package of maps that show some demographic and industry data overlaid by zip code. We would also produce worksheets that show the same infor-

mation. We cranked these out using the Equifax system, which is a specialized program that displays demographic information geographically. We use our own databases as well to bring in more information.

I did that for about a month or so. Then, I was assigned to work with one market demographer in the department, and as that person got an assignment, he would give me parts of it to do. I began by doing worksheet reports. He would give me a stack of information and say, "Put this into worksheet format." They were more complicated than the initial ones. Every time I was given a new responsibility, I still had to do my old ones. Then [the market demographer] would give me a report to read and summarize and give the highlights.

We moved into more and more complex work. After a while, I was collecting first-hand information on different areas by calling Chambers of Commerce and state planning agencies, things like that. Right now, I'm producing more complex maps. I can go in and outline different areas that may not be a standard geography. I can do a map based on those kinds of outlines.

Advice to Liberal Arts Grads

Be really ambitious; let them know you like to take on challenging tasks. You have to be very flexible. You can't be set in your ways. When they tell you the priorities have changed, you have to roll with the punches. We change priorities by the hour. You drop what you're doing and do another one.

I would suggest just standing back and observing for a while to see how things work before you start adding your own input. That's what I did. I would watch everybody and see how things ran. After awhile you'll find your own niche.

A Major Plus

The main thing I like about working here is the wide range of experience I've gotten using all the different pieces of computer equipment and the knowledge of marketing in general. I've learned a lot about the industry from the people I work with. They are real helpful and will take time to help you and give you answers.

What I Want

I'm ready to become a market analyst. Other grads would start as a market analyst, too, but I will be at a higher grade level because of my internship experience. I would hope to start at a grade nine at about $26,000. Other graduates would probably start at a grade seven or eight [$22,000].

If there is no opening in this, the property and casualty side as a market analyst, my next choice would be in the marketing department on the life insurance side. I would also consider going into life and health. They do the same types of market analysis, although the marketing criteria may be different.

My next choice is in investment product operations. I would try to get a research analyst position, which would require a lot of computer work in ana-

lyzing data. They take care of all of the company's investment products, from guidelines to underwriting.

Working Conditions

Sometimes its high pressured . . . off and on. It's kind of cyclical. Sometimes the deadlines seem impossible, but you just have to tell them, "Say, I can't get it done by then, can you give me a later deadline?"

I have really enjoyed working here. I accidently fell into it. It is challenging and yet the job changes from day to day. I like dressing up to go to work. And I like the people in the department. That makes a big difference.

I will stay in the insurance industry, even if I don't get a permanent job at Nationwide. I have this knowledge now, and it will set me apart, I think.

PAYLESS DRUG STORES

9275 S.W. Peyton Lane
Wilsonville, OR 97070
(503) 682-4100

Other Employment Centers
Stores in 10 states: Oregon, Washington, California, Idaho, Montana, Nevada, Wyoming, Arizona, Utah, and Colorado

Products/Services
Retail drugstore chain

Number of Employees
16,000

Job Opportunities
Management trainees

Starting Salary
Low 20s

Major Pluses
+ Training (six-month management training class with classroom and on-the-job learning on the nuts and bolts of retail, PayLess style)
+ Advancement potential (all promotions are job-performance based; hot shots can make it to store manager in five to seven years)

Drawbacks
− Retail hours means working nights, weekends, and holidays.
− Relocation is possible whenever a new store opens (around 90 did in 1991).
− Being a store manager for PayLess is not exactly a prestige position; it may have limited applications if you jump ship to another industry.

Corporate Philosophy

Highly customer-motivated: "We are a team of highly motivated, self-managing associates driven to provide service and top-quality products that keep customers returning."

Atmosphere

This is not walk-around-with-a-clipboard style management. The emphasis is on *doing*. Members of a management team are constantly working with customers or merchandising.

Working Conditions

High-pressured, long hours. You'll spend most of the time on the floor.

Tips for Getting a Job

- Give them a clean-cut look, an upbeat attitude, and a firm grip on the work ethic.
- Organize your thoughts, and articulate them well.
- Put all job experience, including dates, on your resume.
- Be genuine and realistic; they don't want to hear that you expect to be CEO in five years.

Profile

Liberal arts grads walking into the management training program at PayLess can put their people skills to work in an industry that isn't dying because of the recession. In fact, PayLess is on a growth plan, with about 90 new stores opened in 1991 alone.

PayLess is one of the largest retail drug store chains, decidedly upscale, with an average store size of 27,000 square feet and average sales of $5.4 million per store. The company is committed to remodeling and new merchandising techniques, so the stores look great. There's a lot more than just medicine and cosmetics: you'll also find cameras, watches, plants, appliances, and more.

Founded in 1939, the company has made some major acquisitions in the past two decades, notably 22 Value Giant Stores in 1976; 61 PayLess (Oakland) stores in 1980; 24 Osco Drugs in 1987; and 52 more Oscos in 1991. Bought in 1985 by Kmart Corporation, the company is a wholly owned, independently operating subsidiary. Sales growth hit a record $1.64 million in 1990.

Customer Service Reigns

Dealing with the public is the bottom line at PayLess. You'll do it six days a week—14 hours a day at Christmas time—so you should have a positive attitude toward customer service. The company values liberal arts graduates because they tend to have better communication and interpersonal skills than do business graduates. Thus, they deal more effectively with the public, says PayLess recruiter Sandra Parker.

Getting the Job

You can't expect to just put in your time and start racking up success here. Seniority doesn't equal promotions—everything is based on job performance.

Qualifications

No minimum GPA or curriculum are required, although some basic business and communications classes might help, as does any retail experience. Whatever jobs you've had, put them on your resume.

"I interviewed a girl who didn't list any work experience, even though she had worked for four years during college at McDonald's. I thought that was very important," says Parker. "PayLess wants to see your stick-to-it-iveness."

Hands-on Management Training

Liberal arts graduates start as trainees in a six-month program that includes four weeks of classroom learning, then it's into the real world: the stores. Each month the trainee completes a project on an aspect of management, such as advertising or developing profit/loss statements. Once the trainee successfully completes all the projects, a promotion to supervisor follows. After that, the trainee's performance determines how fast (and how far) he or she is pushed up the ladder.

If you are a superstar, you can make the next steps—floor manager, assistant manager, and store manager—in seven years. But most can't do it quite that quickly, and there is no typical time frame, since it all comes down to performance. There is great potential to move up to corporate from the store manager level; most of the people there came up the ranks the same way.

Report from the Trenches

TIM IREY
Position: Management Trainee
Age: 22
Earnings: Low 20s
School: Washington State University, Pullman, Wa.
Major: Communications

Tim Irey graduated in December 1990, facing the communications recession. He used a placement agency from April through mid-July, looking at a lot of career possibilities before deciding retail was a good bet.

Tim is very pleased with his work so far in the management training program. He's been working as a supervisor at a PayLess store in Kent, Washington, for several months, doing everything from directly supervising cashiers to rearranging displays, stocking shelves, and handling customer service problems. Here's what he has to say:

He Did His Research

I pushed for an interview with a retail drug store chain. The main reason? I did research on my own through business journals and magazines to investigate what companies were having success. PayLess was very open with me about expectations and values, and it fit with how I like to treat people and how I like to be treated. And I liked the job security. Recession or not, people will always need to go to the drug store.

Wearing a Smile

What I think got me my job was my attitude—I walked in with a smile, clean-cut. PayLess has the mold of what they want. If you go in with a good attitude, you have a good shot. Their attitude is: We always have room for one more good person.

No Rest for the Wicked

I'm in charge of one-third of our store, in terms of merchandising, filling stock, and so on. I help throughout the store on a lesser scale. I handle all rainchecks, and I'm responsible for all calls from the cashiers. A typical day lasts 12 to 13 hours. Constantly, you're reworking displays and merchandise. I always feel like I'm not productive enough because there's always something more you can improve.

A Reward, At Last

A customer came in a couple of weeks ago, and I was called to the camera desk. He said, "I tried to get in here yesterday for your ad. I wanted to buy this watch for my wife. Is there any way you can give me the price a day late?" I gave him the price. When he left he said, "You made my day." I wish there were more like that. I feel like I just won a customer for life.

Wear the Hats, Juggle the Batons

I'd say it's a high-pressured environment, from the point of view that you're being pulled in so many directions: employees under you always need something, as well as motivation. There's a constant need to watch them plus do more on my own, so I can get bumped up. You have to wear all the hats and juggle all the batons.

It's teamwork 100 percent. Everyone helps each other in the store and even in the company. They're real high on praise. It's an unwritten expectation that you put in as many hours as it needs. If you love customer service, it's worth it. I'm looked favorably upon for the way I deal with customers. I've been asked my opinion on things many times, like suggestions on what people might buy on impulse.

The Right Stuff
I would pick PayLess again for the friendliness, professionalism, stability, and upward mobility. You can become CEO if you work for it. The best thing about working here is the customers and the employees. For the most part, everyone has fun and is not afraid to joke around and roll with the punches. People around me care about me and my home life. There's a genuineness about the company.

What's Ahead
The next step for me is being promoted to floor manager. I plan to keep going up the path from there. Ten years from now, I expect to be at least a store manager. Then, I would prefer to be in the main office, doing public relations or management training.

PC CONNECTION, INC.
6 Mill St.
Marlow, NH 03456
(603) 446-3383

Other Employment Centers
Some customer service and inventory areas in Keene, New Hampshire, a TV studio in Newport, Rhode Island and a distribution facility in Wilmington, Ohio

Products/Services
Sells computer equipment and software by mail

Number of Employees
A little more than 300, but one of the fastest-growing businesses in the country

Job Opportunities
Non-commissioned sales, primarily over the phone

Starting Salary
$18,000 to $22,000

Major Pluses
+ Excellent benefits package
+ Company cultivates warm, family ambience
+ Work in beautiful, picturesque setting

Drawbacks
− Very small company, but this may be your chance to get in on the ground floor
− Very structured system not conducive to the independent worker

Corporate Philosophy
Need a high energy level to work with team. Owners have an open-door policy and they regularly interact with employees. Down-to-earth ambience due to owners' disbelief at amount of success they've already generated.

Atmosphere
A professional, but laid-back team environment. Interact with unassuming owners every day. Ties and jackets for meetings, but not Wall Street stuffy.

Working Conditions
Restored Victorian building. High employee morale.

Tips for Getting a Job
• Be articulate and able to work in a fast-paced environment.
• Show ability to change and adapt to new environment.
• Show an interest in the company and work by asking pointed questions about business.
• Demonstrate ability to work well on computer keyboard.

Profile

The second-fastest growing privately held company in the United States, PC Connection began as the brainchild of two computer novices who met while hiking on the Appalachian Trail. When they found out how difficult it was to get computer software in northern New England, they started their own company and the rest has been very pleasant history.

What They Want
Since the company primarily looks for salespeople, good communication and computer keyboard skills are most important. Exuding a lot of positive energy is also important. A high GPA isn't as necessary as being a well-rounded person who either has a lot of different interests or has shown the ability to work his or her way through school. You must also be willing to change what you're doing at a moment's notice.

The Hiring Process

It begins with an on-campus interview. If suitably impressed, the company will call you back for a second interview—a casual prescreening during which you fill out an application. A third interview is held on site, where you'll meet with a supervisor of the department, tour the facilities, and possibly meet the director.

Training

Training depends on the department. In sales, it is very structured, encompassing classroom training, videos, sales simulation, and customer scenarios, observing senior sales consultants, going to vendor demonstrations and seeing new products. There's also a lot of ongoing training during and after work.

Career Path

What's interesting about PC Connection's promote-from-within policy is that employees never know quite where they'll be placed. There are frequent openings. They can become buyers or sales supervisors, or they can end up in training and development or technical support.

Report from the Trenches

PAT BERGLUND
Position: Supervisor, Order Desk
Age: 30
Earnings: Mid 30s (est.)
School: Keene State University, Keene, N.H.
Major: Biochemistry

Pat Berglund originally wanted to work in a hospital. Then she read some intriguing stories in the local papers about this small, successful company that was hiring and promoting regularly. So she went in for an interview, got the job, and doesn't have one regret about that career move. Here's how it all turned out:

Getting the Job

While finishing college, I was getting ready to move out of the area when I heard about this company in the paper. All these people were getting hired and promoted; it sounded like a neat place to work. On just a whim, I decided to apply. I had about three or four interviews, and the next thing I knew, there I was.

Career Progress

I started as a salesperson in the IBM PC division; I was very intimidated by the whole thing. At that time, there was no specific training. You basically sat with people, listened, and learned from them. I actually started training others after a couple years on the job. About three years later, I took over the training and developed a very specific program.

When we added a new order-taking division, I went there. It was a bit different from sales; it was for people who knew what they wanted and didn't need any information. It was developed in November of 1989. At the time, I got back from maternity leave, and I saw a posting for an order supervisor job. I applied for it and got it. I now work in the evenings, from 4:30 P.M. to 1 A.M. We're not a 24-hour operation, by the way.

The Typical Day
I basically oversee my department, answering procedural questions and any other problems with the system or the hardware. I also field calls from unhappy customers if they need to go beyond the agent they're dealing with. I have to keep communication lines open between all the other departments so we all know what's going on.

The Work Environment
The workload is ever changing. Every day I come to work, never knowing what's going to be new today, what we have announced, and what we did accomplish. Some days I come in and it's almost relaxing. The next night it can be total chaos. The phones are crazy, but the support is so good that the stress usually goes away after five or 10 minutes. My colleagues are very helpful. Since there's no commission, it's very team-oriented and upbeat.

Best and Worst
The people are the best thing about this company. They're very selective about who they hire, so we know we're going to work with educated people who are interested in the company. They're able to really examine employees and set them on the right career path, and the benefits are great.

On the downside, it's very structured here. You have to be in sales for one year before you move on—no exceptions. That can be frustrating for someone who already has that experience and who likes to work independently.

The Future
I'd like to get into a more customer-oriented area like customer affairs (which is a couple of levels beyond here). I'd like to work directly with the owners of the company. With the supervisory experience I've gained here, I know I can go up another level or two.

Tips
Be more open-minded and don't set specific, all-or-nothing goals. Leave as many avenues open as possible and don't set limits. Don't limit yourself to your area of study. People come here with art and teaching degrees.

People conducting interviews here look for openness and candor, for people who are well-rounded, have stories to tell, and enjoy neat hobbies. Let everyone know about you and what you can offer—not only on the computer but also as a whole person.

THE PRUDENTIAL

1111 Durham Ave.
South Plainfield, NJ 07080
(908) 412-4590

Other Employment Centers
Offices in more than 200 locations throughout the United States and the world

Products/Services
The largest American mutual life insurance company, offering a broad line of insurance products, including Keogh plans, IRAs, mutual funds, mortgages, and credit cards

Number of Employees
Almost 100,000, with a field force of 40,000

Job Opportunities
Management trainees for a variety of fields such as actuarial, under-writing, claims, and human resources

Starting Salary
$25,000 to $27,000

Major Pluses
+ Strong training program available throughout career
+ Salary reviews every six months during the first two years; annually thereafter
+ Opportunity to work flexible hours

Drawbacks
− Expect to relocate often as you move up the ladder.
− It takes considerable study and work to move beyond entry level.
− Hugeness of the company makes some people feel lost.

Corporate Philosophy
Stated shared values: "The utmost integrity and truthfulness, the courage to take a stand for what you believe, to take pride in who we are and what we do and to be personally committed to taking the initiative and finding innovative solutions to problems."

Atmosphere
Prudential stresses a personable attitude between employers and with clients. A first-name basis prevails.

Working Conditions
Not the stereotypical suit-and-tie look. Dress code is "appropriate" for
the particular place or professional class.

Tips for Getting a Job
- A good GPA and accounting and computer knowledge are especially
  helpful.
- Demonstrate evidence of leadership ability.
- Have a good idea of what you want to do within the company; state
  your goals.
- Be spontaneous and show your personality, but don't be cocky.

Profile

Few business entities present themselves more effectively than The Prudential and its Rock of Gibraltar logo. As the world's fifth-largest corporation and the largest American insurance company, Prudential, boasting assets in the neighborhood of $200 billion, is able to withstand the
longest recession or deepest stock market crash. In its current position,
it can afford to build on its strength by hiring, developing, and paying
for top-dollar talent.

What They Want
They're looking for intelligent people (who proved it in school) with leadership ability, strong verbal and written communication skills, and the
ability to think analytically, says Joyce Goldstein, vice president for
administration.

Why They Like Liberal Arts Grads
"We once interviewed somebody who said he wanted to go to Harvard
Business School, but he was a philosophy major," says Goldstein. "Somebody said, 'So, if you knew you were going to go into business, why didn't
you become a business person?' He said, 'Because I wanted to learn how
to think. Once I learned how to think, I thought I'd learn my skills.' "

"That is why we hire liberal arts people. We look upon thinking skills
as analysis, being able to assess situations, look at the big picture, design
and organize work, and generate ideas. I think liberal arts graduates have
a much better foundation than technical people."

The Hiring Process
The main avenue for hiring is through college recruitment. "I like to say
each grad may be the future CEO from within," states Goldstein. Students
are put through rigorous interviews and are flown to corporate head-

quarters where they have dinner with the executives. They then go through an entire day of interviews with two separate departments that they chose beforehand. They also take math tests and are asked to provide writing samples.

Training

New employees are immediately put into an intensive training program that begins with one week of orientation classes that provide an overview of the company and departmental roles. Although trainees start working after that, the training continues.

New employees may become part of the management development program, which is specifically geared toward liberal arts graduates. This program includes five weeks of up-front training with instruction in company organization, the financial reporting system, business writing, and understanding the company's values. This is followed by on-the-job training and monthly classroom instruction with heavy involvement from department advisors.

Career Path

This is a very decentralized company, which means there are a plethora of career paths one can take. For example, there are 12 different non-management levels. The professional entry level is number eight; they expect people to be promoted to level nine within a year. Confused? Join the club. You can go into fields as diverse as marketing and sales, administration (which includes claims, actuarial, and human resources) and accounting and finance. "Once you get into The Prudential, you could be anything," Goldstein concludes.

Report from the Trenches

JOHN SUTTON

Position: Management Intern, Public Affairs
Age: 25
Earnings: Mid 30s (est.)
School: Swarthmore College, Swarthmore, Pa.
Major: Political Science/Economics

John Sutton was a typical liberal arts grad who was just looking for a steady paycheck when he was hired by Prudential. Fortunately, he was hired by a corporation boasting one of the country's best training programs, which allowed him the opportunity to develop and find a challenging position. Here's how it all happened:

The Training Program
I spent the first nine months in the group auditing area as a comptroller. I had at least one month of actual training for the job. The first week was a staff auditor training course, taught by Prudential employees from around the country. The second week featured a program where I performed a mock audit, which was an excellent preparation for the real auditing I would do. Throughout those nine months, I performed six or seven audits that focused on "manage-medical" profit groups and networks.

Career Progress
For the next six months, I moved to legislative tax work, then I spent six months working in securities. That was a fast-paced and stressful environment, but I learned a lot. I had to interview for each of those positions.

The Typical Day
My typical day involves a lot of meetings. I work with governmental affairs, especially concerning health-care issues. I also interact with other insurance companies and businesses, lobbyists and other health-care groups. I read and write information about new bills and proposals to Congress. I help Prudential build its own position on the issues through interaction with all these people.

The Work Environment
You have to be on your toes and be receptive to change here. After a few years, people are practically encouraged to move around. It's almost like you get a brand new job every nine to 12 months. It provides great exposure to different people, management styles, and different areas of the company.

Best and Worst
People are very committed to the new employees here mainly because they want to keep them around. The bosses really care about your development. You are intentionally put into positions that aren't your strengths to help you develop. The one big drawback is being moved around so much so fast. It can be upsetting at times.

The Future
To be honest, I haven't had time to think of this as a career because I haven't been here that long. But I am surprised at the amount of responsibility I've been given so early on.

Tips
Stick with it, and don't rule out any area. Initially, it's not what you do, but whom you work for, so look for someone who's interested in your development. Don't just be happy to get any job, because you won't learn as much about the

job as you could. Find out about the various opportunities beforehand. I made
the mistake of just being happy I had a job. Fortunately, I was lucky enough to
be hired by Prudential.

SCOTT PAPER COMPANY

Scott Plaza 1
Philadelphia, PA 19113
(215) 522-5000

Products/Services
Consumer paper goods

Number of Employees
27,000

Job Opportunities
Consumer sales representative

Starting Salary
In the mid 20s, plus commission of $4,000 to $5,000

Major Pluses
+ One of the best sales-training programs in the country
+ Company car and expense account
+ No set office hours
+ Tuition assistance

Drawbacks
− Sales (you either love it or hate it)
− Time spent driving from store to store
− Earnings from commission are based on group rather than individual achievement.
− Because sales associates work independently, it can be lonely.

Corporate Philosophy
Consumer sales mission: "Talented people moving as one toward acquiring more and better space with customers."

Atmosphere
Sales are by nature competitive, but the company is known for nurturing its employees to achieve their potential (for example, it has developed a Performance Improvement Plan for this purpose). Promotions are always from within the ranks.

Working Conditions
As part of the consumer sales force, you'll spend most of your time traveling by car in your own sales territory. Overnight travel is rarely required, except in Western territories.

Tips for Getting a Job
- Avoid giving prepared answers (or at least ones that appear to be prepared).
- Highlight any past experience in sales, no matter how seemingly innocuous.
- Emphasize how you demonstrated leadership and teamwork in any extracurricular activities.

Profile

If you have ever considered a career in sales, then the Scott Paper Company, the world's largest producer of paper products in the United States, should be high on your list of possible employers. The company's consumer sales division consistently ranks at or near the top of the best sales forces in its industry, as judged by *Sales & Marketing Management* magazine.

What's more, Scott's comprehensive, 12-week training course is designed to teach the novice everything about selling, at least in terms of consumer packaged goods—a skill easily transferred to many other industries.

Why Sales?
Throw in the freedom of not having to sit behind a desk, then a company car, and an expense account, and the sales job that Scott typically offers looks pretty good.

But the crux of any sales job is the potential financial reward. While the starting base salary might seem relatively low—mid 20s—in two years you can expect to be earning close to $40,000.

If management is your ultimate goal, then you will start in sales at Scott—a career path that's typical in a consumer products company.

Everybody Needs It
Scott has grown from a modest Philadelphia company producing coarse paper goods in 1879 to a worldwide operation in 21 countries with more than $5 billion in sales in 1991. The company invented toilet paper and thus has been among the most recognizable names in consumer paper products. "We are in a unique situation in that everybody has to use the products we make," quipped Phil Vitale, human resources manager.

Even a seemingly recession-proof company such as Scott has been impacted by the downturn in the economy. Its S.D. Warren printing and publishing operation experienced a precipitous 90 percent decline in the second quarter of 1991, and that was coming off a depressed 1990 base.

The decline in Scott's printing division and sluggish sales in its domestic consumer products division have been somewhat mitigated by healthy sales of its European consumer paper products. In 1983 Scott restructured its operations to take advantage of potential regions of growth, opening new headquarters in London, Hong Kong, and Mexico City. Branching into Europe turned out to be particularly prescient with profits jumping 80 percent in the second quarter of 1991.

What Liberal Arts Grads Should Offer

Scott's position with regard to liberal arts grads is neutral—the type of a degree a job candidate holds is not paramount to Scott recruiters. Rather, the ideal candidate should demonstrate strong leadership skills, a high standard of success in and out of the classroom, a commitment to winning, and pride in whatever organization for which he or she has worked.

"We have individuals from a variety of educational backgrounds who have reached high levels in our company," says Vitale.

In addition, candidates should possess strong questioning and listening skills, creative thinking ability, and a knack for solving problems.

Training

When the consumer sales division's mission statement says "more and better space with customers," it means retail store space, advertising, *and* mental space. "We believe that our people are our greatest asset and give us our most valuable competitive edge," says Vitale.

New employees in the consumer sales division are enrolled in a 12-week program that includes classroom instruction as well as field days with sales representatives and district managers.

Once the initial training is completed, employees can take refresher courses through the company's Performance Improvement Plan. Participation in the plan is mandatory if sales goals are not met.

Recruitment

Scott recruiters look for job candidates in several ways, including advertising and on-campus efforts. "We truly believe that the talent we're looking for does exist in college," says Vitale. If you can't find announcements of Scott openings through your placement center, then send a resume to Vitale.

Candidates are screened initially either by phone or in person. Top candidates then continue through an extensive interviewing process. The sessions start with tough "situation" interviewing, where three Scott managers present 10 to 12 questions to candidates, asking them to resolve problematic situations. Finalists then spend a day out in the field.

"Scott's not a hard company to work for," says Vitale. "It's just a little demanding because we search for the best talent."

Career Path

New hires begin immediately as sales reps with their own territories, where they will spend the next 18 months to two years before moving up to senior sales reps.

After another two years or so, the next promotion is to account representative. Account reps focus on large corporate accounts, and do very little if any calling on retailers.

Employees can reach management level after five to seven years, becoming territory or district managers. And Scott promotes almost exclusively from within.

Report from the Trenches

JIM FARRELL
Position: Sales representative
Age: 29
Earnings: $39,000 ($32,000 base plus $7,000 commission)
School: La Salle University, Philadelphia, Pa.
Major: Criminal Justice

Jim was a U.S. Marine Corps officer from the time he graduated from college until 1989, when he accepted a position with the Philadelphia police force. Even though he had an opportunity to use his criminal justice degree, he was unhappy with the job and decided to look for a position in manufacturing. Here's his report after a year-and-a half on the job:

After I made up my mind to leave the police force, I remember sending out a great deal of resumes. I actually was offered another job—with McCormick Spices—but decided ultimately to accept Scott's offer.

I had a total of three interviews before they gave me an offer. The second was with a district manager and third with seven other sales reps.

Training

I was really quite impressed with the three-month training program. It begins with a two-week introduction during which you are indoctrinated into the organization, just like in the Marine Corps. You learn everything about Scott, the history, the way it's set up and so on. It's very structured, something I felt very comfortable with.

Basically the program teaches you everything you need to know about selling. But perhaps the most important thing you gain from the program is the right attitude about your job. Before, I was very anti-sales; I felt that all salesmen just try to sell you something you don't want or don't need. But the program really informs you that Scott's products do fill a need, and that's something I sincerely believe in now.

The Life of a Traveling Salesman
My territory includes New York City and parts of New Jersey. I can drive to and from my house in a single day anywhere within the territory, which is typical in the more urbanized areas. However, in the West I understand that some sales reps have accounts that are as far as a three-day drive.

My day consists of servicing accounts and reconfiguring shelf space. I try to speak with my clients at least once a week. At first being a salesman was hard for me. You're calling upon very busy store managers who really might not have time for you that day. And I was surprised how much sales is a good old boys' network. I really strive to be well-liked by my customers.

It was also quite lonely at first, especially after spending five years in the Marine Corps where you were always surrounded by people. You're on your own most of the time as a sales rep. But now I enjoy the freedom of setting my own schedule.

Bonus
The company offers generous bonuses, which of course is a nice benefit. Bonuses are also awarded for group effort. So even though I was the top performer in my district in 1991—and 1991 was a tough year for everyone—I got as much as everyone else.

Corporate Culture
The company is conservative but dynamic. Management sincerely cares about its employees and is always encouraging us to reach our potential. For instance, we have an audiotape library composed of leadership and motivational tapes. Sales reps are assigned tapes and then issue a report to other sales reps on what they learned from them.

The Future
Right now I am pursuing an MBA. I take two courses in the evenings and one on Saturdays. I am figuring that it will take me about four years to earn the degree. The company is reimbursing me for my tuition.

Ten years from now I would either like to be a senior account representative or district manager or even possibly go inside the organization for a position in marketing.

SEAFIRST BANK
701 Fifth Ave.
Seattle, WA 98104
(206) 358-3000

Other Employment Centers
More than 200 branches throughout Washington state

Products/Services
Retail Banking

Number of Employees
7,000

Job Opportunities
Management trainee

Starting Salary
Low 20s

Major Pluses
+ Quarterly bonuses based on performance
+ Training (4 to 6-month personal banker training program, with class-room and hands-on experience)
+ Discount privileges (free checking and savings; reduced credit card fees and personal loan rates)

Drawbacks
− Must live or move to Washington state; may be forced to relocate within the state
− Demanding hours

Corporate Philosophy
Aggressively customer service–oriented, as exmplified by its Excel Service program (round-the-clock customer service phone line) and a guarantee of less than five minutes in teller lines

Atmosphere
Professionalism is a top priority in all areas, particularly in dealing with customer relations. Diplomacy is mandatory. Teamwork prevails.

Working Conditions
"Bankers' hours" is a myth. To serve customers, branches are open from 9 A.M. to 6 P.M. weekdays. Branches are mini-franchises, with modern customer service centers and drive-up services.

Tips for Getting a Job
• Look and act professional.
• Prepare a list of questions that demonstrate your interest in and knowledge of the company.
• Don't hound recruiters after your interviews.

Profile

New Seafirst employees should erase from their minds any images of the lazy banker kicking back after a tough day of arranging a few foreign loans by phone. Seafirst employees work hard to offer the best new services to the bank's most important and loyal customers, the residents of Washington.

Bought out by San Francisco–based Bank of America in 1982, Seafirst soon suffered from too many bad loans. In the next 30 months it pulled itself out of a financial quagmire with the aid of local depositors, who never abandoned the ailing bank. Not wanting to lose touch with these customers again, Seafirst turned its sights back to Washington State.

McBankers

Washington's largest bank has turned itself into a market-driven financial institution, one in which sales and satisfied customers are top priorities. Seafirst's new "franchise" system, whereby each branch is sort of a McDonald's of banking, is partly responsible.

Since branch managers knew the customers better, Seafirst top management reasoned, the franchise system would allow managers to make their own decisions about how to sell services and attract new customers. And the system, combined with a widespread incentive program for employee performance, gives newer employees a voice in sales strategy and a reason to work hard.

Consumers enjoy the newest ideas in customer satisfaction. The bank has redesigned some of its branches, adding a service center near the entrance to answer customers' questions. This attention to consumer need is part of the reason Seafirst serves nearly one million customers every day.

The Liberal Arts Advantage

Seafirst recruiters look for people who can deal with a variety of people and situations. It's what Jean Lim, an employment services officer, calls the "liberal arts advantage."

"We're usually not looking for any particular types of majors. In general we're looking for people who are great with people. If they're well rounded, they have a good advantage. They have the ability to deal with situations and have flexibility."

Training

Training programs continue to change, but an ongoing one is the Personal Banker program. It offers trainees four to six months of classroom and hands-on experience in handling customers' financial portfolios. Because sales and customer service are the lifeblood of Seafirst, liberal arts graduates should have some kind of sales experience before entering the program.

Recruitment Process

Seafirst recruiters look for another important quality in college graduates: professionalism. Degrees and work experience won't work miracles for graduates who demonstrate carelessness, impatience, or ignorance when applying. Retail banking's livelihood depends on employees who attract new clients, and keep old ones, through wise financial decision making and personal diplomacy.

Seafirst's application process is designed to detect those flaws. The bank screens graduates over the phone or during short interviews. After a full-length interview, the top candidates are referred to a hiring manager for additional evaluation.

The process can be rigorous, but graduates should not crack under the pressure as one candidate did. "We had one person who called over and over again about a couple of jobs," Lim said. "We're looking for enthusiasm to a certain point. But you've got to know protocol."

Report from the Trenches

MELVIN BRADLEY
Position: Personal Banking Officer
Age: 29
Earnings: Mid 30s (est.)
School: Eastern Washington University, Cheney, Wa.
Major: Communications

Melvin Bradley played basketball for Eastern Washington University, and when he graduated in 1986 he dreamed of coaching at a college or high school. He hadn't even thought about how his degree in communications could launch him into the competitive and fast-paced world of retail banking.

Melvin was working as an account executive for the Seattle Supersonics, handling ticket sales and public relations, when he heard about the personal banker training program at Seafirst. Now, a little more than three years later, Melvin handles more than 1,000 financial portfolios totaling more than $10 million.

He reflected on the success he's found at Seafirst:

In His Own Medium
I was definitely in my own medium at Seafirst with the communications degree, something that helped me out with the Supersonics. Seafirst asked me to write a one-page essay titled "What I Can Bring to Seafirst as a Personal Banker." I keyed in on my sales experience and customer service with the Supersonics. They gave me scenarios and I told them how I would handle customers. And I gave them presentations and speeches I had made to corporations buying tickets.

Training

The training was kind of fast, kind of slow sometimes. Three weeks of it was in-class training with computers, terminology, discussions. We were all assigned to a branch for hands-on training. The managers knew you were learning, and they helped you apply your knowledge.

The nicest part about the whole training was that they expected you to make mistakes. You learn from the mistakes.

On the Job

The atmosphere is definitely not relaxed. I wouldn't say high-pressured, but definitely stressful. When you deal with peoples' life savings, they tend to get a little touchy. But customer service is the number one key to our success, and we're pretty much trained to handle clients' complaints.

There could be some days when I'm handling the portfolios of my counterpart, so between us there's no real competition to speak of. "Teamism" definitely plays a big role in our success. The branch is a team. But branches do compete all the time. We had a CD [certificate of deposit] promotion once when both branch managers got their people together and explained the goals. The losers had to buy the winners breakfast.

Banking can be a really serious job at times. The competition we have with other branches and the camaraderie makes it all a little more fun.

Bigger and Better Things

All of us have to sell ourselves. Don't think of yourself as a braggart—you're a salesperson. I have to keep selling myself, even here. I want to stay with Seafirst and go to the corporate level. I like the direction I'm going now.

ITT SHERATON CORPORATION

World Headquarters
Sixty State St.
Boston, MA 02109
(617) 367-3000

Other Employment Centers
Hotels in 61 countries, including Argentina, Australia, Belgium, Canada, China, Denmark, Japan, Saudi Arabia, Soviet Union, Spain and, Thailand

Products/Services
Hotels

Number of Employees
125,000

Job Opportunities
Management training (after one year of staff work)

Starting Salary
$22,000

Major Pluses
+ Credit union
+ Tuition reimbursement
+ Chance to work all over the world
+ Company is secure (no lay-offs even during recession)

Drawbacks
- Must work for one year on line staff in a hotel at a salary of $15,000 to $18,000 before entering the management training program
- Demanding hours, demanding customers
- Must work many weekends and holidays

Corporate Philosophy
Service, service, service. Sheraton's stated goals for the 1990s are to be the clear worldwide leader in hospitality and service and to extend its commanding lead and global presence to a minimum of 75 countries.

Atmosphere
While employees wear either uniforms or suits for the most part, the working atmosphere—in the hotels and at the corporate office—is a warm, family-like atmosphere.

Working Conditions
Sometimes frantic and demanding, the working conditions in the hotels can be very frustrating. You need to have patience and a strong customer-service personality.

Tips for Getting a Job
- Demonstrate a friendly, open personality and excellent grooming. Image is important in the hotel industry.
- Show evidence of successful teamwork and cooperation.
- Demonstrate some knowledge of ITT Sheraton and of the hospitality industry as a whole.
- Demonstrate a good customer-service attitude. Read up on the latest theories of corporate quality service.

Profile

The Sheraton Corporation began in 1937 with the acquisition of the Stonehaven in Springfield, Massachusetts. By the end of its first decade, the company owned hotels from Maine to Florida and became the first hotel chain to be listed on the New York Stock Exchange.

Over the years, Sheraton's innovation and expansion have been marked by a number of firsts. Its "Reservatron," launched in 1958, became the industry's first automated reservations system, making Sheraton the first chain to centralize and computerize the reservations function.

Sheraton was also the first consumer company to develop a toll-free telephone system for direct consumer access. In 1985, the chain became the first international hotel chain to operate a hotel in the People's Republic of China bearing its own name—The Great Wall Sheraton Hotel Beijing. Then, in 1986, it signed the first Western management agreement in the Eastern Block for the Sheraton Sophia Hotel Balkan in Bulgaria. In 1989, ITT Sheraton announced the first U.S./Soviet joint venture to own and operate two hotels in Moscow.

With nearly 500 properties, including luxury hotels and resorts, business and convention hotels, inns, and all-suite hotels, ITT Sheraton serves 22 million guests each year at hotels in 65 countries on five continents. It is the leading hotel company in international coverage.

Liberal Arts Grads Wanted

College Relations Manager Brett Hutchens firmly believes liberal arts graduates are desirable management candidates: "Liberal arts graduates usually have a broader business exposure than technical school graduates. They can relate to the hospitality part of the business more readily."

On the other hand, grads do need to master certain specific skills to succeed at Sheraton "Liberal arts graduates lack the technical knowledge of the hospitality business. They require more training than technical school graduates," says Hutchens.

That's why Sheraton requires that before getting into the management training program, recent grads must pay their dues by either getting a masters degree in a hotel-training school or by working for Sheraton as a staff employee in the food and beverage or rooms divisions of one of the hotels. After that, they are eligible to enter the management training program.

General Management Training

This program is for those people who haven't yet chosen an area of specialization. It allows them to spend time in each hotel department to gain a comprehensive understanding of operations. The twelve-month training program usually focuses trainees in the Rooms Division. However, in the final months of the program, trainees can choose other areas of specialization, such as food and beverage, human resources, or systems management. Following completion, they are placed in an area of specialty in a hotel where they are needed.

Food and Beverage Management Training

Trainees who have already spent a year in a hotel food and beverage department can enter this program. Again, they work in all areas of food and beverage to develop culinary and management skills and knowledge and then are placed in entry-level management positions at a hotel.

Systems Management Training

This program is designed specifically for those people with experience in information systems. During the year-long program, trainees gain a working knowledge of the automated functions of each hotel department. Upon completion, they are asssigned a systems analyst position in a hotel.

Career Path

Hutchens says one of the advantages of working for the company is its expansion program, which presents advancement opportunities for employees.

It usually takes someone about seven or eight years to work his or her way up from line staff to the corporate office. After working for a year on staff, either for Sheraton or another hotel, employees spend one year in a management training program. Typically, they then become department specialists, department managers, department directors, and then regional directors with responsibilities for several hotels. After that, they may move to the corporate office in Boston.

Internships

One way to qualify more quickly for the management training program is to get a part-time internship before you graduate. Almost every department in each hotel has internships available to beginners in the summer and during the school year. To apply for an internship, contact the individual hotel's personnel office directly.

Report from the Trenches

PEGGY BENUA
Position: Executive Housekeeper, Sheraton Los Angeles Airport Hotel
Age: 32
Earnings: High 30s
School: University of North Florida, Jacksonville, Fla.
Major: Art History

Before going to work for Sheraton in 1989, Peggy Benua had already worked for eight years for a restaurant chain and had received her masters degree in hotel and food service management. Even though she started in the Sheraton Masters Training Program and was placed in a higher level job than she would have been if she were right out of college, Peggy's experience with the company gives you a good idea what a career there is like.

When I was graduating with a masters from Florida International University, Sheraton came along with this management training program for masters degrees and MBAs. It was the only opportunity like it.

It's a training program where you learn all aspects of the hotel business, but you learn it from a top-down approach. Instead of going into the accounting department in accounts payable, you go in with the controller and do an outlook. It's more of an executive focus.

Career Path

For the first year I was in that program at the Sheraton in San Diego going from department to department and learning the operation, following a manual. It's formal but structured so you can concentrate on your own strengths and weaknesses. Most of it is on-the-job training.

After the training, I decided to go into the rooms division, because it is less demanding and more business-like than food and beverage. I was the assistant front office manager. My duties were to oversee check-in, reservations, the bell desk, and the concierge. I assisted in managing all of the employees in those areas, plus I had forecasting and financial reporting responsibilites.

I did that for several months and was asked to take a position as assistant front office manager at the Sheraton Los Angeles Airport. It was much busier, a bigger hotel with different situations. I was in that position for a year when I was asked to take over the housekeeping department, which is where I am now.

My duties are to manage about 130 people who clean the rooms and do the laundry. It is the largest department in the hotel and most of the employees are Hispanic. I am taking Spanish classes now and the hotel is offering English classes to all Spanish-speaking people.

People-Oriented Management

This is a very people-oriented business, and upper management is very concerned with individual employees as well as guests. When you move, you go where it's good for the company, but they consider what's good for you, too. You never have to move, but I've moved twice. They gave me a choice of 120 hotels and asked me where I wanted to go.

Advice to Grads

Try to get some experience during school or during the summer. Work at the front desk or in a restaurant waiting tables.

Remember, you have to be service oriented, you have to enjoy that kind of work and to think it's fun. Sometimes you have to deal with difficult people and not everyone can do that. You have to be flexible.

Exciting Career

You have camaraderie and a sense of teamwork with the staff. When you're in a seasonal hotel, you work hard and when it's over, you have that sense that you made it. It's a fun, exciting job. There's always something going on. It's different every day. You meet people from all over the world, some of whom are pretty funny.

Once when I was working in the front office, we had an older couple who had a layover one night in L.A. They had adopted a small kitten in Hawaii. The next morning after the man opened the door to get his paper, he couldn't find the kitten. He thought it had run out when he had his back turned. Our security supervisor was walking up and down the hallways looking for the kitten. Another assistant manager and I went all the way up to the 15th floor looking down the halls. The couple had to postpone their flight because we couldn't find the kitten. When the second flight came, we still hadn't found it, so they left.

I went across the hall from the room they were in, looked under the bed, and saw a piece of fabric ripped from the bedspring. I felt around inside the little hole and felt the cat up there.

There were 10 people in the room with the bed on its side trying to get the kitten out. We finally got it out, ran downstairs, and jumped on a shuttle bus to try to catch the Delta flight the couple was on. A valet parker told us the couple was still in the restaurant. We ran into the restaurant with the kitten and they were there with long faces, depressed. But when we gave them their kitten, they were all smiles.

A Secure Company

I feel confident being an employee of the Sheraton Corporation. It offers more opportunities for me and I feel more secure working here than I would with a hotel that's in financial trouble. With the recession, there are a lot of companies downsizing, while Sheraton is still putting money into hotels. It's very strong financially; there have been no lay-offs.

STAPLES, INC.
100 Pennsylvania Ave.
Framingham, MA 01701
(800) 888-2422

Other Employment Centers
83 retail stores in 13 states, including New England, the Eastern Seaboard, Ohio, and California. One regional office in Fountain Valley, California

Products/Services
Discount retail office equipment and supplies

Number of Employees
Approximately 4,000

Job Opportunities
Management trainee

Starting Salary
Low 20s

Major Pluses
+ Fast-growing company, lots of opportunities to advance quickly

Drawbacks
- Long hours, 45-hour work week (nights, weekends, early morning hours, and holidays are a regular part of work schedule)
- Changes occur rapidly (demands high degree of patience and flexibility)

Corporate Philosophy
Business devoted to "developing and implementing bold new ways of customers to save money" by volume buying and slashing selling prices

Atmosphere
Young company, young employees, fast-paced. Conservative, business dress

Working Conditions
You're out on the floor. Think "Price Club" with more sophisticated customers.

Tips for Getting a Job
- Demonstrate that you like being in the public eye.
- Do your homework on the company.
- Show you understand the concept of customer service.
- Don't make mistakes on your resume.
- Emphasize your skill at handling multiple tasks and your ability to change quickly to changing demands.

Profile

This is a youth-oriented company known for its rapid growth and rapid advancement of management trainees. What's more, the company plans to hire more than 100 liberal arts graduates this year.

Staples was founded in 1985 to fill the gap between traditional retail office products stores and their warehouse-club competitors. Founder Tom Stemberg's solution to the gap was deep-discount office superstores, sort of a Toys R Us of office supplies.

Opened in May 1986 in Boston, the first store was an instant success. Now with more than $300 million in annual sales, 114 operating stores, and 150 more scheduled to open by 1995, Staples has been called the largest and fastest growing new venture in retail.

Liberal Arts Connection

One of the reasons liberal arts graduates are valued and do well with Staples is that the clientele is more professional, unlike that of most retail companies, and company management believe that those with a broad education can communicate well with doctors, lawyers, accountants, and CEOs.

Training

Management trainees are schooled in all aspects of operations from customer service to specific product information (being able to operate all office equipment one sells is requisite). Trainees learn marketing techniques, systems operations, including cash reporting, inventories, special orders, corporate office functions, and promotional marketing.

Although the training program is structured, it can begin at any time and is tailored to the needs of each trainee. Ninety percent of the training is on the job; the rest takes place off-site on topics such as management development, motivation, and so on.

Training rotates throughout store departments. When you reach the goal for one, you progress to the next step. It's up to you to achieve the prescribed goals.

To encourage further training and education, Staples reimburses employees for tuition and expenses, starting at 50 percent after one year of employment, increasing to 75 percent after two years, and reaching 100 percent after three years.

Qualifications

You don't have to be a scholar to get into management at Staples. However, you must demonstrate a sense of responsibility, such as a consistent work history. Many management trainees worked as waiters and waitresses during high school and college.

"Grades aren't real important to us," explains corporate recruiter Amy Resnick. "If someone has been to college and is going to graduate, they have obviously worked hard. However, work history is very important because retail is a hard industry. A consistent work history shows that students are responsible and know what it's like to work on different agendas and to budget their time."

Career Path
The average liberal arts graduate starts as a management trainee and within six to eight months progresses to line management with actual supervisory responsibility over other trainees. He or she becomes an assistant manager by the end of the first year. Assistant manager responsibilities include scheduling, needs assessment, and training and development of new employees.

The next step is to a manager position, overseeing a whole department with responsibility for meeting set objectives, hiring, and training. Finally, within three or four years of being hired, the person will become a general manager responsible for an entire store.

Report from the Trenches

NICK TSEPLIS
Position: Merchandising Manager
Age: 26
Earnings: Low 30s (est.)
School: University of Pennsylvania, Philadelphia, Pa.
Major: Economics

Nick missed the Staples recruiters when they interviewed on his campus. Later, he sent the company a letter and was invited for an interview. At that time the company was only two years old, so his interview was conducted on the back of a car in the parking lot of an unopened store. Here's what happened:

The interview lasted about an hour and 15 minutes. They asked questions like Why do you want to work for Staples? What do you know about our company? What was your favorite class? But most of the questions focused on what my reactions would be in certain situations. It was my only interview with Staples, and the job offer came four weeks later.

Career Progress
Since I started with the company in 1988, I have been moved or promoted six times, all within the same geographical area: I started as an office consultant (customer service rep) for five weeks and then moved to the service department for five more weeks. Then it was onto merchandising (where I helped open a new store) for four months.

Then I was promoted to merchandising manager and stayed in that position for eight months, during which time I received two salary increases.

I got a third raise when I was promoted to cash department manager, a position in which I stayed for six and a half months. Then I became a service manager for three months and progressed to service manager in a higher-volume store for five months.

Next, I served as merchandising manager in a higher volume store where I am now.

Whew! What's Next?

I expect to be promoted shortly to general manager. Then it's onto corporate office as a buyer. Longer term . . . who knows? Maybe president!

The Typical Day

Hectic! Part of the day is spent planning, making lists, and delegating. This is a good portion of the day. The rest is devoted to handling customer-related and inventory problems, but it is fun. I like the constant change; it's not the same thing day in and day out.

There is always a different crisis or new set of problems. I am always trying to improve display techniques. The people are great. The hours change from week to week and are sometimes long. Inventory is done every six months, and then you can count on several 12-hour days.

Deliveries are made five days a week on weekdays, so mornings are consumed with stock-related duties. I have responsibility over approximately six people who are mini-department or aisle heads or assistant managers.

Best and Worst

The best things about working at Staples are the opportunities for advancement and growth. The worst is keeping track of the changes—everything changes so quickly. This would probably not be the place for someone who is inflexible and does not adapt well to change.

Advice

Start early! Make sure you know what you want. I've seen a lot of management trainees start and if they don't have a clear understanding of the industry, it may not be right for them. Knowing the company you are applying to and what you are applying for is also important. Have a realistic idea of what is expected. It's very important to have all the facts.

STATE FARM INSURANCE COMPANIES

One State Farm Plaza
Bloomington, IL 61710-0001
(309) 766-6200

Other Employment Centers
26 regional offices in the United States and Canada serve as operation centers for more than 850 field offices around the country

Products/Services
A multiple-line insurance carrier providing protection to more than 53 million policyholders

Number of Employees
More than 58,000

Job Opportunities
Management trainees in a variety of disciplines such as claims, underwriting, and data processing

Starting Salary
Low 20s (Varies, depending on living conditions and labor market of specific office. A claims rep in Bloomington won't make as much as one working out of an office in New York City)

Major Pluses
+ Excellent benefits package includes health, dental, life, and long-term disability insurance as well as retirement and profit-sharing programs
+ Flexible career growth offers employees chance to change career path as it suits him/her through job opportunities programs
+ Stable company with plenty of room for growth
+ Cost-of-living adjustment ties salaries to Consumer Price Index

Drawbacks
− Company not yet equipped to adequately facilitate employees' constant relocations

Corporate Philosophy
The corporate philosophy has been one of "insurance agents on Main Street." Personal contact with policyholders is the rule, not the exception.

Atmosphere
Very family-oriented. An activities association at corporate and at the regional offices provides an opportunity for employees to get to know each other through intramural sports and other activities.

Working Conditions
A home-town atmosphere prevails. Employees work with higher-ups on a first-name basis. "You'd feel just as comfortable sitting down, talking with the president of the company as you would with anybody else here," explained Wesley B. Little, personnel specialist.

Tips for Getting a Job
• No. 1 priority: Good communication skills.
• Research the positions you're interested in ahead of time. Really get to know the company.

- Offer a balance of good grades and outside activities.
- Ambitious and goal-oriented interviewees always fare better.
- Mobility is an asset.

Profile

Sometimes called the Fort Knox of insurance companies, few would deny that State Farm is one of the most stable and financially secure insurance companies in the country. Its conservative investment policies, and its independent contractor relationship with its agents, are responsible for its steady, spectacular success—even during a tough economy and more than a few natural disasters.

State Farm is richer than most U.S. companies and the leader by far in auto and homeowner insurance. In 1990 it earned almost $26 billion in premiums, second to Prudential (which had about $28 billion). Yet in equity capital—or wealth—State Farm beats Prudential by a mile ($18 billion to $8 billion).

What They Want

State Farm likes candidates who display a balance between intelligence (through school work *and* life experience) and communication skills. A graduate's exact major is of little difference, except for certain technical positions.

"I'd like to see someone who is assertive and goal-oriented," says personnel specialist Wesley B. Little. "We want someone with a well-rounded educational background who's able to communicate with the public and shows ambition. Mobility is also very important as far as qualifications because we're growing so quickly in so many areas that we need folks who are able to relocate well."

The Hiring Process

Submit a resume, a job application, and a copy of your college transcript. The next step is a personnel screening interview with a person in a specific department. Some pre-employment testing is given, depending on the position. This can be done in any of the 28 regional offices around the country. Those who pass the screening process join a pool of qualified applicants. When an opening comes up, prospective employees are interviewed by the department manager and have a meeting with upper management. The selection process goes from there.

Training

Training includes a combination of on-the-job training and specific educational programs. Most liberal arts majors train for claims and underwriting departments. For auto claims, for instance, all reps are flown to

Bloomington for a three-week training program in a classroom setting. For fire claims, there are two two-week training sessions. Underwriters, on the other hand, are trained in an educational program and a self-study course.

Career Path

There are several different levels of progress, depending on the individual department, until you reach a supervisory level and, after that, management. From a management position, you can continue as high up the ladder as your ability and desire allows.

Report from the Trenches

VIC PLYMOUTH

Position: Personnel Specialist
Age: 26
Earnings: Low 30s (est.)
School: West Liberty State College, West Liberty, W.Va.
Major: Art/Music/Communications

Vic Plymouth combined one of his hobbies (automobiles) and one of his talents (working with people in a service situation) and landed in a very comfortable position at State Farm. Here's how he parlayed his strengths into a great career:

I was a working musician and a sales rep for a music company when a friend, who worked at State Farm, told me about a couple of openings there. He gave me an application, which I filled out, and I later was called in for an interview. Three or four weeks after that, I was interviewed again. I have an interest in automobiles, and I have a good track record at being service-oriented, so they hired me.

Training

I started out as a claims trainee. I attended a three-week automobile claims school. There were daily tests, except for the first day. If you didn't pass a majority of the tests, you wouldn't get a job. You were paid during this training period. They give you three to six months to get some general training, and then they kick you out of there.

Career Progress

After that, I became a claims rep, which is the first level. After a two-year period, I was promoted to the next level—senior claims rep. From that point, I could have continued in claims to be a specialist or supervisor and then move into management. However, I got a call to come out to corporate and interview in personnel. So I started as a personnel assistant doing everything, doing off-street hiring and working in the transfer relocation process. I also got involved in salary administration, assisting or counseling management as far as working with their employees.

The Typical Day
A lot of it depends on the season. I essentially do everything in-house except anything that is employment-related. I don't hire off the street anymore. I'm still involved with the job-posting process. I have done recruiting; I've gone to colleges.

The Work Environment
The work style is more individualized. You're given a project, and it's your responsibility from start to finish. I'm responsible for all the personnel services–related items. We have an activities association that promotes tennis, volleyball, and softball leagues. A lot of people utilize that, but it's not my bag.

State Farm's corporate philosophy is very traditional. Essentially, it revolves around providing the best service to our policyholders, giving them the best value for their dollar. And that's very instilled in the culture.

Best and Worst
The stability is the best thing here. I can work here for the rest of my life, and I will be taken care of when I retire. I get satisfaction from the work that I do, the people I work with, and then I can go home.

On the down side, as an employee who likes to take things into my own hands and do it for myself, this isn't the best career choice. The work structure is very traditional here. People who come in with a "set the world on fire" attitude gets their jets cooled. Entrepreneurship is good if you want to be an agent; I wish that had been available to me a lot sooner.

Tips
Accept the fact that Plan A is not always going to work, so always have Plans B and C ready, and make sure they're acceptable. But never forget about Plan A.

STRAWBRIDGE & CLOTHIER
801 Market St.
Philadelphia, PA
(215) 629-7817

Other Employment Centers
Besides the Philadelphia headquarters store, there are 13 department stores in New Jersey, Pennsylvania, and Delaware. The Clover division encompasses 25 mass-merchandising stores in the region.

Products/Services
One of region's most renowned retail clothing department stores

Number of Employees
More than 12,000

Job Opportunities
Entry-level positions as assistant buyers and department managers

Starting Salary
Low 20s

Major Pluses
+ Good benefits package (includes company-funded pension plan, tuition reimbursement, and 20 percent store discount)
+ Family atmosphere; begins with training program and continues into workplace
+ 95 percent of management was promoted from within

Drawbacks
− Long retail hours
− Physical work involved in putting merchandise in store

Corporate Philosophy
"Give the customer the best you can" is the overriding philosophy, both in quality and in prices.

Atmosphere
A close-knit atmosphere keeps turnover quite low. Loyalty at upper levels is quite high.

Working Conditions
Like all retail sales work, it comes down to meeting people and the physical work of stocking merchandise. Ability to deal with higher-ups on a one-to-one basis.

Tips for Getting a Job
• Strong communication skills and an enthusiastic and positive attitude are important.
• Show a commitment to work in this industry.
• Look sharp. This is an image-perception business.

Profile

Established in 1868, Strawbridge & Clothier has become an integral part of the Northeast retail scene. Now with two divisions and 12,000 employees, Strawbridge generates almost $1 billion in annual sales.

What They Want

A high GPA is not essential in a retail environment. However, a 2.5 is the minimum. "We are looking for liberal arts graduates who have had some business exposure," says Strawbridge & Clothier's Manager of Executive Recruitment and Placement, Charlotte Waterbury. "This can be as little as one or two courses, or as much as a minor in business."

Eighty-five percent of the employees have had some exposure to the retail industry. Far more important, however, is the ability to communicate effectively and to convey an enthusiastic, warm personality. Looking sharp is also paramount. You must be confident and persuasive and look the part.

The Hiring Process

It begins with an on-campus interview, then a trip to a store, which includes a tour, lunch with executive management, and interviews with buyers and divisional merchandise managers.

Training

A comprehensive executive development program complements hands-on, day to day, in-store experience. Meetings with management are interspersed with specialized seminars to develop a solid understanding of the various aspects of the retail clothing business.

Trainees take courses in retail mathematics, merchandise reports, supervision, inventory control, and customer service. They also receive lectures by top management on the organization of the company and its structure. From these learning opportunities they gain an understanding of what each department and area does. During the first year, trainees are in class two days week, the rest of the time learning on the job.

Career Path

According to Waterbury, it's possible to be promoted within six months of your employment. "Initial movements can begin after six months to a year. The first placement can happen before training ends and would be based on merit, not necessarily time with the company."

After becoming a department manager or assistant buyer, the typical liberal arts graduate would move to the next levels of senior assistant buyer, assistant merchandise manager, and then buyer, receiving a pay increase at each step. New employees are reviewed after six months and annually after that.

Report from the Trenches

MELBA GALAMORE
Position: Department Manager
Age: 25

Earnings: High 20s (est.)
School: Pennsylvania State University, University Park, Pa.
Major: English Literature

Melba Galamore started visiting the Penn State Career Placement Center at the beginning of her senior year, attending workshops and signing up for interviews with corporate recruiters. She interviewed with a variety of companies for such jobs as industrial sales, management training, and retailing. That's when she had her first interview with Strawbridge & Clothier. Here's her story:

I was very impressed with Strawbridge & Clothier's training program. They seemed a notch above the other retailers. My second interview was on-site in their Philadelphia flagship store, and I was sold. I toured the store, I talked with buyers, and I had a lot of meetings with people at varied levels. I knew at that point I wanted the job. When they offered me the position, I accepted right away.

Career Progress
You're called an "executive trainee" when you spend your first four weeks trailing a department manager. You learn what sales are like, how customer service policies work, how the register works, etc.

A few months later, I was placed in the better sportswear buying office, and I was there for six months. Then I went to better sportswear in Philadelphia, where I was in charge of 25 sales associates. This was more personnel-type work, dealing with the receiving department, buyers, store manager, and customers. It's a juggling routine—one day paperwork, the next day in jeans moving merchandise. It's very fast-paced and exciting.

I worked as a department manager from May until December 1990 and helped in recruiting until May of the next year. Now I am working as a men's department manager until a personnel opening becomes available.

The Typical Day
I deal a lot with customers. The philosophy is that when you see customers, you smile, say hello, and ask if they need help. Receiving the figures and making comparisons with last year (are there decreases and increases?), budgets, scheduling salespeople, constantly checking stock, and talking with buyers, are also some of my responsibilities. I also deal a lot with store management regarding any needs, problems, good and bad things.

The Work Environment
The feeling of the company is very family-oriented. Any branch will give you that feeling, and it all ties together. It's easy to give a number one commitment to the customer when you feel like family. It's a very traditional company where

you give the customer the best customer service you can, the best selection and best price. There's a strong feeling of pride that's nice. You're not just a number; the president, CEO, and VPs who visit the stores call the department managers by name.

Best and Worst
The best part is the family atmosphere and the training program. That, along with the support you get, go hand in hand. The worst part are the retail hours. You can love retail as much as you want, but the hours around the holidays are tough, yet the commitment has to be there.

The Future
I could spend the rest of my career here because I know I'm not going to be stuck in one position forever. I can leave my options open and go in other directions. There's no threat of someone from the outside coming in and taking my job.

Tips
Know what you want to do, but explore a lot of different things. Be confident in selling yourself and your activities, and draw from those. Show your confidence and enthusiasm; don't close yourself off to anything; you never know where it will take you. The main thing is the ability to think, reason, analyze, explore, and communicate. You can learn any type of technical things with those basics.

T.J. MAXX
770 Cochituate Road
Framingham, MA 01701
(508) 390-3632

Products/Services
Discount clothing retailer

Number of Employees
30,000

Job Opportunities
Merchandise analyst

Starting Salary
$20,000 to $28,000

Major Pluses
+ Company's rapid expansion can mean opportunity for quick advancement
+ Fast-track executive training program
+ Profit-sharing
+ Tuition assistance

+ Merchandise discounts
+ Fitness center
+ On-site children's day care
+ 9 to 5 hours (unusual in the retail industry)

Drawbacks

− Despite the euphemistic name for the "off-price apparel retail" industry, there remains the aura of "bargain basement."
− Salaries on the low side compared to same jobs in department stores

Corporate Philosophy

The company is young, aggressive, and optimistic. We were hard-pressed
to find a mission statement; management's energies apparently are
focused primarily on growth. But there does appear to be a proactive
interest in employee welfare.

Atmosphere

Down-to-earth. Everybody is on a first-name basis, including the CEO.
Associates and management have a sense of ésprit de corps. The people
who work for the company have seen the future and it looks bright.

Working Conditions

The headquarters are in a contemporary, well-designed building that
houses 1,500 employees in a suburb 30 minutes outside of Boston. You
will work in a cubicle, but that environment will be somewhat mitigated
by an on-site cafeteria, fitness center, and childcare center. Dress is professional but not formal. Associates wear the clothes the company sells.

Tips for Getting a Job

• Present a "we-oriented" rather than a "me-oriented" attitude.
• Use "team player" to discuss your experience.
• Highlight experience that relates to a job in retail, especially cus-
  tomer service.
• Express enthusiasm at the prospect of working for the company.

Profile

T.J. Maxx has ridden the crest of the fast-growing off-price segment of
the retail industry that surfaced in the seventies and captured 9 percent,
or $14.3 billion, of the $198.9 billion retail apparel and footwear industry.
The company has recorded 14 consecutive years of sales and earnings
growth, finishing 1991 with sales of $2.45 billion, a 14 percent increase
over the previous year.

Although T.J. Maxx began with just two stores outside of Boston in
1977, it now operates some 400 discount retail apparel stores in 44 states.
The company is part of TJX Companies, which also owns the 600-store

Hit or Miss off-price women's apparel chain and Chadwick's of Boston, an off-price apparel catalog. In 1990, TJX acquired Winner Ltd., an off-price family apparel chain based in Toronto.

The combined sales of all TJX subsidiaries make it the largest off-price retailer in the United States, with the T.J. Maxx banner accounting for the vast majority of sales.

Recession-Proof

Despite the recession, T.J. Maxx continues to operate in a growth pattern. If anything, T.J. Maxx and the off-price industry in general appear to be flourishing in hard economic times, with T.J. Maxx planning to open approximately 45 to 50 stores annually in the foreseeable future. Its main competitors are other major off-price apparel retail chains, such as Marshall's and Ross Stores.

The off-price concept that T.J. Maxx and others pioneered is simple: Offer consumers much of the same name-brand merchandise available in department stores but at prices that are 20% to 60% discounted. If the stores tend to be spartan and the displays plain, well, many customers tend to think the discounts are worth it.

Management Training

T.J. Maxx offers the Corporate Executive Training Program, a self-paced, on-the-job training program that is designed to give a total perspective on retail merchandising. The seven-step career path has three levels: merchandise analysis, planning, and buying.

As a merchandise analyst and then senior merchandise analyst, your responsibilities will include analyzing sales and inventory, making appropriate shipping decisions, and inspecting merchandise for quality and value.

The planning division is described as the "ears and eyes" of the buyers. As an assistant planner, you will help identify the latest fashion trends and help execute seasonal buying plans. Eventually, as a planner you will also assume full managerial responsibilities.

The buyers are described as the major players in the company's merchandising strategies. They ultimately decide what goes to the store. A good deal of price negotiating with vendors required as well as constant travel to New York City and other retail centers in the United States and abroad.

Other Opportunities, But . . .

There are other job opportunities as well, in store management and distribution. But the road to top management is clearly the fastest along the merchandising route.

Report from the Trenches

KATHY DOONAN
Position: Planner
Age: 25
Earnings: $30,000 (est.)
School: Boston College, Chestnut Hill, Mass.
Major: Psychology

Kathy knew she did not want to further her education in psychology. While working as a volunteer in her college recruitment office—"I forced myself," she recalls—brochures from several retail businesses came across her desk, and she began to explore executive training programs in the industry.

After only three years at T.J. Maxx, Kathy has already risen to a mid-level management position. Here's her report:

After I became interested in a career in retail, I had a few interviews with department stores. But the more I learned about the industry, the more I realized that the real growth potential was with the discount retailers. In fact, at the time, department stores were already beginning to have financial problems. I could have gotten a higher starting salary with a department store but I didn't want to take the risk. I've never regretted that decision.

Recruitment
I had one interview on campus with a recruiter and then two back-to-back interviews at the company's headquarters. That was followed by three, more in-depth group interviews. In one exercise, candidates were divided into teams, and we had to create a marketing plan for a new business, including its location, name, and the number of employees to be hired.

It was pretty challenging. There were people from different schools and different backgrounds. Two employees from T.J. Maxx observed. I think they were less interested in the final outcome of the marketing plan than in how we interacted in a group.

Working as a team here is very important.

Career Path
I began as a merchandise analyst, responsible for allocating and distributing merchandise. Basically, my job was making sure the right merchandise got to the right stores at the right time. I had to be aware of sales trends and react quickly so that I could maintain the proper balance of inventory with our vendors. After six months I was promoted to senior merchandise analyst, which included additional responsibilities.

Ten months later I was promoted to assistant planner and then eventually to planner, which is where I am now. I work in the girl's division of the children's department. I'm responsible for creating and monitoring sales inventory plans for all (400 plus) of our stores.

The next rung up the career ladder is associate buyer, but I have decided to stay in planning. I really like the analysis that's involved in the job. It's a good balance of technical and people-oriented tasks.

Corporate Culture
It's essentially a nine-to-five schedule. You aren't made to feel as if you must work late to get ahead.

There are lots of opportunities to brainstorm and come up with ideas. Management encourages creative solutions to problems. Ideas are listened to. Everyone's opinion is respected.

My peers are fairly down-to-earth, but because it's merchandising many people are very ambitious. The mentality is definitely upwardly mobile.

The Future
Eventually, I might like to have my own business, maybe a bridal consultation service. But that's very long-term. Our company is really strong, and I can see myself being here a long time.

I have always been really hard on myself in terms of getting ahead, but I never thought it would be this fast. Here I am 25 years old and making million-dollar decisions.

TOTAL SYSTEMS SERVICES
1200 Sixth Ave.
P.O. Box 1755
Columbus, GA 31902-1755
(404) 649-2310

Other Employment Centers
None, although employees frequently travel to clients in 34 states, Canada, and Puerto Rico

Products/Service
The second-largest independent credit card processor in the United States

Number of Employees
1,300

Job Opportunities
Public relations and customer service

Starting Salary
$18,000 to $22,000

Major Pluses

+ Excellent benefits package including profit sharing, stock option, fitness plan, and tuition assistance
+ Employees are treated by the higher-ups like they're supposed to treat their customers.

Drawbacks

− A very technical company, so you must have an aptitude for details

Corporate Philosophy

Employees are challenged to effectively deal with both the banks they serve and the individual credit cardholders. To serve both parties adequately and effective, the staff must work as a team and be open to change.

Atmosphere

Life in a computer-driven world. It's a hard-working, yet positive, atmosphere.

Working Conditions

Parallels a bank environment; the stress level rises at the end of each month. Hours can be long and hard.

Tips for Getting a Job

• Appearance makes a difference here. Look sharp, act sharp.
• Exhibit strong analytical and communication skills.
• Show an interest in the company and the work by asking questions.
• Display an energetic confidence and strong eye contact.
• Show an interest in building a long-term career.

Profile

With more than 16.5 million credit cardholder accounts and 300,000 merchant accounts in more than 33 states, Total Systems Services is the second largest independent credit card processor in the United States. Annual sales add up to about $84 million with $13 million in earnings.

Founded in 1983, TSS gives what it calls "Total System" treatment to primarily financial institutions that issue Visa and MasterCard. Its services include recording transactions, mailing bills, and relaying customer information.

What They Want

Being customer service–oriented, Total Systems believes that liberal arts grads have the communication skills necessary to relate to their clientele. The technical stuff can be taught. They want well-educated, committed graduates with either technical or analytical talents and the ability to communicate those talents to others. A knowledge of computers and programming is especially beneficial.

"They need to be creative, analytical, confident, and mature and have a high energy level," says recruiting manager Joyce Fowler. "They'll work more than eight hours a day and on weekends for special projects in the most work-intensive environment that I have ever worked in."

The Hiring Process

Liberal arts grads initially send in a resume highlighting their skills, then go for multiple interviews, which weed out candidates. The real interviews come when you meet a division manager, who looks at your skills and determines where you would fit in. Expect to take a drug test as well as a background and credit check. Programmers may be asked to take an aptitude test.

Training

The type of training depends on the area you were hired for. Computer training is essential, since every aspect of the company uses computers. The rest of the training is on the job. Everyone is trained, and once training is completed, they become trainers for new employees.

Career Path

Total Systems is currently building a career planning program so any employee can set up a logical career path early on. There are many opportunities for upward mobility. Within five years, the company expects employees to move into supervision.

Report from the Trenches

BEN STAHL
Position: Process Manager
Age: 23
Earnings: Mid 20s (est.)
School: Columbus College, Columbus, Ga.
Major: Political Science

Ben Stahl was simply looking for a challenging, fast-paced job when he applied for a position at Total Systems. His dedication and experience enticed the company to create a new position for him, in which he has excelled. Here's his take on his smooth entry into Total Systems.

I was working in the training and development department for Blue Cross/Blue Shield, and a woman who worked at Blue Cross knew the personnel manager here. I went in for an interview and got the job basically on the interview. They created a position for me as a training assistant on a part-time basis. I'd go to school in the mornings and come back and work in the evening.

Career Progress
Eventually, I started looking a lot harder for an internal job because I wanted to stay with the company. I had a talk with one of the VPs, who was starting a new department. They were reformatting in a couple of areas and redoing the way they did certain things. So I became process manager, which was nonexistent before I was hired for it.

The Typical Day
Every day is different. For instance, I just spent the last two weeks trying to get a feel for the production mode building. I spent two weeks looking at the entire process on an internal audit basis. I took my notes to Quality Assurance, which has a big pool of resources.

The Work Environment
Basically, we follow everybody else. Our closing dates parallel the banks'. The end of each month is a stressful time in some departments. Personally, I don't work a lot of overtime, and the end of the month doesn't affect me as much as others, some of whom work 10 hours a day. My problem is that a lot of errors become evident during this time of the month. I have to identify why these errors occur and who is causing them.

Best and Worst
The best things are the variety of work and the people. Everyone is positive and open to change, and things change daily here, so people are very receptive to it.

With so many different personalities in the company, there can be problems if you happen to be matched up with someone who is very negative or isn't easily adaptable to change. This is a fast-paced company, and if you can't change, you're going to have problems.

The Future
Hopefully, I'll move upward in the company. I'm participating in a stock purchase deal and I'm trying to build myself up by working on a master's degree. By the time I'm done, I'll have an MBA and be in middle or upper management. But there's no telling where I'll end up.

Tips
A lot of people won't take a job unless it's exactly what they're looking for. It pays to be flexible in this company. Since a lot of jobs are posted internally before they're made public, it's best to get some entry-level job and work your way up.

You'll have a lot more luck doing that than trying for that position from the outside.

Don't give up or develop a real negative attitude if you aren't automatically promoted after a month or two. Stay positive and work twice as hard, which shows the company you're serious about staying with them for the duration. If you work hard and work smart, they might create a position for you, too. It may take longer to get a job that way, but in the long run it might be better. This company will be receptive to people who can come up with ways to improve the business.

THE TRAVELERS INSURANCE CO.

One Tower Square
Hartford, CT 06183
(203) 277-2980

Other Employment Centers
Scattered throughout the United States

Products/Services
Life, health, and property insurance and managed health care

Number of Employees
32,000

Job Opportunities
Management training (customer service, claims)

Starting Salary
Mid to high 20s

Major Pluses
+ Advancement potential within six months of starting
+ Profit-sharing; company matches up to 5 percent
+ Flex-time
+ Tuition reimbursement
+ Fitness center at headquarters

Drawbacks
− Most jobs in Hartford
− Ultra-conservative
− Requires a sunny attitude that may be too much for some

Corporate Philosophy
Teamwork is the golden rule at The Travelers. Most employees work on projects in groups, and all members of the team are thanked for their input.

Atmosphere

Conservative, corporate. Because Travelers is so teamwork-oriented, the competitive scrambling up the ladder is not as cutthroat as may be expected. But employees are still expected to be serious about their jobs. Travelers does not provide cushy jobs.

Working Conditions

Relaxed, suburban surroundings with fitness center on premises

Tips for Getting a Job

- A professional image is important. Look like you belong in the business world.
- Show that you were active in nonacademic programs in college.
- Do your research about the company before the interview.
- Know what type of job you want or what area you would like to work in.

Profile

Travelers, one of the largest U.S. insurance companies offering property, casualty, life, and health insurance, began about 128 years ago with a two-cent insurance policy on train travel. The company has grown from just one guy asking a friend if he would pay two cents to be insured for a train to an insurance giant with more than $50 billion in assets.

Qualifications

The Travelers looks for people who want to be part of the action, and despite its conservatism, it does not want timid types.

"We're not interested in people who just want to be comfortable," says Cheryl Kozak of corporate staff and recruiting. "We want somebody who's going to take the initiative, somebody who is going to take risks, and somebody who is going to ask why."

A recruiter who interviews many liberal arts graduates, she says one of the worst things a candidate can do is come to an interview unprepared, without knowing what the company is all about and where he or she might fit in.

Travelers also looks for people who are well rounded and determined. Your undergraduate history and resume should include classes in computers and business. An internship in the business world is also very valuable.

The Liberal Arts Advantage

Travelers has found that liberal arts graduates can bring a lot to the company. Recruiters like Kozak are impressed with the well-rounded characteristics of those who studied liberal arts. "They have good communication skills," she says. "They can see the bigger picture . . . they are creative and not so specialized, and they bring in some new ideas." But without some classes in computers or business, Kozak says, graduates lack the focus in business needed at The Travelers.

Where You Might Fit In

Liberal arts graduates often start as customer service reps in departments like Managed Care and Employee Benefits (MCEBO). Others start as field representatives and underwriters and at entry-level jobs in the law department.

It is also possible to end up on a fast-track program like the Managed Care and Employee Benefits Associate Program, if you are the type of person who thrives on being on the go. This accelerated program, which requires an outstanding academic record as well as demonstrated leadership abilities, combines field office rotations, home office rotations, and classroom instruction.

Report from the Trenches

KAREN PURCER

Position: Administrative Assistant
Age: 22
Earnings: Mid 20s (est.)
School: Bucknell University, Lewisburg, Pa.
Major: Math

Karen took a different route to finding a job: networking. Thinking that her math degree wouldn't open many career doors except perhaps teaching, she began talking to friends and quickly landed a job she never dreamed she would be doing. As an administrative assistant to the vice president of Managed Health Care Marketing, Karen works on marketing projects and proposals to promote Travelers' insurance plans to companies that are changing policies. Here's her report:

Great Expectations

I think that I'm going to be on a fast track because the area of marketing that we're in is very fast-paced, and I'm sure I'm going to get thrown into it as soon as we move to the new building. Managed Health Care and Insurance is one of the only areas at this time that is actually growing. I saw this and I grabbed it. After a year as an administrator you can probably go pretty far.

The Typical Day

A typical day is working on marketing projects, arranging meetings, working on proposals, lots of phone calls. I expect to be assigned to do certain marketing projects with certain people along with working on specific projects directly for the vice president.

Companies that provide benefits look at all the insurance companies for the best deal. We hear about companies that are changing insurance companies or are running out on a contract, and we try to get them the best deal. Our department also makes all the materials used in presentations: the literature, slides, and videos.

Lots of Atmosphere

It is very fast-paced. Of the people I work with, everyone is very dynamic, energetic, on the go. It is also very team-oriented. When a project goes well, the recognition goes to everyone who worked on it.

It's a pleasant atmosphere. They welcome new people. A lot of times you go into a new company and you wonder, "Who am I going to go to lunch with?" I didn't have that problem here. People called me up to invite me to lunch or to introduce themselves to me since we would be working together.

Advice

Don't limit yourself geographically. Don't rule out any industries. I talked to banks, law firms, computer companies. A lot of people think that the only job you can get as a math major is as an actuary, but I was amazed at what was really out there.

Climbing

I was nervous at first. I was finally getting a job in the bad economy. I was afraid I would be just a glorified secretary. But then I heard a story about someone who started out as an administrator and three days later she became a sales rep. If you can prove yourself, you go. You climb up the ladder.

With Travelers in particular, one of the goals is to gear salary toward potential. They can see how you're doing. They look at the type of skills you can bring with your degree, not just at your degree. I didn't even take any business courses in college.

The Future

I can see myself doing this for a good number of years. I see a lot of potential for growth here for me and for the department I'm working in. I'll just follow this route and see where it takes me. I'm up for relocating, if that happens.

Nothing ever goes the way you planned. I never expected to be working in insurance and especially not as an administrator. But it's encouraging when things that you wouldn't expect to be so great can be so great.

I like the fact that I'm working towards something. I'm not just going to be a robot.

WALGREENS
2100 Wilmot Rd.
Deerfield, IL 60015
(708) 405-5886

Other Employment Centers
1,568 stores across the country, with nine distribution centers

Products/Services
Retail drugs and health and beauty aids

Number of Employees
50,000

Job Opportunities
Management trainee

Starting Salary
Depends on location of work (can run anywhere from $20,000 to $26,000)

Major Pluses
+ Outstanding insurance, stock purchase, and profit-sharing programs
+ High employee loyalty to store
+ Lots of room for promotion

Drawbacks
− Typically long retail hours

Corporate Philosophy
Very goal-oriented. Requires a lot of no-nonsense, hard work.

Atmosphere
A very employee-oriented company that emphasizes new ideas and ways to make work more productive

Working Conditions
Long retail hours, but employees are well compensated for retail

Tips for Getting a Job
- Be assertive, but not aggressive, in the interview. Without exaggerating, play up your strengths and experience.
- Exhibit good communication and people skills.
- Show that you balanced a decent GPA with extracurricular activities.
- Describe the wide variety of course work you took.

Profile

Despite the recession, Walgreens continues to be one of the fastest-growing companies in the drugstore business. With more than 1,600 stores operating in 29 states, the company has targeted 100 new store openings per year through the 1990s.

With such lickety-split growth and annual sales of more than $6 billion, Walgreens must be doing something right. One thing is generating intense customer loyalty through its emphasis on convenience and customer service. Dun & Bradstreet says Walgreens is one of the best managed companies in American business.

What They Want

Walgreens needs extroverted, outgoing people who don't get flustered by things like long hours and customer complaints. Naturally, a strong work ethic and good communication and people skills are necessary in the retail environment, too. An open mind and the ability to work with the latest in high technology—such things as laser scans and new computerized inventory management systems—are also key characteristics of the ideal Walgreens employee.

The Hiring Process

It begins with either an on-campus or corporate headquarters interview. Then comes another interview with a district manager. "We try to recruit in the markets we have the need for," noted Donald Moseley, a Walgreens management recruiter. "We don't believe in relocation. So if we are opening a new store in a certain area, that's where we'll recruit."

Training

Trainees are sent to a store right away, yet they also go through one to two years of classes and book work. During that time, they'll work one-on-one with the store manager and rotate through the various departments to learn the complexities of daily operations.

The second phase is the Initial Management Training Program, a self-study plan that complements on-site training. Next is the Applied Drug Store Management Program—classroom sessions that cover a variety of subjects.

Career Path

After 18 to 24 months of training as an assistant manager, you move up to the next level, executive assistant manager, a co-manager position where you have direct input on how the store is run. Within 12 to 18 months, you become a full-fledged manager of your own store. Next on the corporate ladder is district manager. Walgreens strongly believes in a promote-from-within policy. "Everyone in upper management at Walgreens has started as an assistant manager," Moseley says. "Promotions happen and we don't wait for death or retirement to do so."

Report from the Trenches

TIM ETTER
Position: Assistant Manager
Age: 25
Earnings: High 20s (est.)
School: University of Minnesota, Minneapolis/St. Paul, Minn.
Major: General Science

Although Tim Etter didn't initially set his sights on the retail drugstore business, he can't say he has been surprised at the work involved and his career progress. As he says, "After they hire you, they lay out the path you're going to follow, and it's pretty accurate." Here's how he has done on that path:

A friend of mine, who was in a Walgreens management training program, told me they were hiring. I had just been laid off from a finance company, so I made an appointment with a district manager. After the interview, I was offered a position as a management trainee.

The Training Program
The training here is real comprehensive; they do a real good job. I was put in a store right away, and after a year or two, I took some classes. The training program lasts until you get your own store. Each district runs its own ongoing training with classes held locally by the company.

Career Path
My next step will be store manager. When they see I'm ready, they'll give me my own store. The general time frame is three to four years until that happens. The next step after that is district manager in approximately five to seven years.

The Typical Day
The general running of the store includes ordering merchandise and displaying it, putting up new displays, and just about everything else. I have a staff of about 15 working under me. There are two assistant managers per store. We work five-day, 44-hour weeks (with four hours of overtime each week).
   They move us around from store to store in the same geographic region, so we don't work with the same assistant managers all the time. They generally

keep you in the same store for about a year before moving you. As manager, you stay until they need you somewhere else or you request to be moved, with the length of time in each store being about five years.

The Work Environment
You've got to be able to work one-on-one with the customers, employees, and vendors. You have to be able to deal with a constant contact with people. Now that we're computerized, you don't have to do all the books, the paying, and the invoicing by hand. The new inventory computer system is satellite-linked to the mainframe in Chicago.

Best and Worst
The benefits program is excellent. They have a really good profit-sharing program as well as the usual stock purchases and all that. All you have to do is have one year of service.

The worst thing about the job is the typical retail hours.

Tips
People should keep an open mind about whom they want to work for. I was all set on working for just one company instead of a broad range of companies. It takes a lot of work to find a good job. Do a lot of networking and use word-of-mouth with family and friends.

WAL-MART STORES, INC.
People Division
702 Southwest Eighth
Bentonville, AR 72716
(501) 273-6441

Other Employment Centers
More than 1,750 stores in 35 states

Products/Services
Discount retailer of apparel, health and beauty aids, household products, electronics, toys, fabrics, etc.

Number of Employees
300,000 plus

Job Opportunities
Management trainee

Starting Salary
$23,000 to $30,000, depending on location

Major Pluses
+ Company-paid profit-sharing program
+ Rapid advancement
+ Extraordinary job security (you'd have to dance naked through the aisles before they would consider letting you go)

Drawbacks
− Frequent relocations, often to small towns, are required to advance.
− Long hours (weekends, holidays) and physical work
− Stores tend to be located in smaller, rural areas

Corporate Philosophy
A reflection of founder Sam Walton, a down-home-kind-of-guy who was America's wealthiest man until his death: Never forget what the common man wants and establish relationships with customers to build store loyalty.

Atmosphere
Team-oriented, even familial if not a little too homey for someone from an urban background. The sales people on the floor are listened to and respected. In fact, Walton considered these underlings more important than top brass.

Working Conditions
Think "Kmart." You'll be on the floor most of the time.

Tips for Getting a Job
• Be enthusiastic, positive, and energetic.
• Know the company.
• Show you have an understanding of the demands of the retail industry.
• Demonstrate a sense of responsibility by describing other jobs or leadership roles you've held.

Profile

While many retailers seemed to be on the economic skids in 1991, Wal-Mart, the fastest-growing retailer in the country, planned to open 150 new stores and hire 900 college graduates to help run them. With more than $32 billion in 1991 revenues, Wal-Mart passed Sears to become the nation's largest retailer.

The company began as a vision of founder Samuel Walton in 1962, beginning with a single store in Rogers, Arkansas. Today, Wal-Mart spans most of the country, with 1,600 stores in 35 states. Along the way, Wal-Mart has become one of the top-rated stocks on Wall Street.

If there is one potential hurdle in Wal-Mart's continued accelerated growth, it may be the competition it faces from other aggressive discount retailers such as Kmart and Target, who are already well entrenched where Wal-Mart might hope to expand.

What They Want

More than anything, Wal-Mart wants employees with lots of enthusiasm (the cheerleader kind). More than your grades, your major, or past work experience, the one thing you must have to work for Wal-Mart is enthusiasm for the retail business in general and for Wal-Mart in particular. You can easily acquire this by working in retail part-time during college or simply by researching the company and demonstrating your excitement during your sole interview. (Wal-Mart has too many openings and too little time for multiple interviews.)

Communication Skills

Company recruiters do, however, look at the bigger picture, especially communication skills. You will be observed and judged by how you communicate one-to-one as well as in a group.

Recruiters also look closely at your collegiate activity with the attitude that "busy students make busy workers." Leadership in school organizations and church activities impress Wal-Mart, too.

Training

Wal-Mart's management training program is recognized as one of the best in the retail industry. Mostly on-the-job, the program covers personnel functions, operations, merchandising, and supervisory skills. After the 20-week training, the employee becomes an assistant manager reporting directly to the store manager.

Internships

Another excellent way to get experience and into the management program is by becoming a college intern. Students have a choice between working full-time during the summers or part-time during the school year. They receive the same management training that graduates receive as full-time trainees. After the 20-week program is completed, trainees become assistant managers. So it is actually possible to complete the 20-week training before graduation and start as an assistant manager immediately.

Career Path

When trainees are promoted to assistant managers, they are assigned to an area of the store for which they manage inventory and merchandise. They rotate to different areas to get total store experience. Within approximately four and a half years, trainees are promoted to store manager, possibly at a different (and smaller) store.

It is possible to become a manager more quickly, because every promotion is based on merit; there is no seniority program. "We are growing at a rate where we need people to develop very quickly," says director of college relations Joey Jones. "The sooner they get themselves ready, the sooner they will get their stores."

Power to the Underlings

What seems unique at Wal-Mart is how much grass-roots power there seems to be. When company founder and chairman of the board Sam Walton used to visit stores, it was common for him to ask the floor people if they liked their store manager or district manager. If the answer was negative, Sam reassured them with, "Don't worry, I'll kick his butt."

As a supervisor, the people under you are the ones who ultimately promote you. If you work well with them, they talk about how good you are and get you where you want to be.

They Want Mavericks?

As a liberal arts graduate, your idea of a maverick is probably light years away from Wal-Mart's. After all, rushing around all day keeping shelves stocked, cash registers full, and customers happy doesn't leave a lot of room for free thinking.

Still, there seems to be room for creative minds here. "We like the mavericks—the people who are on the leading edge who try things that have not been tried before," says Jones. "Wal-Mart people are highly motivated and have a very strong work ethic. They are given the flexibility to experiment or try things on their own—the things that work are welcomed in the company. When you make a mistake, we tend to view that as a learning experience."

The Hiring Process

Hiring is not complicated. There is only one interview, conducted at any of the 100 universities at which the company recruits. During the evening before interviews, a company shows a video and has a question and answer period. At the interview, Wal-Mart tries to find out everything about the candidate. This 30-minute interview will be your only chance to sell yourself to the company.

Report from the Trenches

BILL MOORE
Position: District Manager
Age: 28

Earnings: Low 40s (est.)
School: University of Northern Iowa, Cedar Falls, Iowa
Major: General Studies

Bill Moore knew very little about the retail industry when he interviewed with Wal-Mart in 1985 during his senior year. But the company's "people philosophy" and long-term benefits, such as profit-sharing, motivated him to accept an offer two days after his interview. He had one month between graduation and relocating to Warrensburg, Missouri. His rise has been rapid. Here's what he says after six years on the job:

Career Progress

I started as an assistant manager trainee. It was a 16-week training course, on the job. I was in every area of the store for a specified amount of time, following "the book"—a very rigid training program. After every placement in a particular area of the store, I took a multiple choice test.

I was then promoted to assistant manager over soft lines (wearables) for eight months. I stayed in that at the Warrensburg position for a little over one year.

I had been talking to one of the assistant managers who had been with the company for about five years, and he was ready to get his own store. I asked him how long it took the average person to become a store manager, and he said about five years. I personally thought it could be done faster than that. So that was always in the back of my mind.

One day I was talking to the regional personnel manager and he said, "Have you ever been to Florida?" And I said, "Yes, we went there for our honeymoon." He asked "Did you like it?" and I said, "We loved it." He said, "Want to go to Florida?" I replied "Well, can I get ahead any faster down there?" He said, "Yes, things are really moving down there." I said, "Let's go." It was a lateral move—I was still an assistant manager.

I started the Milton [Florida] store from the ground up. I would go anywhere in the store where I was needed to help start putting up counters. I did everything—all of the interviewing, hiring, building check-out registers, training personnel, stocking. I stayed in the Milton store for two years and two months.

His Own Store

Then I became store manager in Crest View [Florida], where I stayed a year and a half. The store at Crest View was 50,000 square feet, which was smaller [than the one at Milton]. When the Panama City store came open, I decided to go to Panama City, which is where I am now.

My duties as store manager are to oversee the total store operation, from inventory level to ordering and stocking, to maintenance, hiring, and firing. I delegate everything. My job entails a lot of training and teaching. My goal is to make money for the company.

My job also is to train assistant managers to be store managers. The training is passed down. Assistant managers should be teaching department managers to be assistant managers.

Long Hours, Good People

The people here are great. They are what keep me going. Being a store manager with Wal-Mart, I hardly ever get a pat on the back or any "atta boys"—hardly any recognition. But I am at the store at 6 A.M. every day, six days a week. My typical work day averages 11 hours. It gets kind of tough.

I do it because I believe in what I'm doing and in my people, the ones on the front lines with customers who are doing the actual work. I have to be here for them, to help them. That's really what it's all about. I'm self-motivated because I like getting people promoted. I like getting hourly people into management. I am very committed to Wal-Mart and don't believe I would ever work for anyone else.

The Future

I have just been promoted to district manager and will be responsible for eight to 11 stores depending upon the district that is established by the corporate office. I am now waiting for the word where to go and when.

Tips

Wal-Mart is very expense-oriented. Low expenses, low prices—that's how we make our money. Successful candidates will be very aggressive, flexible, hard-working, and very people-oriented and think of themselves last. Unsuccessful candidates will be clock-watchers, complainers, and selfish—not team players.

JOHN WILEY & SONS, INC.

Human Resources Department
605 Third Ave.
New York, NY 10158
(212) 850-6718 or (212) 850-6295

Other Employment Centers
Somerset, N.J.; Colorado Springs; Etobicoke, Ontario; Sussex, England; Milton, Queensland, Australia; Singapore; New Delhi; Moscow

Products/Services
Publisher of education, professional, reference, and trade books and periodicals

Number of Employees
More than 2,000

Job Opportunities
Editorial, production, marketing, or publicity assistant

Starting Salary
Low 20s

Major Pluses
+ Opportunity to work with very bright, creative, talented people
+ Plenty of opportunity to grow and advance
+ Bonus incentive program (rare for the publishing industry)
+ Satisfaction and fulfillment from producing high-quality, well-respected products

Drawbacks
− Heavy competition, both in getting hired and on the job
− You must pay your dues as an assistant offering clerical support to editors
− Requires patience (first promotion will take a year or two)

Corporate Philosophy
Wiley's stated purpose is to find and select the best authors and achieve the widest possible distribution of its books. It operates on the principle of collaboration between authors, suppliers, and staff, with each adding value and all working together to satisfy the needs of customers around the globe.

Atmosphere
Professional, but friendly and casual. Senior management is very supportive and encouraging in career development of lower-level staff.

Work Conditions
High-rise in Midtown Manhattan. Everyone's busy but not overworked; 40-hour work week is the norm.

Tips for Getting a Job
• Unless you attend one of the better universities in New York City where Wiley focuses its recruiting efforts (they feel it's too difficult to get students in other areas to relocate to New York), you'll have to take the initiative and contact the company directly. Or you can go through one of the placement agencies that specializes in the publishing industry.
• Do your research; know how Wiley is organized and what it publishes. Know what's going on in publishing as a whole. To really wow them, demonstrate your familiarity with Wiley's most recent list of new books.
• Have an idea where you might fit in.
• Be very focused and articulate.
• Don't be shy; say what you think and what you want.

Profile

Founded in 1807 as a printing company, John Wiley & Sons began publishing the fiction of such novelists as Hawthorne, Melville, and Poe in 1814, and by mid-nineteenth century, had become a leader in scientific and technical publishing.

Today, the company is a publicly held international leader in the publishing of college, scientific, technical, professional, trade, and reference books. Wiley is known for its high regard for and protection of the rights of its authors.

Highly respected by publishing professionals, Wiley's growing Professional, Reference, and Trade division won the 1991 *Literary Marketplace* corporate award for professional publishing for its "diversity of product while maintaining its long-established level of quality."

With revenues of almost $237 million in 1991—up three percent from 1990—the company is holding its own, even during a recessionary period that has hit the publishing industry hard.

Opportunities

Most of the approximately 200 liberal arts graduates hired by Wiley in a typical year begin as administrative assistants in the editorial, production, marketing, or publicity departments, either in the college division or in the Professional, Reference, and Trade division.

Although entry-level opportunities exist on both sides of Wiley's business, the two are distinctly separate. The college and educational side markets its text and other educational books to colleges by getting professors to "adopt" books to be used in the classroom.

On the professional, reference, and trade side, books such as the *Ernst & Young Tax Guides* are marketed directly to bookstores.

The Ideal Candidate

Director of Staffing and Training Lynne Salisbury says the company likes very poised, articulate candidates who have strong verbal and written communication skills. Wiley also wants people who have good computer skills (a basic editing test on a word processor will be given).

In the interview you should take the initiative and ask insightful questions, because creativity is highly valued at Wiley. "We are looking for people who have ideas and are creative and resourceful," says Salisbury.

Salisbury also suggests that you have well thought out answers to the questions "Why do you want to work in publishing?" and "Why do you want to work for Wiley?" Her advice: "Research the company and the industry."

Entry-Level Duties

Most administrative assistants are required to provide general administrative support, including preparing correspondence; tracking manuscripts; proofing; acting as liaison between authors, editors, and departments; and compiling lists and reports. In the publicity department, trainees coordinate publicity and interviews, prepare press releases, and send out books.

Training

One of the greatest benefits of working for Wiley is the commitment of senior management to developing its staff. "We do feel that one owns one's career, but we feel an obligation to provide support and resources, such as workshops," Salisbury explains. "We are interested in growing our own talent and I think statistics would bear that out. We promote from within as much as possible."

Most training is on the job with some in-house training sessions and seminars. According to Salisbury, entry-level employees are expected to take the initiative and develop their own careers. "We are in the process of developing a formal career development program, but they are responsible for managing their careers. Promotions are tied to their performance as well as to the needs of the company."

Editorial Career Track

A typical editorial assistant would, after a year or two, move into a senior marketing assistant or senior editorial assistant position. From there, the next step would be to the position of supplements editor or assistant editor, then to an associate editor position. (The salary range for an associate editor is in the mid to high 30s.)

A supplements editor works on supplements or ancillaries—teaching aids or student aides, such as guidebooks that accompany textbooks. "This is a good way to work on a manuscript without having full responsibility for a full text," says Salisbury. "It's a much smaller piece. So the editor will go through a lot of the mechanics in what's involved and learn quite a bit. It's a stepping stone to becoming an editor."

Other Tracks

Wiley offers many opportunities besides editorial ones, and many liberal arts graduates end up in marketing and sales. The company recently created a sales internship for administrative assistants to spend some time in a sales capacity. "We really do stress the need for outside sales experience on the college side," says Salisbury. "We have carved up a piece of the New York territory, and it gives an assistant an opportunity to get some of that market knowledge."

Salisbury stresses the fact that all employees, from editorial to sales, need to know a lot about business. This is a business with finance, marketing, sales, production . . . but, we make books, not widgets. That's an attraction to many people. It's an opportunity to work with very bright, talented, creative professionals. The industry attracts those kinds of people."

Report from the Trenches

LAURA LEWIN
Position: Associate Editor, Professional/Trade Division
Age: 26
Earnings: Low 30s
School: Tufts University, Medford, Mass.
Major: English

After graduating in 1987, Laura decided to take some time off to travel across the country, so she didn't bother with on-campus interviewing. Knowing that she wanted to go into publishing, she returned to New York and immediately contacted a personnel agency that specialized in publishing. Bingo! Her first interview was with Wiley, where she received and accepted an offer to become an editorial assistant. She doesn't regret her decision. Here's her story:

The last year of college, Tufts offered an elective that concentrated on careers. I took an editing course that was taught by a manager at Houghton Mifflin. She told us about the industry and the positions available, from production to manufacturing to editing. At that point it really piqued my interest.

I contacted a personnel agency that advertised in the New York Times. *I told them I wanted an editorial position.*

I went to only one interview, and it was with Wiley. I interviewed first with a personnel person and then with two acquisitions editors. One was a computer books editor, and the other a general trade editor. I felt as though we really understood each other from the start. But the computer line intimidated me. I remember asking "Are you sure I don't need to know anything about computers?" I didn't even use a word processor in college. I did all my papers on a typewriter.

First Job: Editorial Assistant
I was hired as an editorial assistant, and was trained on the computer by one of the editors. At that point, our division was much smaller. I knew that in publishing I was going to have to pay my dues . . . a few years of clerical work in one area.

Training was mostly on-the-job. I did do clerical work for about a year but there was some introduction to editing work. I segued into that end of it by getting more involved in manuscripts before they went into production. This is how I progressed, I think.

Promotions

From editorial assistant I was promoted to editorial program assistant and given a few more responsibilities. This job is kind of a reward for editorial assistants who do a lot . . . an interim step. In this capacity, I took on more individual projects, and had a lot more interplay with authors.

Then, I was promoted to assistant editor. I became solely responsible for the computer books. This is a good spot because it's a training spot. They don't expect too much from you at this point, but you have the chance to learn a lot. I was given an office and particular goals to attain, like a specific number of contracts to sign. I was lucky to have a good manager who threw a lot of projects my way.

After a year I was promoted to associate editor, and I have been an associate editor for almost a year. As an associate editor, your goals become much higher. My present goals are to publish 14 books, put 15 manuscripts into production, and sign (or contract) 15 books. Also, you have a projected number of dollar sales you need to make in a year. It's like you're a mini editor. I get credit for my books, and all the questions come my way. As an assistant editor, I worked on books within another editor's program. Now I work on my own program.

Why She Loves It

What I like about Wiley is that there's a lot of support and team effort here among marketing, editorial, and production.

In our division it's very positive and exciting; during my time here it has grown tremendously. We're always hiring new editors for new lines.

Advice

At Wiley a big thing is to make your career happen. To move up from editorial assistant, you have to work pretty hard and have a lot of patience to get through the clerical aspect of the job. Once you're an assistant editor, it becomes a bit easier because you're already in the niche and there's a structure that you can grow in.

Keep your mind open. If I hadn't been open-minded, I don't think I would have this job. I had no interest in computers in the beginning, but I really enjoy computer books now.

I took the job on my first interview, but it's a good idea to get a feel for what else is out there, because you always wonder. One thing I do know is that I am challenged all the time in this job. That's a pretty good sign.

Surprises

What I didn't expect were the business things required that aren't really my thing, the financial aspect—like spreadsheets for quarterly sales projections, and gross margin worksheets. I never imagined I would be doing any math on my job but I am.

You always have to ask questions, never be afraid of asking questions. No one knows how to do something until he or she is introduced to it. You can't be embarrassed to ask, "What is this?" I try not to feel at a disadvantage when I don't know how to do something. I just ask. Gradually, I've come up to speed on the business stuff.

The Future

My next step is editor. After that? I just may stay an editor forever. I don't have a goal past that; right now it's too soon to say. Some editors become associate publishers and run publishing groups with a bunch of editors under them. Then some become senior editors and don't get into management.

FOUR

Uncle Sam as Boss

While somewhat similar to working for a mega-corporation with separate divisions, working for the federal government requires a fundamentally different mind-set. If you're highly ambitious and innovative and have little patience with rules, regulations, and procedures, forget about civil service.

On the other hand, if the idea of overseas assignments, serving your country, job security, and a guaranteed pension sound appealing, Uncle Sam should be your boss.

Whether you go to work for the CIA or the Social Security Administration, you'll probably never have to worry about losing your job. It practically takes an act of God to cause a major government lay-off. And you'll end up with more money for retirement than almost any other employee.

A recent story in the *Philadelphia Inquirer* estimated that the average pensions for federal workers ($12,966) are almost double those of workers in the private sector ($6,512), with state and local government employees about halfway in between ($9,068).

Even though some people find a mind-numbing sameness to the vast majority of civil service jobs (in terms of the working conditions, pay scale, benefits, and advancement opportunities), careers with government agencies can be as different as information management for a D.C. bureaucracy and filling out passports in Botswana.

In researching this book, the following 10 government agencies appeared to have the most and best opportunities for liberal arts graduates. However, if you're interested in government service, consider all government agencies, even the ones that don't appear in this book. You will notice that we do not include any "Reports from the Trenches" entries for these agencies—the reason is that most government employees are not permitted to discuss their positions publicly.

UNITED STATES FOREIGN SERVICE

U.S. Department of State
Recruitment Division
Box 9317
Arlington, VA 22209
(703) 875-7490 or (800) JOB-OVERSEAS

What Does It Do?
The Department of State implements foreign policy and operates diplomatic missions around the world.

The United States Information Agency (USIA) explains U.S. foreign policy and actions to the world, engages in "public diplomacy," operates academic exchange, cultural, and other people-to-people programs, and is responsible for the press and cultural sections at American diplomatic missions.

The Department of Commerce supervises the Foreign Commercial Service (FCS), which provides commercial attaches to American diplomatic missions.

Number of Employees
16,000 Foreign Service Officers

Job Opportunities
Within each branch of the Foreign Service, a wide range of opportunities exist in the following fields:
- Embassy and Consular
- Administration
- Economics
- Political Analysis and Reporting
- Information and Cultural Affairs
- Commerce and Business

Starting Salary
Typically between $23,700 and $31,700

Major Pluses
+ Travel and living experience worldwide
+ Families may usually accompany FSOs at government expense
+ When FSOs are assigned overseas, their salaries are enhanced by a wide range of benefits

Drawbacks
− Little control over assignments and you will be transferred routinely according to the needs of the service
− Slow hiring process (a wait of a year or more between application and assignment is not uncommon)
− Very extensive background investigation of applicants

Agency Purpose/Philosophy
A commitment to serve the political and economic interests of the U.S. government, and especially to promote U.S. policies in the realm of international relations, are of the utmost importance to an F.S.O.

Working Conditions
Work conditions vary greatly depending on assignment; many overseas posts are in remote locations where harsh climates and health hazards prevail. American-style amenities may be unavailable. Service at some posts may involve security risks for FSOs and their families.

Although the majority of careers in the Foreign Service do not involve much of the glamour and luxury experienced by ambassadors and other top service officials, they do provide unique opportunities and benefits for those willing to make the necessary adjustments.

What Does It Want

No specific educational background is required. Most successful officers have a broad knowledge of international and domestic affairs, U.S. and world history, government and foreign policy, and culture. In recent years, about 65 percent of successful FSO candidates have had advanced degrees in international relations, economics, business administration, law, journalism, or other areas. When necessary, language training is provided.

Although most FSOs are still generalists, a growing diplomatic emphasis is being placed on what Secretary of State James A. Baker III has called "transnational issues" (the environment, AIDS, drugs, international business, etc.). Consequently, the Foreign Service will be looking for more candidates with relevant technical skills.

The FSO must accept political and policy direction from the President and his top appointees. The professional FSO is expected to place loyalty and obedience over personal opinions and preferences.

Hiring

As with all federal jobs, the standard application for federal employment (SF 171) must be filed. It is available through the Office of Personnel Management and often through campus career centers.

Candidates must pass a written exam, an oral assessment, and an extremely thorough background investigation, all geared toward determining eligibility for a security clearance as well as suitability for appointment to the Foreign Service. Medical clearances are required for overseas candidates and their dependents.

People who successfully complete these requirements may be offered probationary appointments as FSO career candidates. During this period, they are reviewed for tenure and commissioning, and depending on the needs of the service, may be offered tenure in a functional field.

Training

Upon entering the Foreign Service, all career candidates receive several weeks of basic orientation. An officer can expect up to seven months of subsequent training prior to the first overseas assignment. Entering officers who are already professionally competent in a foreign language may spend a significantly shorter period in Washington, D.C., before leaving on the first overseas assignment.

Advancement
The changing needs of foreign policy and departmental responsibilities make it difficult to predict individual career patterns.

USDA FOOD AND NUTRITION SERVICE (FNS)
United States Department of Agriculture
National Headquarters, Personnel Division
3101 Park Center Dr.
Alexandria, VA 22302
(202) 447-3585

Other Employment Centers
Seven regional offices

What Does It Do?
The FNS directs the following USDA programs:
- Food Stamp Program
- Special Supplemental Food Program for Women, Infants, and Children (WIC)
- National School Lunch and Breakfast Programs
- Food Distribution Program
- Child Care Food Program
- Summer Food Service Program

Number of Employees
1,800 nationwide

Job Opportunities

Program Administration:
- Program Specialists
- Food Stamp Investigators
- Program Analysts

Management:
- Information Specialists
- Personnel Specialists
- Management Analysts
- Contract Specialists
- Office Management

Starting Salary
Typical liberal arts graduates would probably start at the federal GS-5 or GS-7 level (in 1991, GS-7–level pay was $21,000)

Major Pluses
+ Serve the public, not your boss. Satisfaction in knowing you are assisting the disadvantaged
+ Good benefits

+ Portable retirement system (easy to transfer in and out of government)
+ Relatively easy to go from one government agency to another, especially for those in administration and management

Drawbacks

− Salaries are not competitive with the private sector
− Huge organization; difficult to find your niche and get individual recognition (things happen slowly)
− Most USDA agencies have formal or informal expectations of mobility, especially early in one's career.

Agency Purpose/Philosophy

Public service is the raison d'etre of the FNS. You are there to provide assistance to those Americans who are most in need.

Working Conditions

Work conditions are those of a very large government bureaucracy. A huge number of employees must coordinate their efforts to get work done within it.

As a liberal arts graduate, you will probably be qualified for work within one USDA agency: the Food and Nutrition Service (FNS). Many opportunities exist for liberal arts graduates within the FNS. Jobs here are well-suited for people who are interested in serving the poor, the elderly, and children.

What Does It Want?

Being a good team player is very important, but leadership capabilities are also stressed, including resourcefulness, initiative, ability to prioritize, organize, and get projects accomplished efficiently and effectively.

The FNS is looking for people who come to the interview knowing something about the agency and its services and are prepared to explain why they are interested in working for the agency. The agency will view your ability to market yourself as an indication of how well you will be able to promote its programs and services.

Hiring

The FNS does a lot of on-campus recruiting. Following preliminary contact at a campus job fair or career center, hiring decisions are usually made on the basis of academic performance, written examinations when the applicant's GPA is below 3.5, and one interview. Your chances are not as good if you go directly to the agency you seek employment with. Competition is very tough, especially among liberal arts graduates without technical experience.

As with most federal jobs, the standard form for federal employment (SF 171) must be filed, and U.S. citizenship is required.

Training
Most liberal arts graduates will come into the FNS in entry-level administrative training programs. These involve a combination of formal and on-the-job training working in various agency programs. Training programs are tailored to the individual employee's needs.

Like many federal agencies, the USDA trains college students at the baccalaureate, graduate, and professional degree levels for government careers through cooperative education programs. These combine academic study with work assignments. Contact your school's placement office for more information.

Advancement
Advancement can be rapid; pay raises are standard at the end of the first and second years. By the end of the second year you should be receiving substantive assignments and participating on team projects, as well as handling some matters on your own. Most professional and administrative positions have promotion potential to the GS-9 or GS-11 level based on performance, experience, and education.

BUREAU OF ALCOHOL, TOBACCO AND FIREARMS (ATF)
Personnel Division—Employment Branch
Washington, DC 20226
(202) 566-7321

What Does It Do?
The bureau investigates violations of the federal Alcohol Administration Act, illicit liquor violations of federal magnitude and interstate smugglers of no-tax-paid cigarettes. It also investigates violations of federal firearms and explosives laws.

Number of Employees
4,341

Job Opportunities

Law Enforcement
- Special Agent
- Criminal Investigator
- Inspector

Administration
- Equal Employment Manager

- Program Analyst
- Personnel

Starting Salary
Enter at GS-5 or GS-7

Major Pluses
+ Good benefits; some opportunities for bonuses; retirement security
+ Jobs in law enforcement can be very exciting at times (for the right people)
+ Agents, investigators, and inspectors are out in the field often; much opportunity for travel throughout the U.S.
+ Tuition reimbursement
+ Flexible hours (for administrative employees)
+ Many opportunities in large number of organizations within the bureau

Drawbacks
− As with most federal jobs, salaries are not competitive with the private sector
− Applicants must pass thorough background investigation
− Law enforcement work has very rigorous physical requirements; can be dangerous
− Routine transfers according to the needs of the bureau

Agency Purpose/Philosophy
Cracking down on the sale and use of unregulated guns, explosives and on trafficking in legal drugs is an important public service.

Working Conditions
Work conditions vary greatly depending on the job; law enforcement can combine mentally and physically exhausting, dangerous work with a lot of paperwork. There's a lot of travel that involves irregular hours.

What Does It Want?
The bureau is another government agency that hires many liberal arts graduates and then provides them with extensive, specific training. Good opportunities exist here for those whose interests lie in the area of federal law enforcement and who can fit in well.
- **Special Agents/Investigators**
    The bureau wants college graduates with very good academic records who are under age 35 at time of appointment and able to undergo a complete background investigation and meet rigorous physical requirements, including drug screening. Women can qualify for special agent and investigator jobs and are encouraged to

apply. Applicants must demonstrate they are prepared to face physical danger as well as mental challenges. They must have a great deal of self-confidence, and the ability to be aggressive yet function well with other agents working on teams. They must be able to prepare case reports and assist attorneys in the preparation and presentation of cases.

* **Inspectors**

    To be an inspector, you should have an excellent academic record, and you'll need to pass a background investigation, drug screening, and other tests. You should have a knowledge of basic accounting procedures; skill in preparation of reports, oral and written communication, and cooperative and persuasive dealings with a wide variety of people; the ability to recognize discrepancies or irregularities in records, reports, and operations at establishments being examined; and the ability to analyze data, weigh alternatives, and reach decisions that require interpreting regulatory requirements.

    Knowledge of the basic laws and regulations relevant to the bureau's work can qualify you to enter at a higher level.

    Inspectors must be versatile; although they usually work in offices, they also travel routinely to various locations to perform a very wide range of duties.

Hiring

An interview is set up with qualified applicants. Hiring is highly competitive at this point. The bureau focuses on grades, test scores, extracurricular activities, and work experience.

Contact the Office of Personnel Management for information about the administration of the Treasury Enforcement Agency (TEA) Examination.

As with most federal jobs, the standard form for federal employment (SF 171) must be filed, and U.S. citizenship is required.

Training

Special Agent appointees undergo approximately eight weeks of intensive training in general law enforcement and investigative techniques. Then they attend New Agent Training, where they are taught more specialized skills.

Inspector trainees acquire basic knowledge and skills through classroom training, a training detail at a regional office, and on-the-job training with a higher-level inspector.

Administrative trainees can take necessary college courses, which are paid for by the government, and take courses run by the Office of Personnel Management. This training varies with position and previous experience.

Advancement
There seems to be a good deal of opportunity for advancement for ATF inspectors and administrators. Career mobility depends on experience, training, self-development, and outside activities for which appointees receive points according to set guidelines.

UNITED STATES SECRET SERVICE
Department of the Treasury
Employment Division
Washington, DC 20223
(202) 435-5800

Number of Employees
Approximately 4,600 (1,900 Special Agents)

What Does It Do?
The Secret Service provides protective services to the President and Vice President and their families, as well as to former presidents, major candidates, important foreign dignitaries, and others.

The other half of its responsibility is the suppression of counterfeiting and the investigation of stolen or forged U.S. government checks, bonds, etc.; fraud and related activity in connection with identification documents; and major fraud cases involving credit and debit cards, computers, automated teller machines, telecommunications, or electronic fund transfers.

Job Opportunities
- Administrative
- Special Agents (rotate between protective and investigative services)

Starting Salary
Special Agents and administrators start at the GS-5 level. GS-7 level entry possible.

Major Pluses
+ Good benefits; retirement programs
+ Interesting, exciting work

Drawbacks
− Very thorough background investigation often involving a long wait
− Routine transfers according to the needs of the service
− Possibly dangerous, very stressful work in protective services
− Salaries are not competitive with the private sector

Agency Purpose/Philosophy
The Secret Service is selflessly dedicated to responsibly planning and maintaining security for individuals and property it is charged to protect.

Working Conditions
Work conditions will vary according to post and experience.

What Does It Want?
Although much of the investigative work performed by the Secret Service is highly technical, there is a place here for liberal arts graduates. There is no requirement for specialized education beyond a B.A. degree, and the service provides extensive training.

Basically, they want college graduates with excellent academic records and impeccable personal credentials. You must prove that you are capable of being trained in the wide range of duties performed by Secret Service personnel. Special Agent applicants must pass a comprehensive physical examination and be prepared to move to duty stations anywhere in the United States. Liaison assignments in foreign countries are also possible during an agent's career. You must demonstrate you are willing to put your life on the line to fulfill your protective duties.

Hiring
All candidates must file the standard federal application (SF 171) and those applying for Special Agent positions must take the Treasury Enforcement Agency Examination before being considered. For all positions, an interview follows agency evaluation of applications and examinations. Opportunities for Special Agent positions are limited because of high competition and low attrition. For up-to-date information on openings in administration, contact the employment division. U.S. citizenship is required.

Training
General investigative training is provided for successful Special Agent candidates in criminal law and state-of-the-art investigative procedures at the Federal Law Enforcement Training Center. More specialized instruction is then given at Secret Service training facilities. Special Agents regularly participate in advanced in-service training programs.

Administrative training takes place mostly on the job, depending on the trainee's position and previous experience/education. Government-provided courses and allowances for college course work when necessary are available.

Advancement
Eligibility for promotion is based on performance. The full performance level for a Special Agent is GS-12. Selection for promotion to positions above the GS-12 level is based on merit and as vacancies occur.

PENSION AND WELFARE BENEFITS ADMINISTRATION (PWBA)

PWBA—Room N–5711
U.S. Department of Labor
200 Constitution Avenue, NW
Washington, DC 20210
(202) 523-6471

What Does It Do?
The PWBA oversees the responsible management of the nation's pension and welfare benefit system. Founded when the Employee Retirement Income Security Act (ERISA) was passed in 1974, PWBA's major activities include: formulating current and future policy; conducting research; issuing regulations and technical guidance concerning ERISA requirements; enforcing ERISA rules; and assisting and educating the employee benefits community about ERISA.

Number of Employees
600

Job Opportunities
- Investigator/Auditor
- Employee Benefit Plan Specialist
- Program Analyst
- Management
- Administration

Starting Salary
GS-5 to GS-9, depending on education and work experience. 1990 GS-9 level pay was $24,705.

Major Pluses
+ Good benefits; retirement programs
+ Satisfaction in protecting the rights of American workers
+ Employee benefits is one of the fastest-growing career fields in the nation

Drawbacks
− Large government bureaucracy

Agency Purpose/Philosophy
The PWBA helps protect the economic future and retirement security of working Americans by managing nearly one million pension plans and 4.5 million health and welfare assets. It accounts for almost 20 percent of all securities traded on the New York Stock Exchange.

Working Conditions

Work conditions are relatively intimate for a federal agency; the agency is currently focusing its recruiting efforts on six offices in Washington, D.C., five of which have staffs of 30 or fewer employees. The remainder of PWBA career staff work in 15 field offices around the country as well as in Washington.

What Does It Want?

This agency is well suited for detail-oriented liberal arts graduates interested in the labor law and financial fields. It promises challenging careers with potential for continued advancement.

For investigation/auditing and employee benefits specialist positions, education and/or work experience in the fields of law, accounting, economics/finance, investigative programs, employee benefit administration, or public administration is very desirable.

The following skills and abilities are called for:

- **Investigator/Auditor**

  Understanding and applying provisions, regulations, and administrative procedures; working independently; conducting interviews; fact finding; analyzing and evaluating legal records; interpreting and drawing conclusions from written and numerical data; and using computers.

- **Employee Benefits Specialist**

  Solving abstract problems; conceptualizing complex legal and policy issues and formulating recommendations; drafting technical opinions, testimony, memoranda, and reports; performing detail-oriented tasks; analyzing and evaluating data; engaging in intellectual challenges and exchanges; communicating orally and in writing; mediating and resolving conflicts.

Hiring

The standard application for federal employment (SF 171) available through Washington or field offices must be filed. Interviews follow for qualified applicants. U.S. citizenship is required.

Training

Most training occurs on the job, but bringing fairly well-developed, specific skills to the job is emphasized.

Advancement

Most positions currently available within PWBA have automatic advancement within the GS classification. For example, for positions listed at the GS 9, 11, or 12 levels, an employee can advance one grade for each year of service. So, within three years you can raise your grade and income substantially with successful performance at each level.

FEDERAL BUREAU OF INVESTIGATION (FBI)
10th St. and Pennsylvania Ave.
Washington, DC 20535
(202) 324-3000

What Does It Do?
The FBI is the principal agency charged with investigating violations of federal statutes. FBI activities include investigations into organized crime, white-collar crime, public corruption, financial crime, fraud against the government, bribery, copyright matters, civil rights violations, bank robbery, extortion, kidnapping, skyjacking, terrorism, foreign counterintelligence, and fugitive and narcotics matters.

Number of Employees
21,000

Job Opportunities
- Language Specialist
- Special Agent Linguist
- Diversified Special Agent

Starting Salary
- Language Specialist: GS-7 to GS-11, depending on experience and education
- Special Agent: GS-10 level

Major Pluses
+ Good benefits and retirement programs; Special Agents can retire after only 20 years of federal law enforcement service
+ Work can be challenging and interesting

Drawbacks
− Thorough background investigation and (for Special Agents) rigorous physical requirements
− Routine transfers according to the needs of the bureau
− Irregular, unpredictable hours and working conditions
− Possibly dangerous work

Agency Purpose/Philosophy
Violations of federal laws, either by individuals or domestic or foreign groups, are among the most serious dangers facing the nation. Investigating and stopping them is the FBI's role, and it will do what is necessary to fulfill that mission.

Working Conditions
Working conditions vary greatly according to job and assignment. Emphasis is on efficiency, toughness, and discretion.

What Does It Want?
Although the majority of FBI agents and support staff have technical and scientific skills, there are opportunities here for liberal arts graduates who can fit in. Fluency in foreign languages that are of special interest to the government can get you a good position in the FBI. Graduates with a B.A. degree plus three years of full-time work experience are eligible for placement in the Diversified Program. Contact the bureau to see if your particular skills and experience can be of use.

As with all government jobs dealing with matters of national security, large amounts of money, the safety of leaders, classified information, and so forth, applicants must meet very rigorous standards. The FBI relies on detailed background investigations, examinations, and interviews. If you meet the basic age and citizenship requirements for federal employment and are found to have no qualities the bureau deems objectionable, you could find yourself on the way to becoming an FBI agent.

Hiring
The FBI actively recruits on campuses, focusing on students in fields that are relevant to its work. If you are a serious student of foreign languages, for example, Russian or Arabic, the FBI or the CIA may have already tried to contact you.

The FBI makes all appointments through a centralized hiring system from its headquarters in Washington, D.C. The application process includes testing in specific skills, an interview, a background investigation, and a physical examination.

The standard form for government employment (SF 171) must be filed, and U.S. citizenship is a prerequisite.

Training
All newly appointed special agents take part in a 16-week training program at the FBI Academy in Virginia. This includes academic study, physical fitness training, and instruction in the use of firearms and defensive tactics. Specialized in-service training is also provided at various times throughout the agent's career.

Foreign language specialists/translators will receive on-the-job training with equipment and procedures used in their work.

Advancement
There is a career development program that includes a variety of supervisory and management assignments.

SOCIAL SECURITY ADMINISTRATION (SSA)

Recruitment and Placement Branch
6401 Security Blvd.
Room G-120 West High Rise Building
Baltimore, MD 21235
(301) 965-4506

Other Employment Centers
Ten regional offices handle applications for positions outside Baltimore headquarters. Contact office above for list of regional offices, or look in your telephone directory under U.S. Government.

What Does It Do?
The SSA administers public funds that are paid when a person's income is reduced due to retirement, disability, or death.

Number of Employees
60,000

Job Opportunities
In Claims
  • Claims Representative
  • Claims Authorizer
In Management/Staff
  • Policy Development
  • Management Analysis
  • Staffing/Personnel

Starting Salary
GS-5 or GS-7, depending on position, education, and experience

Major Pluses
+ Good benefits; retirement programs
+ Potential for satisfaction
+ Wide choice of work locations

Drawbacks
− Huge government bureaucracy
− Salaries are not competitive with the private sector
− Agency processes controlled by myriad rules and regulations

Agency Purpose/Philosophy

The Social Security system serves the public by protecting the financial security of the working Americans who contribute to it. Dedication to this service is emphasized; this is what should keep you going. Claims jobs require much contact with the public; management/staff positions are more behind-the-scenes.

What Does It Want?

Social service/public policy–oriented liberal arts graduates may find challenging, satisfying careers in the SSA. A fairly wide range of positions exist in this huge agency.

The SSA seeks out liberal arts graduates. It needs versatile, independent, dedicated, service-oriented people who are able to master the large body of laws, rules, and regulations covering the administration of Social Security benefits. Claims workers must be able to deal tactfully and diplomatically with the public when necessary. This requires excellent communications skills; having compassion is important. Computer literacy is necessary for nearly all positions.

Hiring

Some recruitment is carried out on campuses; the SSA participates in the Administrative Careers With America program as well as in college cooperative education programs. The SSA also welcomes inquiries at district personnel offices regarding career opportunities. Depending on the applicant's GPA, a civil service examination may be necessary.

As with most federal jobs, the standard form for federal employment (SF 171) must be filed, and U.S. citizenship is required.

Training

Claims representatives and authorizers go through 13 weeks of intensive classroom training. Training for management/staff positions varies according to position, experience, and education.

Advancement

Claims jobs are for the most part career-ladder jobs, with opportunity for yearly advancement and increased responsibility based on performance, training, awards, outside activities, and so forth.

Management/staff jobs are usually filled, and advancement is controlled, by an internal merit system. Opportunities for moving from claims to management are limited.

INTERNAL REVENUE SERVICE (IRS)

U.S. Department of the Treasury
Washington, DC 20227
(Contact local IRS offices for specific information on how to apply)

Other Employment Centers
The IRS has hundreds of locations nationwide.

What Does It Do?
Collects tax revenues

Number of Employees
110,000

Job Opportunities
- Revenue Officer
- Tax Auditor

Starting Salary
Comparable to other government agencies

Major Pluses
+ Good benefits; retirement programs
+ Most work is done on an independent basis
+ Wide choice of work locations

Drawbacks
− Huge government bureaucracy
− Interaction with taxpayers in certain circumstances could be very unpleasant

Agency Purpose/Philosophy
The stated mission of the IRS is to collect appropriate tax revenues at the least cost to the public. "We do this in a manner that warrants the highest degree of public confidence in our integrity, efficiency and fairness."

By collecting tax revenues, the IRS ensures that virtually all vital federal programs remain funded.

Working Conditions
Revenue officers work mostly outside the office, attempting to collect delinquent taxes and tax returns from companies and individuals. On-the-spot judgments must be made and presented in a tactful manner. Tax auditors do most of their work in local IRS offices, working closely with taxpayers.

What Does It Want?
Liberal arts graduates whose interests and abilities include the law and working with numbers, and who possess excellent diplomatic skills, may find satisfaction in a career with the IRS. And the IRS claims to be one of the more "progressive" federal employers.

It wants sharp people who are capable of mastering tax law and applying it to individual circumstances, often working independently. Officers as well as auditors must possess excellent communications skills, since complex rules and decisions must be explained to taxpayers. Employees must also be very diplomatic in dealing with often-unhappy taxpayers.

Hiring
Most hiring takes place in the 63 district offices. These offices have established relationships with schools in their areas; the IRS participates in cooperative education programs. Hiring processes vary slightly from office to office, depending on the job sought. Most applicants will interview with a panel that will evaluate their communication skills.

As with most federal jobs, the standard form for federal employment (SF 171) must be filed, and U.S. citizenship is required.

Training
The IRS provides extensive classroom and on-the-job training for its entry-level employees. Its internal training organization is one of the largest in the federal government. When necessary, the IRS provides funds for employees to take college courses or other training opportunities provided by the Office of Personnel Management.

Advancement
The IRS awards good employees with promotions; those who perform well can move all the way up to senior management.

CENTRAL INTELLIGENCE AGENCY (CIA)
Director of Personnel
Washington, DC 20505
(703) 351-2028
Washington recruitment office: (703) 351-2141

What Does It Do?
The CIA collects, analyzes, and interprets foreign intelligence information. It then provides this information to U.S. policymakers. Three arms of the agency hold career opportunities for liberal arts graduates.
- The Directorate of Operations, also known as the Clandestine Service, is charged with the primary responsibility of collecting intelligence. Through clandestine service's activities, the CIA also seeks "to change adversaries into friends or neutrals" through covert actions by political, psychological, and paramilitary means. It works with friendly intelligence services toward mutual goals.
- The Directorate of Intelligence (DI) analyzes and interprets foreign intelligence information collected by various methods, and then provides this information to U.S. policy makers, the military, etc.
- The Directorate of Administration (DA) supports the agency with a wide range of administrative services.

Number of Employees
Classified, but in the thousands

Job Opportunities
In the Directorate of Operations
- Clandestine Service Aagents
- Case officers (operations officer)

In the DI:
Political analyst in the fields of political science, history, international relations and foreign area studies.

In the DA:
Career appointments in: banking operations; business administration; communications; human resources; information management; international relations; journalism; personnel management; polygraph; security; training; and transportation.

Starting Salary
$21,000 to $25,000

Major Pluses
+ Good salary, benefits
+ Opportunities for living and working overseas

Drawbacks
- You can't talk about what you do
- Hiring process is very slow, due to the extensive investigations of applicants
- Routine international transfers according to the needs of the agency
- Depending on job and location, possibly dangerous work
- Irregular, often long hours

Agency Purpose/Philosophy
The CIA serves the U.S. government by providing the intelligence information the government needs to pursue international goals. The agency also serves and supports the government by carrying out covert international political, paramilitary, and counterintelligence missions through nonconventional channels.

Working Conditions
Working conditions will vary greatly, according to job, post, and so forth. The agency emphasizes that employees have loyalty to the U.S. government and its policies, flexibility, and secrecy.

What Does It Want?
Few CIA careers are as glamorous and thrilling as many spy movies portray. However, if playing an active role in the U.S. government's efforts to maintain the so-called New World Order through covert actions and

intelligence operations appeals to you, a career with this very interesting government agency may prove exciting and fulfilling.

It wants stable, dedicated, and trustworthy American citizens who can meet extremely strict standards relating to political beliefs and personal history, with unquestioned loyalty to the U.S. government. The CIA likes risk-takers, not thrill-seekers.

This agency, like most, is now recruiting more people with specific technical skills. However, the CIA continues to need generalists. Broad, up-to-date knowledge and an understanding of international affairs, politics, current events, foreign cultures and languages is stressed. You should be able to demonstrate this knowledge with excellent communication and writing skills. The desire and ability to work anonymously and smoothly as part of a team is very important. There aren't many "stars" in the CIA.

CIA employees must be versatile, flexible, and willing to move anywhere in the world on short notice. Their personal beliefs and morals must remain subordinate to those of the agency, and they must be capable of maintaining secrecy regarding their work when necessary, even with close friends and relatives.

Hiring

Very few applicants are finally accepted into the CIA because of its extremely strict standards and very low attrition rate (the lowest in the government). The standard application for federal employment (SF 171) must be filed with the Office of Personnel Management. Interested college students should see a campus career placement officer (preferably six to nine months before graduation) and request an interview with a CIA representative. The interview will probably be held at the school or at a nearby regional office.

The Clandestine Service bases its hiring on the personal and educational requirements described above, proven through testing and investigation. Send a resume and letter describing your goals and qualities to: Chief, Career Training Program, P.O. Box 12002, Arlington, VA 22209.

The DI and the DA each request a comprehensive resume outlining your relevant qualifications, education, and work experience. They will then send you preliminary application forms. For the DI, write to the CIA Director of Personnel at the address above; for the DA, write to: Personnel Representative, P.O. Box 12406, Arlington, VA 22209-8406.

Training

Each arm of the CIA provides extensive and ongoing training programs in a wide range of fields relevant to its work. Courses offered each year by the CIA's Office of Training and Education number in the hundreds, and the agency also arranges for its employees to pursue graduate studies at leading universities.

Training and education for most employees also involves a stint overseas.

Advancement
A few CIA employees will be selected to enter the Career Training Program. Successful graduates of this intensive training and education program will go on to become the elite of the agency.

Promotions for all employees are competitive and based on accomplishment. You will be given additional responsibilities as soon as you are able to assume them.

BUREAU OF THE CENSUS
U.S. Dept. of Commerce
Personnel Division
College Division
Washington, DC 20233
(800) 638-6719

What Does It Do?
The Bureau of the Census collects and provides basic statistical information about the people and the economy of the United States to the government and the public. Besides the decennial enumeration of the population, the bureau conducts censuses of housing, manufacturers, agriculture, mineral industries, governments, business, and transportation, among other sectors.

Number of Employees
10,500

Job Opportunities
- Administration
- Social Science
- Public Administration
- Business Administration
- Demography
- Social Science Analysis
- Data Collection and Processing

Starting Salary
Comparable to other government agencies

Major Pluses
+ Good benefits; retirement programs
+ Flexible work schedules available
+ Possibly very interesting, educational work

Drawbacks
 − Salaries are not competitive with private sector
 − Large government bureaucracy
 − Very limited choice of work locations

Agency Purpose/Philosophy
The Bureau of the Census is at the forefront of developing and using the latest scientific systems to obtain statistics used in planning and implementing all Census Bureau policies. These statistics inform the nation about its demographic makeup and many of the ways in which it is constantly changing.

Working Conditions
Working conditions will vary greatly according to the job and the time, depending on what phase the censuses being conducted are in. Most Census Bureau jobs promise variety, and there is an expectation that employees should follow new developments in their fields and adapt their work methods to take advantage of such developments.

What Does It Want?
Although the majority of Census Bureau employees are statisticians, computer scientists, and mathematicians, liberal arts graduates can find opportunities interpreting information for the nonscientific public and government, assisting in effectively planning research, and keeping the Bureau running smoothly.

The ability to interact effectively with the scientific community is very important. You should have the desire and ability to learn something about the mathematical and scientific methods widely employed by the bureau. You should demonstrate skill at interpreting data and translating statistics into the language of politics, social science, etc. A genuine interest in the bureau's work is highly desirable.

Hiring
The Bureau recruits on campuses, at job fairs, and through its cooperative education program. If you are out of college, write to the bureau for specific application instructions and up-to-date employment opportunities. The standard application for federal employment (SF 171) must be filed, and U.S. citizenship is a requirement.

Training
The bureau provides on-the-job training tailored to the needs of the employee.

Advancement
Opportunities for advancement exist, both within the bureau and throughout the government.

FIVE

Next Best Companies

While the following companies didn't make the cut of the 50 best corporate employers featured in Chapter 3, they offer excellent prospects for liberal arts grads. Our research revealed that all of them have a record of recruiting and employing liberal arts grads.

If you really want to cover your bases, you might consider sending a resume to each one. Alternatively you might select only those in your geographic area or those in an industry that especially interests you.

Allstate Insurance Co.
Allstate Plaza South G1C
Northbrook, IL 60062
(708) 402-5000

Amerada Hess Corp. (petroleum)
1185 Avenue of the Americas
New York, NY 10036
(212) 997-8500

American Drug Stores/Sav-On/Osco (retail drug stores)
1818 Swift Dr.
Oak Brook, IL 60521
(708) 572-5294

American Stores, Inc. (retail food & drug stores)
709 E. Temple
Salt Lake City, UT 84102
(801) 539-0112

AT&T
101 JFK Parkway, Rm. 1L-332
Short Hills, NJ 07078
(201) 221-2000

Ball Corp. (heavy mfg.)
345 S. High St.
Muncie, IN 47305-2326
(317) 747-6100

Banana Republic (retail clothing)
1 Harrison St.
San Francisco, CA 94105-1600
(415) 952-4400

Bank of America
555 California St.
San Francisco, CA 94104-1590
(415) 622-3456

Bank of New England
One Washington Mall, 4th Fl.
Boston, MA 02108
(617) 573-7447

Bank South Corp.
55 Marietta St.
Atlanta, GA 30302
(404) 529-4111

Bankers Trust (commercial banking)
280 Park Ave.
New York, NY 10017
(212) 454-1790

Banta Corp. (printing graphics, video services)
Harbour Place
100 Main St.
Menasha, WI 54952-8003
(414) 722-7777

Barnett Bank, Inc.
50 North Laura St.
P.O. Box 40789
Jacksonville, FL 32203-0789
(904) 791-5278

BBD&O (advertising)
1285 Avenue of the Americas
New York, NY 10019
(212) 459-5000

Bear Stearns (securities)
245 Park Ave.
New York, NY 10167-0024
(212) 272-2000

Blue Cross/Blue Shield (health insurance)
150 E. Main St.
Rochester, NY 14647-0001
(716) 454-1700

Booz Allen & Hamilton, Inc. (business consulting)
101 Park Ave.
New York, NY 10178-0053
(212) 697-1900

Boston Consulting Group, Inc. (business consulting)
Exchange Place
Boston, MA 02109-2800
(617) 973-1200

Bristol-Myers Squibb Co. (pharmaceuticals)
345 Park Ave.
New York, NY 10154
(212) 546-4000

Carnation Co. (food mfg.)
5045 Wilshire Blvd.
Los Angeles, CA 90036-4396
(213) 932-6000

Champion International Corp. (sports products mfg./paper)
One Champion Plaza
Stamford, CT 06921
(203) 358-7000

Chemical Bank
277 Park Ave., 2nd Fl.
New York, NY 10172
(212) 820-6867

Citibank (financial services/commercial banking)
399 Park Ave.
New York, NY 10043
(212) 559-1000

Chase Manhattan Bank
1 Chase Manhattan Plaza, Fl 27
New York, NY 10081
(212) 552-2222

Clairol, Inc. (cosmetic products)
1 Blachley Rd.
Stamford, CT 06902-4351
(203) 546-5000

Condé Nast (publishing)
350 Madison Ave.
New York, NY 10017-3799
(212) 880-8800

Cushman & Wakefield (real estate, insurance, leasing, consulting)
1166 Avenue of the Americas
New York, NY 10036
(212) 841-7500

CVS/Pharmacy (retail drug stores)
One CVS Dr.
Woonsocket, RI 02895
(401) 765-1500

D'Arcy Masius Benton & Bowles (advertising)
909 Third Ave.
New York, NY 10022-4731
(212) 468-3622

Dayton Hudson (department stores)
777 Nicollet on the Mall
Minneapolis, MN 55402-2055
(612) 375-3951

Louis Dreyfus Corp. (investment banking)
10 Westport Rd.
P.O. Box 810
Wilton, CT 06897-0810
(203) 761-2000

Dean Witter Financial Services (stock brokerage)
Two World Trade Center
New York, NY 10048
(212) 392-2222

DDB Needham Worldwide (advertising)
437 Madison Ave.
New York, NY 10022-7099
(212) 415-2000

Dunn & Bradstreet (marketing/business info)
299 Park Ave.
New York, NY 10171-0074
(212) 593-6800

Empire Blue Cross & Blue Shield (health insurance)
Staffing Dept.
622 Third Ave.
New York, NY 10017
(212) 476-1000

Fingerhut Corp. (catalog mail order)
4400 Baker Rd.
Minnetonka, MN 55343
(612) 932-3100

First Interstate Bank
707 Wilshire Blvd., W29-43
Los Angeles, CA 90017
(213) 614-3001

First Union National Bank
1400 One First Union Center
Charlotte, NC 28288-0953
(704) 374-2410

Foote Cone & Belding (advertising)
101 E. Erie St.
Chicago, IL 60611-2897
(312) 751-7000

E. & J. Gallo Winery
P.O. Box 1130
Modesto, CA 95353
(209) 579-4361

The Gap (retail clothing)
900 Cherry Ave.
San Bruno, CA 94066-3010
(415) 952-4400

General Mills, Inc. (food mfg.)
1 General Mills Blvd.
Minneapolis, MN 55426-1348
(612) 540-7504

W.R. Grace & Co. (pharmaceuticals)
1114 Avenue of the Americas
New York, NY 10036
(212) 819-5500

Great West Life Assurance
8515 E. Orchard Rd.
Englewood, CO 80111
(303) 689-3000

Grey Advertising
777 Third Ave.
New York, NY 10017-1344
(212) 546-2000

Hallmark Cards, Inc. (greeting cards, curios)
2501 McGee Trafficway
Kansas City, MO 64108-2615
(816) 274-5111

John Hancock Mutual Life Ins.
P.O. Box 111
Boston, MA 02117
(617) 572-6000

Harcourt, Brace, Jovanovich (publishing)
1250 Sixth Ave.
San Diego, CA 92101
(619) 231-6616
6277 S. Harbor Drive
Orlando, FL 32887
(407) 345-2000

Hardee's Food Systems (fast food)
1233 Hardee's Blvd.
Rocky Mount, NC 27804
(919) 977-8536

Harris Trust & Savings Bank
111 W. Monroe St.
Chicago, IL 60690
(312) 461-6452

Hartford Insurance Group
690 Asylum Ave.
Hartford, CT 06115
(203) 547-5000

Hills Department Stores
15 Dan Road
Canton, MA 02021
(617) 821-1000

Howard Johnson & Co. (hotels and restaurants)
111 Third Ave., Suite 1700
Seattle, WA 98101
(206) 256-9030

Hyatt Hotels Corp.
200 W. Madison Ave.
Madison Plaza
Chicago, IL 60606
(312) 750-1234

Kay Jewelers Inc. (retail jewelry)
320 King Street
Alexandria, VA 22314-3283
(703) 683-3800

Kemper Financial Services, Inc.
120 LaSalle St.
Chicago, IL 60603-3473
(312) 781-1121

Kidder Peabody and Co.
10 Hanover Sq.
New York, NY 10005-3593
(212) 510-3000

King Broadcasting (communication)
333 Dexter Ave. North
Seattle, WA 98109
(206) 343-3000

Kmart Apparel Corp.
2300 W. Higgins Rd.
Hoffman Estates, IL 60195
(312) 643-1000

Knott's Berry Farm (amusement park)
8039 Beach Blvd.
Buena Park, CA 90620-3225
(714) 827-1776

Kraft, Inc. (food mfg.)
1 Kraft Ct.
Glenview, IL 60025-5066
(708) 998-2000

Kwasha Lipton (food mfg.)
2100 North Central Road
Fort Lee, NJ 07024
(201) 567-8000

Eli Lilly & Co. (pharmaceuticals)
Lilly Corporate Center
Indianapolis, IN 46285-0001
(317) 276-6321

Limited Inc. (retail clothing)
2 Limited Pkwy.
Columbus, OH 43230-1445
(614) 479-7000

MacMillan Publishing Inc.
866 Third Ave.
New York, NY 10022-6221
(212) 702-2000

Manufacturers National Bank
411 W. Lafayette Blvd.
Detroit, MI 48226
(313) 222-4000

**Manufacturers Hanover Trust (financial services/
investment banking)**
P.O. Box 3732
Grand Central Station
New York, NY 10163
(212) 286-6000

Marriott Corp. (hotels, restaurants)
1 Marriott Dr.
Washington, DC 20058-0001
(301) 380-9000

Marsh & McLennan (insurance brokerage/risk management)
1166 Avenue of the Americas
New York, NY 10036
(212) 345-5000

McDonald's Corp. (fast food)
One McDonald's Plaza, Dept. 137
Oak Brook, IL 60521
(708) 575-3000

McKesson Corp. (pharmaceuticals)
One Post St.
San Francisco, CA 94104
(415) 983-8300

McKinsey & Co. (management consulting)
55 E. 52nd St.
New York, NY 10022
(212) 446-8843

McMaster-Carr Supply (international product distribution)
600 County Line Rd.
Elmhurst, IL 60126
(708) 834-9600

The Mead Corporation (paper mfg.)
Courthouse Plaza NE
Dayton, OH 45463-0001
(513) 495-6323

Meijer, Inc. (retail groceries and merchandise)
2727 Walker, NW
Grand Rapids, MI 49504
(616) 453-6711

Mercantile Stores Co., Inc. (retail)
128 W. 31st Street
New York, NY 10001-3401
(212) 560-0500

Merck Pharmaceutical/Mfg. Div.
Sumneytown Pike
West Point, PA 19438
(215) 661-5000

Merrill Lynch & Co. (brokerage)
225 Liberty St., Fl. 11 South Tower
New York, NY 10080-6111
(212) 449-1000

Michigan National Bank
27777 Inkster Rd., P.O. Box 9065
Farmington, MI 48333-9065
(313) 473-3000

Minnesota Mutual Cos. (insurance)
400 N. Robert St.
St. Paul, MN 55101
(612) 298-3500

Morgan Stanley & Co. (investment banking)
1251 Avenue of the Americas
New York, NY 10020-1181
(212) 703-2387

Mutual of Omaha/United of Omaha (insurance)
Mutual of Omaha Plaza
Omaha, NE 68175
(402) 342-7600

Nestlé Foods Corp. (food mfg.)
100 Manhattanville Rd.
Purchase, NY 10577
(914) 251-3000

New York Life Insurance Co.
51 Madison Ave.
New York, NY 10010
(212) 576-7000

Oppenheimer & Co. (brokerage/investment banking)
Oppenheimer Tower
World Financial Center
New York, NY 10281
(212) 667-7000

Pacific Bell (telecommunications, utilities)
140 New Montgomery St.
San Francisco, CA 94105-3799
(415) 542-9000

PaineWebber, Inc. (stock brokerage)
1285 Avenue of the Americas
New York, NY 10019-6093
(212) 713-2000

Parke-Davis (pharmaceuticals)
201 Tabor Rd.
Morris Plains, NJ 07950
(201) 540-2000

Pier 1 Imports, Inc. (retail imported housewares)
301 Commerce St., Ste. 600
Ft. Worth, TX 76102-4182
(817) 878-8000

Pillsbury Brands (food mfg.)
200 S. 6th St.—MS 38RS
Minneapolis, MN 55402
(612) 330-5154

Pitney Bowes, Inc. (postage meters mfr.)
Walter H. Wheeler Jr. Drive.
Stamford, CT 06926
(203) 356-5000

Prentice Hall (publishing)
Route 9W
Englewood Cliffs, NJ 07632
(201) 592-2000

Price Waterhouse (public accountancy consulting)
1251 Avenue of the Americas
New York, NY 10020
(212) 819-5028

Procter & Gamble Co. (food, groceries mfg.)
Two Procter & Gamble Plaza, TE-3
Cincinnati, OH 45202
(513) 983-1100

G.P. Putnam & Sons (publishing)
200 Madison Ave.
New York, NY 10016
(212) 951-8400

The Quaker Oats Co. (food mfg.)
321 N. Clark St.
Chicago, IL 60610-4790
(312) 222-7111

Random House, Inc. (publishing)
201 E. 50th St.
New York, NY 10022
(212) 751-2600

Saatchi & Saatchi Advertising
375 Hudson St.
New York, NY 10014-3660
(212) 463-2000

Safeco Corp. (insurance)
Safeco Plaza
Seattle, WA 98185-0001
(206) 545-5000

Salomon Bros, Inc. (securities)
One New York Plaza
New York, NY 10004
(212) 747-7000

Sears & Roebuck (retail)
Sears Tower D/707-4, BSC 33-41
Chicago, IL 60684
(312) 875-2500

Simon & Schuster (publishing)
1230 Avenue of the Americas
New York, NY 10020
(212) 698-7000

Southwestern Bell Corp. (telecommunications, utilities)
One Bell Center, 38-P-01
St. Louis, MO 63101
(314) 235-9800

St. Martin's Press (publishing)
175 Fifth Ave.
New York, NY 10010
(212) 674-5151

Sybex Publishing, Inc.
2021 Challenger Dr.
Oakland, CA 94501
(415) 523-8233

Tandy Corp./Radio Shack (computers, home electronics)
500 One Tandy Center
Ft. Worth, TX 76010
(817) 878-6893

Target, Inc. (retail discount stores)
33 S. 6th St.
Minneapolis, MN 55410
(612) 370-6948

United States Surgical Corp. (surgical & medical instrument mfg.)
150 Glover Ave.
Norwalk, CT 06856
(203) 845-1000

The Upjohn Company (pharmaceuticals)
70001 Portage Rd.
Kalamazoo, MI 49001-0199
(616) 323-4000

Wells Fargo Bank
420 Montgomery
San Francisco, CA 94104-1298
(415) 396-3849

Ziff Davis Publishing Co.
1 Park Ave.
New York, NY 10016-5898
(212) 503-3500

Index